REFLECTIONS
ON
THE
CHANGING
WORLD

NAVEED QAZI

Typeset in Adobe Caslon Pro

www.naveedqazi.com

ISBN-13: 9781077576490
ISBN-10: 1077576498

Paperback & digital editions available from Kindle
Direct Publishing, an Amazon unit.

UK | US | Australia | Italy | Spain | India | Netherlands
Japan | Brazil | Canada | Germany | Mexico | UAE
Singapore | Turkey | Poland | China | Saudi Arabia

kindle
direct
publishing

ABBREVIATIONS

ADF Allied Democratic Forces Ugandan
AASU All Assam Student's Union
AoA Agreement on Agriculture
AIKSCC All India Kisan Sangharsh Coordination Committee
AK47 *Avtomat Kalashnikova (Russian)*
APHC All Parties Hurriyat Conference
AFP *Agence France Presse (French)*
AKP *Adalet ve Kalkınma Partisi (Turkish)*
ATCA Anti-Terrorism Clarification Act
APC All Progressive Congress
AQIM Al Qaeda in the Islamic Maghreb
ATM Automated Teller Machine
ASEAN Association of Southeast Asian Nations
AIUDF All India Union Democratic Front
AIPAC American Israel Public Affairs Committee
AWACS Airborne Warning and Control System
BBC British Broadcasting Corporation
BJP *Bharatiya Janata Party (Hindi)*
BN *Barisan National (Malay)*
BNP Bangladesh National Party
CIA Central Intelligence Agency
CFR Council of Foreign Relations
CCTV Closed Circuit Television
CDU *Christlich Demokratische Union Deutschlands (German)*
CLSR Committee of Land Reforms, and State Agrarian Relations
CHRD China Human Rights Defenders
CNN Cable News Network
DNA Deoxyribonucleic acid
DPRK Democratic People's Republic of Korea

DRC Democratic Republic of Congo
DSB Dispute Settlement Body
DPS Democratic Party of Socialists
EAS East Asia Summit
ETIM East Turkestan Islamic Movement
ECOWAS Economic Community of West African States
EU European Union
FDLR Democratic Forces for the Liberation of Rwanda
FTA Free Trade Agreement
FM Future Movement
FPM Free Patriotic Movement
FBI Federal Bureau of Investigation
FATF Financial Action Task Force
FLN *Front de libération nationale (French)*
FATA Federally Administered Tribal Area
FCR Frontier Crimes Regulation
FPO Farmer Producer Organisation
GCC Gulf Corporation Council
G5 Group of Five
GDP Gross Domestic Product
GMR Grandhi Mallikarjuna Rao
GFA Good Friday Agreement
GIEI *El Grupo Interdisciplinario de Expertos Independientes (Spanish)*
HRW Human Rights Watch
HKUPOP Public Opinion Programme at The University of Hong Kong
HDP *Halkların Demokratik Partisi (Turkish)*
HM *Hizbul Mujahideen (Arabic)*
ICBM Intercontinental Ballistic Missile
IDP Internally Displaced Persons
IGAD Inter-Government Authority on Development
IMF International Monetary Fund
INEC Independent National Electoral Commission
IOR Indian Ocean Region

INSS *Instituto Nicaraguense de Seguridad Social (Spanish)*
ISIS Islamic State in Iraq & Syria
IRA Irish Republican Army
IAEA International Atomic Energy Agency
IACHR Inter American Commission on Human Rights
IAF Indian Air Force
IRGC Islamic Revolutionary Guard Corps
JCPOA Joint Comprehensive Plan of Action
JeM *Jaish e Muhammad (Arabic)*
JNIM *Jamaat Nusrat al Islam wal Muslimeen (Arabic)*
J&K Jammu & Kashmir
JKNC Jammu & Kashmir National Conference
JKPDP Jammu & Kashmir Peoples Democratic Party
JKPC Jammu & Kashmir Peoples Conference
JKLF Jammu & Kashmir Liberation Front
KGP *Komitet Gosudarstvennoy Bezopasnosti (Russian)*
LTTE Liberation Tigers of Tamil Eelam
LT *Lakshar-e- Toiba (Arabic)*
LAS League of Arab States
M23 March 23
MORENA *Movimiento Regeneración Nacional (Spanish)*
MGNREGA Mahatma Gandhi National Rural Employment Guarantee Act
MoEFCC Ministry of Environment, Forests and Climate Change
MINUSMA United Nations Multidimensional Integrated Stabilisation Mission in Mali
MNLA National Movement for the Liberation of Azawad
M5S *Movimento 5 Stelle (Italian)*
NAFTA North Atlantic Free Trade Organisation
NABARD National Bank of Agriculture and Rural Development
NPC National Party Council
NDR *Norddeutscher Rundfunk (German)*
NIS *Naftna Industrija Srbije (Serbian)*

NATO North Atlantic Treaty Organisation
NCPO National Council for Peace and Order
NGO Non-Governmental Organisation
NRC National Register of Citizens
NACLA North American Congress on Latin America
NDTV New Delhi Television Limited
NZD New Zealand Dollar
OSCE Organisation for Security and Co-operation in Europe
OPEC Organisation of Petroleum Exporting Countries
OPCW Organisation for the Prohibition of Chemical Weapons
OIC Organisation of Islamic Countries
PRI *Partido Revolucionario Institucional (Spanish)*
PAN *Partido Acción Nacional (Spanish)*
PAN Permanent Account Number
PAF Pakistan Air Force
PLO Palestinian Liberation Organisation
PKK *Partiya Karkerên Kurdistanê (Kurdish)*
QCG Quadrilateral Coordination Group
RSPO Roundtable and Sustainable Palm Oil
RTBF *Radio Television Belge Francophone (French)*
RAW Research and Analysis Wing
SSHF South Sudan Humanitarian Fund
SDBZ Safe Demilitarised Border Zone
SDU *Sozialdemokratische Partei Deutschlands (German)*
SPA Sudanese Professional Association
SNP Scottish Nationalist Party
SBP Southern Border Provinces
SLOC Sea Lines of Communication
SUV Sports Utility Vehicle
TV Television
ToR Terms of Reference
TRP Television Rating Point
UK United Kingdom
US United States

UN United Nations
UNHCR United Nations High Commissioner for
Refugee Agency
UNOCHA United Nations Office for the Coordination
of Humanitarian Affairs
UNMO United National Malays Organisation
USD United States Dollar
UPA United Progressive Alliance
UDD United Front for Democracy Against Dictatorship
UNP United National Party
UNISFA United Nations Interim Security Force for
Abyei
UAE United Arab Emirates
VG *Verdens Gang (Norwegian)*
WDR *Westdeutscher Rundfunk Köln (German)*
WTO World Trade Organisation
3Ts Tin, Tungsten and Tantalum

CONTENTS

PART I

WAR ZONES

PART II

ELECTIONS

PART III

PART IV

PART V

ENVIRONMENTAL ISSUES

PART VI

UNREMEMBERED HISTORY

PART I

WAR ZONES

1

WAR CRISES IN SOUTH SUDAN

THE FOREBODING EVENTS OF GENOCIDE have compelled eighty thousand South Sudanese to leave their homes beginning in 2013. The refugee population has made Sudan the second-largest host of South Sudanese in the region.

Since the eruption of civil war in 2013, peace has remained absent for over five years. Various forces in the region have often been accused of killing villagers, burning homes, and stealing food. The Bentiu massacre in 2014 was regarded by The Economist as the worst massacre in the civil war. Since then, seven more major war offensives have happened in South Sudan.

Journalists have often observed buildings in various South Sudanese cities without iron roofs. The doors and windows of these homes have often been taken away by looters for their own means.

Humanitarian aid groups have estimated that around $1.72 billion is required to save the 5.1 million population. Save the Children, a UK non-profit agency, has sponsored one of the programmes. As there is very limited access to markets and farms, an acute food shortage is in the offing. It is believed that 2018 will be worse than 2017.

Despite the presence of seventeen thousand UN peacekeepers in the country, more than 1.9 million people have been internally displaced and 2,300 children have been killed. The internal displacement figures stood at three hundred fifty-five thousand in 2014 alone.

Many South Sudanese have often lived inside tents that have been damaged by the baking sun. Around 19,000 child soldiers are associated with the rebel groups. Recruited child soldiers have received a hundred lashes for not waking up on time and have been detained forcefully. Some children have been sold for twenty cows. In other words, a scenario like this happened only during the Rwandan genocide in Africa.

Independent UN experts have reported to the UN Security Council that South Sudan's government has spent millions of dollars on weapons. It had been one of the reasons why the country descended into a serious famine-ridden condition.

As the rebels have been using hunger and sexual violence as weapons against the population, the UN Refugee Agency (UNHCR) has been appealing globally to support the local population. Officials working for the UN agency believe that large quantities of weapons are being smuggled into South Sudan through Kenya and Uganda.

In 2015, despite a peace agreement, the war spread to stable regions such as the Equatorias and Western Bahr e Ghazal. A ceasefire announced on 26 December 2016 ended some hours later, and fighting has continued since then.

South Sudan won independence from Sudan in 2011, but a little over two years later its leaders began a fresh civil war, pitting President Salva Kiir against his former deputy Riek Machar. It seems that war weariness in the country remains constant and threatening.

One of the most challenging things during the ongoing war has been road transport, which is difficult to undertake. Drivers often sleep in remote locations. The journeys often take several days, and cars are not allowed to travel during the night. Due to bad road conditions, cars and trucks often face mechanical problems and tyre punctures.

The logistical cluster facilitated the biggest inter-agency convoy in 2017. It was organised to reduce reliance on costly airlifts. Around 99 vehicles transported cargo on behalf of nine organisations. They moved enroute on the western corridor, with multiple destination points. This corridor is extremely important to the humanitarian community, as it provides access to some locations. This logistical cluster will only close during the rainy season.

In the Ethiopian capital of Addis Ababa, the IGAD (Inter-Government Authority on Development) sponsored peace talks have been resumed after rejecting the procrastination of the South Sudanese government.

The South Sudanese government has been demanding more representation, but the current rule of IGAD states that the government can have only 12 seats. The resolution committee is urging all parties to desist from breaking the ceasefire. They are stressing a revised and realistic timeline, and a schedule towards general elections in the country at the end of the interim period.

The United States is set to announce an arms embargo against South Sudan to end the country's civil war and humanitarian crises. Previously, the Obama administration had urged the UN to back an arms embargo against South Sudan.

During the final quarter of 2017, UNOCHA released the South Sudan Humanitarian Fund (SSHF), allocating

US$11.1 million to 12 core pipeline projects. The funding enabled the procurement of life-saving supplies and dry season assistance, and ensured continuity of distributions during the wet season.

To quell the violence in South Sudan, the African Union High-Level Implementation Panel, with the participation of UNISFA in Addis Ababa, has put forward a proposal on a 2000 km joint border known as the Safe Demilitarised Border Zone (SDBZ) between Sudan and South Sudan. The plan will also include border monitoring and regulatory controls.

Preventing famine and ending the civil war is a daunting task, but if powerful nations exert a positive influence, things might improve. It seems the aid can come in late.

Before also, in 2011, when drought struck in the Horn of Africa, humanitarian aid came late too. If a response comes late repeatedly, the conditions might aggravate to fatal proportions. An ambiguity arises in these situations because if peace-loving countries make promises for a better world, then why does action fail, and if preventive action happens, why does that preventive action get delayed?

February 6, 2018

2

SURGING REFUGEES
OF DRC CONFLICT

THE DEMOCRATIC REPUBLIC OF CONGO
had one of the largest numbers of people displaced
in 2016. A report by the International Displacement
Monitoring Centre of the Norwegian Refugee Council
puts it at around nine hundred twenty-two thousand in
2016. This figure was more than that of Syrian and Iraqi
refugees within the same year.

In 2017, around one hundred twenty thousand DRC
Congolese fled to neighbouring countries. According to
the Global Conflict Tracker, as of February 2018 there
have been up to 4.1 million internally displaced people,
signifying that a significant number of people are in
statelessness. Also, there is a presence of around twenty-
one thousand UN soldiers in the Democratic Republic of
Congo.

Since the beginning of 2018, around twenty-two thousand
DRC Congolese crossed via Lake Albert to Uganda,
bringing the total number of DRC Congolese refugees to
thirty-four thousand the same year.

The refugees, along with their luggage and fishing nets,
use canoes or overcrowded fishing boats, often carrying
around two hundred fifty people on average. The journey
takes them up to ten hours.

Since December 2017, there has been a renewed outpour
of violence where around a thousand houses have been

burned in the Ituri province. In the North and South Kivu provinces of the Ituri region, the militias hold large areas.

The roads of the villages in the Kasai province are called 'hunger roads,' where around forty-two per cent of people risk starvation. As of now, more than six hundred schools have been damaged in attacks, and one hundred fifty thousand children in the Greater Kasai region need emergency support. The cholera outbreak also spread in the Bukama territory in 2016.

Around $368.7 million has been requested by the UNHCR for the DRC Congolese refugee situation, but only one per cent has been funded so far for building shelter, food, and other vital support.

UNHCR spokesman Babar Baloch believes that the situation seems to be the biggest exodus of refugees from Ituri in two decades. In the past, around four hundred thousand people were also displaced and tens of thousands were killed in clashes between the Hema and Lendu tribes over cattle and grazing rights.

The DRC conflict has largely been aggravated due to ethnic conflicts and frequent skirmishes between the armed groups such as the Democratic Forces for the Liberation of Rwanda (FDLR) and the Ugandan Allied Democratic Forces (ADF), who control weakly governed areas of the country and finance their groups with DRC's rich natural resources (diamonds, gold, cobalt, zinc, and coltan estimated at around $24 trillion).

It is estimated that around two hundred fifty ethnic groups live in the Democratic Republic of Congo. Between them, innumerous greedy businessmen, unscrupulous corporations, warlords, and corrupt government officials are trying to have their piece of the cake by trying to gain lucrative advantages arising from the conflict.

As of now, it is believed that almost all of DRC's gold is smuggled for export from Dubai. The leaders sitting in Kinshasa have not become serious about these smuggling practices yet.

Since its independence in 1960, most of the provinces in DRC have disintegrated. Since the war was over in 2003, its eastern province has remained very volatile. Deaths are estimated at around forty-five thousand per month.

Going back to history, British, Dutch, Arab, and Portuguese merchants engaged in the slave trade until Belgians colonised DRC.

When the Second Congo War (also known as Africa's World War) started in 1998, eight African nations and twenty-armed groups were involved. It had been regarded as the deadliest war since World War II, where two million Africans were internally displaced and over a thousand Africans died every day from malnutrition and disease.

Historically, there was also trade of the conflict minerals at a sheer scale, including tin, tungsten, and tantalum (3Ts), sold by the armed groups. The war eventually ended through the Sun City Agreement and the Pretoria Accord, but hostilities continue through the Lord's Resistance Army insurgency, mainly in the eastern DRC and in the Kivu and Ituri conflicts.

In 2015, DRC faced a constitutional crisis. It eventually led to massive demonstrations. The looters had attacked Chinese national-run businesses in the capital for resentment of their low selling prices. Around twenty-six activists, journalists, diplomats, and civilians were arrested in Kinshasa while attending a workshop on freedom of expression. It included journalists from the BBC, AFP, and RTBF. These journalists were beaten by the army and interrogated by the national intelligence.

In DRC's political timeline, it was only in 2006 when the first free elections were held.

Quite recently, the Ugandan government has been investigating allegations of gross mismanagement, malpractices in registration, and trafficking of girls and women from the DRC Congolese refugee crisis in the country.

Rwanda has been accused of financing M23 militia members, a mainly ethnic Tutsi rebel group in eastern DRC. The M23 militia, defeated in 2013, believed that the DRC government did not respect the peace accord signed in 2009.

In 1996, Rwanda and Uganda invaded DRC to rout out the remaining perpetrators in the First Congo War. It eventually led to the downfall of the DRC dictator Mobuto Sese Seko. Rwanda and DRC both have had bitter relations since the infamous 1994 Rwandan genocide.

Coming back to the time when fighting occurred at the Rwandan border at the foot of Mount Nikeno in North Kivu province, the DRC army had exchanged fire with the Rwandan army, whom they initially thought of as ex-M23 members.

February 15, 2018

3

SYRIA'S NEWEST GRAVEYARD

Eastern Ghouta, once a fertile agricultural belt on the outskirts of Damascus, became a symbol of devastation during the Syrian civil war. In February 2018, the enclave was described as 'Syria's newest graveyard' after one of the deadliest bombardments in years. According to the Syrian Observatory for Human Rights, at least ninety-eight people were killed in a single day, marking the deadliest attack in Syria's three-year war history at that time. Over five days, the death toll rose to 229, including fifty-eight children and forty-three women, underscoring the indiscriminate nature of the assault, as reported by The Guardian and BBC News. The United Nations estimated that around 400,000 civilians were trapped in Eastern Ghouta, half of them children, with UNICEF and Save the Children warning of acute malnutrition and psychological trauma among the youngest.

The enclave had been under siege since 2013, with food, medicine, and humanitarian supplies severely restricted. Rebel groups such as Jaish al-Islam, Faylaq al-Rahman, and Hayat Tahrir al-Sham controlled different pockets of the territory, occasionally engaging in peace negotiations but often fractured by rivalry, as noted in New York Times coverage. The humanitarian crisis was compounded by relentless airstrikes: over four days in February 2018, more than 700 civilians were injured. Photojournalists captured paramedics carrying children through neighbourhoods reduced to rubble, while the volunteer organisation known as the White Helmets intensified rescue operations amidst collapsing buildings, according to Reuters and Associated Press.

Survivors described emerging from twisted metal and debris as dark smoke rose over the enclave. The United States accused Russia of imposing strict curfews in areas under its control, preventing civilians from leaving through humanitarian corridors, reported Washington Post and Wall Street Journal. Doctors and nurses resorted to using WhatsApp to communicate with foreign media, while children and activists turned to Twitter to broadcast the shocking realities on the ground. Despite a thirty-day truce announced by the UN Security Council, fighting resumed almost immediately, as Al Jazeera observed.

The siege of Eastern Ghouta was particularly alarming given its designation as a 'de-escalation zone' under a May 2017 agreement signed by Iran, Russia, and Turkey. Yet by early 2018, Syrian government forces had regained control of 10–25 per cent of the enclave, citing its strategic importance due to proximity to Damascus and Assad's residence, reported Financial Times and Foreign Policy. Around 30,000 people were internally displaced from villages such as Beit Sawa, Otaya, and Douma, further straining humanitarian relief efforts, according to Amnesty International.

Syria's notoriety for chemical weapons use added another layer of horror. The use of chlorine and other agents violated UN Security Council resolutions and the 1997 Chemical Weapons Convention, according to Human Rights Watch and UN Human Rights Council reports. Although Syria agreed in September 2013 to destroy its chemical arsenal under a US-Russia deal following the sarin gas attack in Ghouta, doubts persisted. By June 2014, 1,300 tonnes of declared chemical weapons had been handed over to the Organisation for the Prohibition of Chemical Weapons (OPCW), yet several nations questioned whether the arsenal had truly been eliminated, as BBC News and OPCW statements confirmed.

A confidential OPCW report, later summarised by Reuters, concluded 'with utmost confidence' that mustard gas had been used in Marea, north of Aleppo, in August 2014. Diplomatic sources suggested the chemical was deployed during clashes between Islamic State and rival rebels, raising fears that ISIS had either manufactured or seized chemical weapons. American intelligence during the Obama administration believed that Sunni extremist groups had mastered the production of sarin. CIA officials pointed to Ziyaad Tariq Ahmad, a former Iraqi army officer linked to al-Nusra, as having expertise in producing sarin and mustard gas, according to New York Times. Further evidence emerged in August 2015 when blood samples from thirty-five Kurdish Peshmerga fighters in Erbil tested positive for mustard gas exposure, reported Washington Post and Kurdish regional authorities. In April 2017, chemical weapons were again believed to have been used in Khan Sheikhoun, Idlib province, killing dozens. The Independent International Commission of Inquiry on Syria reported thirty-four documented incidents of chemical weapons use by various parties as of January 2018, condemning such acts as violations of international law, noted Guardian and International Crisis Group.

Despite limited access for investigators, UN reports compiled credible evidence of chemical attacks targeting Syrian soldiers as well. In December 2013, then-Secretary-General Ban Ki-moon noted that chemical weapons were used in Khan al-Asal on 19 March 2013 against both soldiers and civilians, in Jobar on 24 August 2013 against soldiers, and in Ashrafiah Sahnaya on 25 August 2013 on a smaller scale, according to UN Secretary-General's Report.

The French government's national assessment of the Douma chemical attack in April 2018 concluded with 'a high degree of confidence' that the Syrian regime was responsible, reported Le Monde and BBC. Civil society groups and medical organisations such as the Syrian American Medical Society and Médecins Sans Frontières documented exposure to chemical agents, reinforcing international outrage. Yet Russia and Syria denied responsibility, accusing rebels of staging the incident. This clash of narratives highlighted the geopolitical stakes: Assad, backed by Iran and Russia, faced calls to step down, while the US framed him as a puppet of Moscow and Tehran, according to New York Times and The Economist.

The question of regime transition loomed large. If Assad were removed, what would follow in a country where ISIS and other extremist groups continued to gain footholds? For many Syrians, the prospect of a US-backed regime raised fears of foreign domination rather than liberation, as Guardian analysis suggested. Meanwhile, Turkey pursued its own offensive against Kurdish forces in northern Syria, complicating the battlefield with yet another actor seeking influence, reported Al Jazeera and Anadolu Agency.

Eastern Ghouta thus became a microcosm of Syria's broader tragedy: a humanitarian disaster, a theatre of chemical warfare, and a geopolitical chessboard where global powers vied for dominance. The siege ended in April 2018 with the Syrian army's capture of the enclave, but the scars remain. As one UN official remarked, 'the scale of suffering in Eastern Ghouta is a stain on our collective conscience', according to UN News.

The events in Eastern Ghouta illustrate the convergence of humanitarian catastrophe and geopolitical rivalry. Civilians withstood the worst of indiscriminate bombardments, chemical attacks, and starvation, while international actors debated responsibility and strategy. The enclave's fall underscored Assad's determination to secure Damascus, but at immense human cost. The legacy of Eastern Ghouta is not only the graves of thousands but also the unanswered question: can Syria ever rebuild trust and stability when chemical weapons, foreign interventions, and fractured political opposition has marked its war landscape?

March 5, 2018

4

WAR AFFLICTIONS IN YEMEN

IN YEMEN, the Saudi-led coalition entered the war in 2015 through Operation Desert Storm. Since then, at least five thousand children have been killed mercilessly as more than nineteen thousand air raids have ravaged the Arab world's poorest country.

It is believed that counterinsurgency operations, part of America's global domination plans, proved pivotal in political instability inside Yemen. The enraged public has often been seen burning the American flag on the streets, showing a fit of collective anger.

Currently, the United States does not approve of the Yemeni army with whom it coordinated before during the USS Cole bombing due to the Yemeni government's illegitimacy and chaos spreading in the US Senate.

As per inputs by offices of the United Nations, many children have been recruited as child soldiers, reflecting the ugly side of war.

After more than three years of fighting, around sixty thousand people have been killed. As per the Yemen Data Project, more than two-thirds of the coalition's air raids have struck non-military and unknown targets.

One of the worst atrocities committed by Saudi-led forces that received worldwide condemnation was in 2015, when one hundred forty mourners were killed who were attending a funeral. There is an alarming cholera epidemic afflicting the lives of common Yemenis as of now. People eat boiled tree leaves for survival as food prices have soared to one hundred fifty per cent since the conflict began in Yemen.

While Crown Prince Mohammad bin Salman gave a financial grant lately, at the behest of the Saudi government, as humanitarian aid, just like the Emirati government, he still, ironically, has been the architect of the Yemen war for over three years. The recent ruling of expelling Yemeni workers from the kingdom makes his political intentions even clearer.

Even now, the Houthi militia has not been defeated yet even though billions of dollars have been invested by the Saudis for the purchase of fourth-generation ultra-sophisticated weapons.

The Houthis are still believed to be working at the behest of Iranian strategic plans because of a common religious affiliation. Iran has been accused lately of supplying missile parts to the Houthis.

For quite a while, a ballistic missile has been targeted at the Saudi kingdom by the Houthis, who had been busy lately retreating against the 'carpet bombing campaign' of the Saudi-UAE air forces.

A $115 billion military deal between the Saudis and the US proved the backbone of their war campaigns inside Yemen.

Regional correspondents have dispersed first-hand accounts where women and old men are seen praying to God while Saudi warplanes have entered Saana.

The oil-rich Saudi monarchy is accused of killing civilians in residential areas, markets, hospitals, and even camps for refugees.

Human Rights Watch (HRW) has accused Saudi Arabia of serious war crimes in the region. They want the United Nations to launch a new probe.

Ironically, a UN Security Council Resolution extended sanctions for a year in Yemen lately, but it did not call for investigations into war crimes perpetrated by the Saudis.

The Kingdom, along with the UAE, seems to have vested interests and possibly wants territorial gains in the war-torn peninsula.

Currently, Yemen is facing famine and twenty-two million people require aid. In terms of the political situation, Aden has become a battleground for southern secessionists.

Economically, Yemen has currently run out of foreign currency reserves. As a result, many regional Yemeni businessmen have collaborated and made their hawala networks. They also have been burdened with extra tax payments at the borders and checkpoints. The problem has increased the cost of goods by around 10–15 per cent.

According to Op-ed writer Peter Salisbury, rebel fighters have been benefitting from poor checks at the borders. These militias now control large swathes of land that have been strategically important, including important trade routes.

To add more fuel to the fire, none of the rebel groups has been allowed to put their opinions in any UN-led peace-making process.

If we look at the blueprint of the UN-mediated peace process, it calls for the Houthi-Saleh alliance to cut some kind of deal with the Hadi alliance to form a 'unity government.'

In the past, when Saleh ruled, he had robbed $33 billion cash, a disbursement by the US to fight al-Qaeda. He had allowed Houthis to gain control of several quarters of government administration during his rule.

During the civil war, not only did Houthis capture Saana but also seized Aden and its airport, which made the ruling President Hadi flee to Saudi Arabia.

Journalists have nicknamed Yemen a 'new Vietnam' emerging inside the Middle East. They see dead coral scattered on the seashores while young Yemeni army men chew raw green tobacco leaves and pose for selfies in UAE armoured vehicles.

Peter Salisbury, a researcher with London-based Chatham House, further reveals: 'In Mareb Province, the main highway is cut off. In the south of this province, there is a less maintained road where lorries drive through anti- and pro-Houthi checkpoints. The country is a region of mini-states at varying degrees of war.'

This fragile situation seems to speak for itself.

Yemen had been a hotbed of extremism since the Afghan civil war in the 1990s. Egyptians also fought an insurgency in the 1960s. But it was Britain that put Yemen on the West's maps, where British warships travelled through its ports to India. The Brits, just like the Ottomans, had partitioned the area into a north-south border.

In 2016, the Saudi-led coalition wanted to seize the port of Hodeidah, which lies on the west coast of Yemen. It is because the alliance believes that the Houthis use this port to bring Iranian weapons. As a political move, it might also have been a plan to squeeze the Houthi faction even further so that they could put something lucrative, in the form of political dialogue, on the table.

During the war at the port, violence had been up to a staggering one hundred and sixty-four per cent.

A regional political analyst believes that if Hodeidah port is cut off the Houthis will survive, but the rest of Yemen will starve.

Currently, nine per cent of imported food comes from the Hodeidah port. This fatal move might even surge traffic problems and increase tax customs collections inside the war-torn territory.

Has the role of the United States and its allies in this war helped in any way, even if one approves of a notion about the hands of Houthis being not clean in this war? It does not seem so.

11 April, 2018

5

MACABRE KILLINGS AT NAKBA DAY

IT WAS A DAY TO SYMBOLISE the sufferings of Palestinian Muslims, who were expelled, from their homeland.

But something tragic happened.

This day of sympathy, for seven hundred thousand Palestinians, expelled during the 1948 war, turned into a mass killing of people. The 70th anniversary, of Nakba, turned into a macabre, a bloodbath.

A 31-year-old Nasser was shot in the chest, about eight hundred meters, away from the fence. At the hospital, his heart stopped beating.

One of the teenagers, an 18-year-old, Bilal al Ashram, son of Nisma Abdelqader, was shot, straight in the head. Bilal's brother, at the local morgue, had been shocked about his death, after he heard about it.

On Facebook, Bilal had written a post, the previous day, where he insisted, to go to Bir Se'ba, a city in the south, from where his family had been expelled, during the *Nakba*.

Factually, these journeys are their birthright, but they have been mostly killed, for their intentions.

Killing sprees, of Palestinians, are often largely unprovoked and serve as an illustration, of perpetual tragedies. It is often observed, in the mainstream Israeli press, where Netanyahu calls the killing of Palestinians, on the border, a 'wise decision'.

Media Lens, a watchdog organisation, critical of the mainstream media, flaked BBC, the leading British media corporation, for calling the massacre, a 'mere clash,' at the border. It was one of those examples of 'crowd correct journalism,' drifting away from reality.

These two were not the only people, who were killed. There were around forty-six people killed, and twenty-seven hundred were injured, including babies and children, on May 14, 2018, at the Gazan border. They had huddled together, against the opening of a US embassy, in Jerusalem, a disputed territory.

Make no mistake, Israel is in control of radical right-wingers. It is for this reason that we keep hearing about the Palestinian slaughter, repeatedly. Aren't these figures, too tragic, to say the least?

Palestinian Muslims, and Israeli Jews, have been fighting with each other, since the beginning of the 19th century, the beginning of post-World War I.

The Muslims, living in Israel, have been barred from making *Adhans,* and live amidst the poorest ghettos, of the world. Quiet lately, protests broke out, near Al Aqsa Mosque, where hundreds of protestors sustained injuries.

The fence, constructed by Israelis, made up of barbed wires, fitted with surveillance cameras, has become an embodiment of sorts, an imposed border on Palestinians, who try to defy it, now and then.

Since March 2018, the Israeli forces, in the Gaza strip, have killed around three hundred Palestinians.

In the region's history, the first fence was constructed, in 1994, after the enactment of the Oslo Accords, to control the Palestinian travel movement.

The Israeli government, believes, that they have voluntarily left Gaza, as they vacated some settlements. But, at the same time, they think that Palestinians, crossing the fence, is a threat to their sovereignty.

In other words, it also means that the Israelis want to wield power, over the fence, and want to control much of the air, and sea routes. They claim to have an argument, although an ambiguous one, while as Egyptians control the land crossing, known as the Rafah.

Much of the food travels through these Israeli-controlled territories. When Hamas took over the realms of power, Egyptians, and Israelis, both, restricted the movement, which included supplies of food. It is because Hamas sanctions human shields and public bombings.

Human Rights advocates call Gaza an 'open-air prison.' In its recent history, many political leaders, have emerged from the Yarmouk Camp, 'the capital of Palestinian diaspora,' who were eventually assassinated, by Israeli intelligence.

David Makovsky, an expert at the Washington Institute, for Near East Policy, wrote in an Op-ed: 'Gaza is not a Palestinian state. Part of the problem is that nobody wants Gaza. Egyptians see it as a political quicksand.'

Over time, *Nakba* has acquired a deep resonance, within

the Palestinian identity. It reminds them, time and again that they are expelled from their land.

Nakba is a part of their collective memory, inherited with time, from father to son, generation to generation.

When this community, largely, does a peaceful protest, against the Israeli occupation, they are labelled as 'suicidal' and 'terrorists.'

But there is a fact that Israel knows for sure: if every exiled Palestinian family comes home someday, that day would be the end of Israel. It is because Jews would then never make a majority, in the region. For this reason, they do not want an ethnoreligious imbalance.

According to Noam Chomsky, Christian Zionism was a popular ideology, among British elites, and American politicians. It had been a vantage point for the drafting of the Balfour Declaration, and it still is yearned by politicians. And above all, there is a powerful Jewish lobby controlling America, right now, including the media corporations, as well.

This lobby would not have been powerful, at all, if it had not been supported, the way it has been. And, it still can be put down, but Western leaders, especially the Americans, do not want to keep it, as part of their agenda, for their national interests.

Despite that, quite lately, there have been Jewish American voices, dissenting on Palestinian oppression, and they no longer want to give Israel their political support.

Azad Essa, wrote in an Op-ed, for Middle East Eye that there are political groups, such as IfNotNow, that want an end to American support of the occupation, in Israel, and it signifies a shift, in their ideas, after a massacre, at the Tree of Life Synagogue, in Pittsburgh, that killed eleven people.

These facts do raise serious questions. The audience, largely belonging to the Western world, should retrospect, what they see, and hear, about Palestine, in their media. It is a region, which has seen innumerable deaths, innumerable acts of violence, innumerable crackdowns, and every act of oppression, imaginable.

Trump, just like Obama, has lied to us. Whereas Obama promised peace in the Middle East, he eventually increased Israeli military aid ten times. Trump also assured, of doing something different, for truce and ceasefire, but his actions have spoken of certain vagueness.

During the inauguration of the US embassy, in Jerusalem, he invited two American pastors, with a history of anti-Semitism, as well as Islamophobia. It was something ironical, on his part, to send them, for public prayers, at the US embassy, in Jerusalem.

In places, such as Boston and Cape Town, thousands of people have protested savage Israeli policies, against defenceless Palestinians.

After this gruesome incident, the OIC also sent a message of solidarity.

20 May, 2018

6

SYRIA'S LAST WAR ZONE

IN SEPTEMBER 2018, RUSSIA AND TURKEY reached what became known as the Sochi Agreement, a deal that temporarily prevented a full-scale assault on Idlib province, home to nearly three million people. As Al Jazeera reported, Presidents Vladimir Putin and Recep Tayyip Erdogan announced the creation of a demilitarised buffer zone, 15–20 kilometres deep, to be established by 15 October 2018, with rebel fighters expected to withdraw heavy weapons while Russian and Turkish patrols, supported by drones, would monitor the area. The Arab Centre Washington DC, in analysis by Joe Macaron, stressed that the deal was always fragile, testing Russian–Turkish relations and hinging on the willingness of radical factions to comply. The Guardian's Martin Chulov added a statement that the agreement was seen by many Syrians as a temporary reprieve rather than a durable peace.

On the ground, the truce offered temporary relief. Farmers began buying seeds and fertilisers, trade resumed among local merchants, and some displaced families cautiously returned to southern Idlib. Parents sent children back to school, and warehouses storing chickpeas and figs sought to re-establish contacts. Even potato chip factories and pistachio farms, which had suffered low yields during the war, looked to restart production. Yet beneath this fragile normality, the threat of renewed violence loomed. The New York Times reported that residents feared the buffer zone would collapse at any moment, given the presence of hardline factions unwilling to compromise.

Civilian suffering remained immense. UN reports confirmed that more than half of Idlib's medical centres were out of service. Protests erupted against the Assad regime, with families holding placards and portraits of detainees demanding their release. Filippo Grandi, the UN High Commissioner for Refugees, warned that further bloodshed could trigger mass displacement, adding to the 360,000 deaths already recorded in the Syrian conflict by its eighth year. BBC correspondents covering Idlib noted that hospitals were overwhelmed, with doctors forced to operate without anaesthetics and children dying from preventable diseases.

Turkey's role was complex. It had supported factions such as the Free Syrian Army and Sham Legion, hoping to weaken Assad and secure influence along its southern border. Ankara deployed around 1,300 troops and established observation posts in Idlib. Yet Turkey also faced the risk of a refugee influx if fighting resumed. Russia and Iran, meanwhile, provided decisive military backing to Assad. Christoph Reuter in Spiegel Online observed that Assad's battlefield successes since 2015 were not due to his depleted army but to Russian air power, tens of thousands of Hezbollah fighters, and militias from Iraq, Afghanistan, and Pakistan under Iranian command. Patrick Cockburn of The Independent similarly argued that Assad's survival was largely the result of Moscow's intervention and Tehran's mobilisation of foreign fighters.

Extremist groups remained entrenched. Around 12,000 fighters from the former al-Nusra Front, rebranded as Hayat Tahrir al-Sham, controlled large parts of Idlib. Comprised of Chechen, Tunisian, and German militants, they sought to impose an Islamic emirate, carrying out kidnappings and killings of businessmen and doctors. Analysts doubted such radicals would surrender heavy weapons, undermining the buffer zone's viability. The Washington Post reported that HTS checkpoints continued to dominate trade routes, extorting merchants and undermining Turkish efforts to stabilise the province.

The United States, once committed to ousting Assad, had shifted focus to dismantling ISIS. With around 2,000 troops in eastern Syria working alongside Kurdish and Arab fighters under the Syrian Democratic Forces, Washington lacked the diplomatic capacity to shape a peaceful settlement. Christopher Bolan, writing for the US Army War College, warned that Assad might resort again to chemical weapons, potentially provoking a stronger response from America and its allies. The New York Times' Anne Barnard noted that Washington's Syria policy had narrowed to counterterrorism, leaving the diplomatic field largely to Moscow and Ankara.

Israel exploited the chaos to strike Iranian targets. Reuters reported that hundreds of airstrikes were launched against Syria to prevent weapons transfers to Hezbollah in Lebanon. Israel also backed counter-insurgent forces in the Golan Heights to curb Iranian influence. Meanwhile, Russia controlled Syrian airspace, bombing Aleppo and Eastern Ghouta in support of Assad, as Al Jazeera documented. Haaretz journalists confirmed that Israeli strikes targeted weapons depots near Damascus and Homs, underscoring Tel Aviv's determination to prevent Iranian entrenchment.

For civilians, the war's brutality was relentless. In Idlib's western city of Jisr al-Shughur, where some of the earliest firefights of the conflict occurred, families sold homes and furniture to finance escape. Many fled with only what could fit on motorcycles or cars, as fighter jets roared overhead. The Guardian reported that families often travelled at night to avoid bombardment, carrying only bread and blankets, while children were traumatised by constant shelling.

The broader geopolitical picture was equally fraught. Iran, Russia, Turkey, Israel, and the United States were the main external actors. Washington demanded Iran's withdrawal, while Moscow insisted on America's departure from eastern Syria. Assad's opposition was fragmented and ineffectual, leaving his regime dominant. Retaking Idlib remained central to Assad's plan to reunify Syria, though he avoided direct confrontation with Kurdish areas protected by US forces. The Financial Times noted that Idlib had become the last major rebel stronghold, symbolising both the resilience of opposition forces and the determination of Assad to reclaim all territory.

The Sochi Agreement thus represented a temporary pause rather than a resolution. Al Jazeera noted that Erdogan hailed the deal as bringing hope to the region, but its implementation was fraught with irregularities. Hardcore militants refused to disarm, and clashes continued sporadically. For Russia, the agreement highlighted its diplomatic leverage, while for Turkey it was a means to avoid a refugee crisis. Yet for civilians, it was a fragile reprieve amid years of devastation. The Guardian's Kareem Shaheen observed that the deal was more about managing tensions between Moscow and Ankara than protecting civilians.

In narrative terms, Idlib symbolises the contradictions of Syria's war. It is a fertile region with warehouses of chickpeas and fig harvests, yet also a battleground where international powers test their influence. It is a place where children return briefly to school, only to face renewed bombardment. It is a province where protests for detainees' freedom echo alongside the entrenched presence of jihadist factions. Journalists from The Independent described Idlib as a microcosm of Syria's tragedy, where daily life and destruction coexist uneasily.

Ultimately, the Sochi Agreement delayed but did not resolve the conflict. Assad's regime, backed by Russia and Iran, remained determined to retake Idlib. Turkey sought to protect its border and influence events, while the United States focused narrowly on ISIS. As Christoph Reuter concluded in Spiegel Online, Assad's victories were not his own but the product of foreign intervention. The fate of Idlib, and of Syria more broadly, continues to depend less on local actors than on the calculations of external powers.

29 September, 2018

7

POLITICAL DISCORDS OF MALI

IT WAS BEFORE DAWN WHEN a militia mercilessly attacked the Mali village of Ogossogou, killing more than a hundred people, in an instant, on March 23, 2019.

The victims included pregnant women, young children, and the elderly. It even included the village chieftain and his grandchildren.

Although there had been some runaway survivors, in the nearby Peulh village, where Muslim Fula tribes lived, it soon became improbable, to probe the number of killed, in the rampage, as per inputs from the President of Peulh group, Tabital Paulaaku.

Some footage of the charred dead bodies appeared, and there was also fire in the village homes. In response to this horrifying episode, Prime Minister Soumeylou Boubeye Maiga said that new military chiefs would be named.

Going back to January 2019, the Dogon hunters were blamed for killing thirty-seven people which had intensified restiveness in Mali. Despite this, the Dogon militia also faced strong drawbacks, in the past, where several of its armed men were killed, alongside soldiers of the Malian Armed Forces, especially in the village of Dioura.

The UN mission, in Mali, had confirmed reports of an

attack but gave no figures. It is believed that a militant group known as Dan Na Ambassagou, splintered from the Dogon group, has been instrumental, in this attack. It was said that the attack was perpetrated because Fulani Muslims, were accused, of grazing cattle, on their land.

In 2013, a largely French-driven military operation happened in the region, but the jihadist violence has escalated, and large areas of the country, are still supposed to be lawless, despite the creation of UN peacekeepers, and the creation of a five-nation military force, in the region. There had been a large terrorist attack on G5 Headquarters, in June 2018, that reflected rising tensions, in the country.

Quite recently, the conflict has escalated, between the Dogon, and Peulth communities. Members of the Dogon militia accuse the Peulth community, of siding with Islamic extremist groups, having ties in Libya and Algeria. Peulth, on the contrary, have accused the Dogon militia, of supporting the Malian army, in its effort, to stamp out extremism. However, now, the government vows to end the operations, of the Dogon militia.

In December 2018, Human Rights Watch warned that: 'militia killings of civilians, in central and northern Mali, are spiralling out of control'. There has been a prominence of Islamic extremists, since 2015, in the region.

In the capital, Bamako, visiting UN Security Council President Francois Delattre, condemned the killing, as an 'unspeakable act'.

In the present scenario, there are conflicts prevalent in northern Mali and central Mali villages.

In January 2012, a Tuareg rebellion erupted in northern Mali, led by the National Movement for the Liberation of Azawad (MNLA). It was in March, that year, when a coup happened, by a military officer called Amadou Sanogo, citing Amadou Toumani Toure's failure, in quelling the rebellion, which had led to sanctions, and an embargo, by Economic Community of West African States (ECOWAS). The MNLA quickly controlled the north, eventually, declaring independence, as Azawad.

Slowly, several Islamist groups including Ansar Dine and Al Qaeda in the Islamic Maghreb (AQIM), took control of the North, to implement Islamic Sharia in the region.

There are reports, from Human Rights Watch, where Tuareg rebels, in the north, included the use of child soldiers, attacked on hospitals, and schools, did abductions, rapes, and uncalled summary executions.

In central Mali, the conflict has mainly escalated, since 2015, as the groups involved, namely Dogon, Bambara, and the pastoral Fula, have been fighting, over access to land, and water. These groups have formed 'self-defence groups', and as per many Human Rights Reports, the fighting has been exaggerated, and instrumentalised, by different actors, for opportunistic ends. The government of Mali has been accused, of acting as a proxy, by supporting some of these groups, in a war against Islamists, in the region.

The UN Security General Antonio Guterres voiced a strong condemnation, of this massacre. According to deputy spokesman, Farhan Haq: 'the secretary-general condemns this act and calls on the Malian authorities to swiftly investigate it and bring the perpetrators to justice.'

Historically, after gaining independence, from France, in 1960, Mali endured decades, of political disorder. Most of the population resides, in the south. The Tuareg and Arab tribes, which sparsely populate the north, rebelled against the government, in 1963, 1990, and 2006, which they named Azawad. It was in 1992, when the Government of Mali, referred its situation, to the International Criminal Court, and consented, to the crimes against humanity, in the Rome Statute.

As per data given by the Council of Foreign Relations, there are around sixteen thousand two hundred twenty-seven UN personnel, situated in the country. There internally displaced persons, have swelled, to one hundred twenty thousand two hundred ninety-eight. CFR cites the number of Malian refugees as around one hundred thirty-six thousand thirty-two. Experts, from the Hague Institute for Global Justice, argue that the reason the Malian government do not effectively tackle the rise of Islamic extremism, and the conflict of Tuaregs, was due to widespread corruption, in the state. For this reason, in 2012, African Union suspended Mali's membership.

The violence against the UN soldiers also seems a norm. UN Security Council extended MINUSMA's mandate for a year, in June 2018. However, in January 2019, a local al-Qaeda affiliate, the Group for Support of Islam, and Muslims (JNIM) claimed a series of attacks, on UN peacekeepers. The capital, Bamaka, also has been targeted, by extremist groups, many times. The group was declared a terrorist organisation, in 2018, by the US State Department.

Some Malians, according to a 2018 US Congressional research paper, at a point in time, wanted the government, to initiate a dialogue with jihadists, but the government and Western donors have rejected the idea. A study of the 2018 US Holocaust Memorial has reflected that if the overlapping violence consisting of jihadists, security forces, and communal self-defence groups does not end, mass atrocities could occur.

Currently, Mali is not a vibrant democracy, and not economically stable, as it used to be, between 1996 to 2011. Its President, Ibrahim Keita won a second term, in August 2015, but only with election irregularities, and low voter turnout, much lower than his win, in 2013. Its economy is mostly confined to the area, irrigated by the Niger River.

In June 2015, the government failed to sign a peace agreement, with the Coordination of the Azawad Movement, and a coalition of Tuareg rebel groups. In the peace agreement, an autonomy proposal was drafted, with some political representation in the north, aiming for the development, and integration of rebel groups, into the Malian Armed Forces. However, all these measures remain unfulfilled, until now.

6 April, 2018

8

A BLOOD SMEARED EASTER

IN POST-WAR SRI LANKA, when two hundred fifty civilians, including forty-two foreign nationals, were killed, in a single day on 21 April 2019 across hotels and churches, in a string of coordinated attacks, it reminded the world of a predatory civil war, which rattled the country, in the past.

The hospitals had struggled, to cope, with a high number of casualties, as suicide bombers, wearing backpacks, caught on CCTV, blew themselves up.

Gory pictures, in the press, appeared, showing debris, spread from ceilings, walls, and burst water pipes, on roads. There were screams, of helplessness around, as survivors got paralysed, with shock. Sometime later, the army was seen looking, for explosives, in the earth, as pallbearers, handling wooden coffins, with mourners around them, were making a way, for mass burials.

The episode received worldwide condemnations, but the world also had scrambled, for answers: Tamil Tigers, the dreaded group, responsible for over one hundred and thirty suicide blasts, in Sri Lanka, had never targeted, the minority Christian communities, before. It was a group that revolutionised the art of suicide bombings, on the Buddhist-dominated, war-torn island. They wore cyanide capsules, under their necks, in the event, of being captured. Even if anyone had whims, about their role, in the multiple bombings, as an initial reaction, they were wrong.

It was only, now, post-Christchurch Mosque rampage, that Sri Lankan officials blamed the Islamic State, for this major attack, on Catholic Christians, on the island, after *Amaq*, the press portal of ISIS, claimed responsibility, for the attack. Perhaps, the ousting of the Islamic State, from Syria, may have been another reason.

During the war, in Syria, ISIS attracted many youths, from neighbouring Maldives, and developed strong transport, and commercial links, with neighbouring Sri Lanka, from where it had recruited, some volunteers. In 2016, the Sri Lankan government was aware that thirty-two Sri Lankan Muslims, had joined ISIS, and about the spread of global jihadist ideologies, in Sri Lanka.

ISIS, quite lately, have used the centre-periphery model for their activities. The caliphate, that it ran, in Syria and Iraq, was the centre, and the rest of the world, was its periphery, where it recruited *mujahideens*, that could carry out attacks.

As the centre came under a sporadic attack lately, it shifted its focus, to the periphery – from the Orlando nightclub to Holey Artisan Bakery, in Dhaka. However, the ideological apparatus will remain intact, and it will continue to inspire more recruits, in the future.

One might ask, why Sri Lanka, this time? It is likely that this blood-smeared Easter attack, was an embodiment, of a soft target approach, where the perpetrators had identified security lapses, in advance. The carnage produced, in the end, vouches upon this fact.

As per Reuters, Indian intelligence had warned the country, about a possible attack, but it seems, a negligent approach was taken. Although, in January 2019, Sri Lankan police seized a haul of high explosives, hidden, in the northwest part of the country, in a wildlife sanctuary.

According to experts, international extremist organisations often find lucrative recruitment grounds, in places, where there is already significant local sectarian tension. Global ideologies thus become powerful tools, and spread quickly, in such fractured environments, as specific community grievances are then expressed, in violent ways. In other words, almost all violent attacks, in the world, will most likely be carried out, by local men, inspired by global ideologies.

Sri Lankan officials believe that all perpetrators were local nationals. Almost nine of them were responsible, for this deadly attack. Some of them came from wealthy business backgrounds, were Western educated, and had degrees, from places, such as Australia.

Investigators have said that National Thowheed Jamaat, involved in the vandalism of Buddhist statues, and Jamathei Millathu Ibraheem, might have been subcontracted, by the Islamic State, for the whole operation.

In a Guardian Op-ed, investigative journalist Jason Burke wrote: 'no one with any knowledge of how extremist ideologies evolve would have expected that its complex mix of conspiratorial politics, radical theology, sectarianism, and apocalyptic prediction would have lost all power to convince overnight. The bombings in Sri Lanka are bloody evidence of this.'

Sri Lankan Muslims, ten per cent of the total population,

have the highest concentration, in its Eastern Province. The province comprises districts, namely Trincomalee, Batticaloa, and Ampara. Batticaloa, is where Zahran Hashim, a preacher turned militant, the alleged mastermind of the Easter attack, hailed from.

Despite condemning the attack, on Christians, the Muslim community, in Sri Lanka, find themselves on the side of the perpetrators, in post-war Sri Lanka.

Historically, Muslims and Christians have largely lived in peace, in the region. Multiculturalism had been a way of life. During Ramadhan, Muslim families often shared their treats, with Christian children, in the neighbourhood, including porridge, made of beef stock. The elder Christian generation also has a nostalgia for co-existence.

Sri Lankan Muslims are mostly Tamil speaking but identify themselves, as a separate ethnic group, distinct from Hindu Tamils, and Christian Tamils. The three-decade of civil wars, not only created rising hostilities, between Sinhalese, and Tamils but also among different ethnic Tamils. Muslims are keener, to prefer a religious identity, over a cultural identity.

Living in cramped homes, they were engaged, in agriculture, fisheries, and weaving, in the past, but now are mostly tradesmen.

Despite being bound by a common language, Tamil-Muslim relations, in Sri Lanka, have not been peaceful. The Hindu Tamils, and LTTE sympathisers, have seen Muslims, in Sri Lanka, as collaborators of state agencies.

The 1990 mosque massacre, in Kattankudy, and Eravur, where LTTE gunned down, more than one hundred fifty

Muslims, offering prayers, have left imprints, of antipathy. Post reactions, against this ghastly act, have appeared, in the form of posters, in Batticaloa, tied to trunks of trees, walls of churches, or gates of mosques. However, the nearby church, in Batticaloa, was cordoned off, where names of victims, had been written, on a banner. The scene was reminiscent of a horror episode, in this scenic coastal town, of lush paddy fields, and enchanting lagoons.

Politicians, in the island country, have been accused, of favouring their communities. Many commentators, and common people, believe that the recent bombings are a reaction, to these political prejudices. Muslim politicians hold key ministerial portfolios, in Sri Lanka, and it had annoyed the Tamil party, in the opposition. The government, in Sri Lanka, were quick to ban radical Islamic organisations but did not show a similar ruse, towards Buddhist organisations, notorious for inciting violence. Hence, the manoeuvres, of vote bank politics, have added a new wave, of insecurities.

At the present moment, Sri Lanka fears a $1.5 billion foreign exchange loss, with a drop of thirty per cent in tourist arrivals.

Sirisena's government had been looking for one hundred forty people, with links, to ISIS. Heavy security was witnessed on the streets, as there were warnings, of further attacks.

The president had asked the people, in possession, of camouflaged military uniforms, to hand them, to the nearest police station.

Revealing his short, and long-term measures, to bring normalcy, President Sirisena, would establish a list of permanent residents, of every house, so that no unknown person could live anywhere.

5 May, 2019

9

KASHMIR'S STRUGGLING PEACE

THE TROUBLED VALLEY OF KASHMIR, is a place, where seasons of peace, do not last long. After the death of more than a hundred thousand people, it has been declared a war zone, which has boiling points, as they have precipitated, out of its historic phases of insurgency. It is also a valley of mass protests, arising out of conditions, that are ripe for anarchy, and revolution-seeking movements. That is why, it is a problem that remains on people's lips, for quite some time, repetitively.

Quite lately, everything turned volatile, since the killing of Burhan Wani, in 2016. The anarchic protests, and the mass blinding that happened on the streets, with pellet guns, mainly used against wild animals, had been widely condemned, by nations, activists, writers, politicians, and common people, all over the world. The practice of maiming youth, and injuring the human body, with small metal spheres, was intended to resent any form of challenge, posed against the statist narrative.

The anatomy of a pellet gun, is such, that it causes serious damage to vital organs, of the human body. This practice of mass blinding was not previously heard, from this part of the world, and the heinous crime went against the UN charter that largely gives impunity to protesters, in a conflict zone.

The renewed political struggle, led by the new generation

of Kashmiris, had come, in the shape of Burhan Wani, who managed to galvanise the mass sentiment, and make his death, a reason to bring the local establishment, to its knees. His death resulted like a spark that leads to a volcanic eruption, but at the same time, it also gave a rise to repression, reflecting that Kashmir's aspirations were at odds, with people, who held the keys to political power.

With time, Kashmiris also saw the death of his associates, slowly, but in a calculated manner, involving a lot of military strategy, and police coordination. Wani's killing resulted in more graves, as he continued to inspire educated, religion-loving youth, some even young boys, willing to die for their ideals.

Youth, in black-clad and military uniforms, with their AK 47s, routinely appeared with audio tapes, mostly giving sermons, warnings, discussing strategies, and giving threatening remarks, against the Indian state, and its machinery, led by police, the army, and their collaborators.

Due to tipped collaborators, who recruited themselves, or were forced into intelligence operations, through coercion, information about the whereabouts of militants, was passed, and there was a flurry of killings, in the valley. There were myriad encounters, mainly in the countryside, but, the reactions, from militant outfits, came instantly.

Militants started kidnapping policemen and interrogating them so that their superiors could restrict their operations, especially against their households, or relatives. Dead bodies were often found, in the jungles, and homes of random neighbourhoods, including of ordinary women, believed to have collaborated against militants. The women, in Kashmir, are also believed to be couriers of militants. There have been cases, when the local police have seized up to twenty grenades, and three sixty-five bullets, from nabbed couriers, reflecting a new development.

Political workers, of leading political parties, associating themselves with the Indian democratic setup, had been either killed or attacked, many of which had resulted in failed operations. JKPDP's Youth President Waheed Rahman Para had claimed that he had escaped unhurt, when he was supposedly attacked, near central Budgam.

There were also cases, where local policemen were killed, in calculated attacks, near police stations. In the Achabal area, of south Kashmir, *Lashkar-e-Toiba* claimed responsibility for the killing of six policemen, involved in the killing of their commander, Junaid Matto. In recent times, a BJP youth member had his throat slit by militants, and the picture of his dead body, in the rich apple orchards of Shopian, created waves on Kashmir's social media. It signified that independence-seeking people, including radical organisations, were not only fighting against Indian democracy, or its politicians, but it was also a war of a Kashmiri, against a Kashmiri. It reminded the days of the counter-insurgency operations and the attacks against them by militants in the past.

Incidents, such as the Pulwama suicide bomb attack, proved to the world, that the art of *al-Qaeda*-styled *Fidayeen* attacks had a space in Kashmir, as well.

Lonely militants, such as Zakir Musa, who survived on biscuits, associated themselves, with the Islamic State, and even saw a breach of trust, from secessionist organisations, such as All Parties Hurriyat Conference. This violent upbringing that escalated the situation had hurt the social, cultural, and spiritual ethos of the valley, but with time, people had to move on, perhaps, waiting for something optimistic to happen, so that sense and resolution would prevail.

As a post-reaction, there had been many instances recorded, about the common people, often blood relatives or near relatives complaining of police brutality against them, that included night raids, and intensive grilling about the aims of militants, who had suddenly run away, from their homes.

South Kashmir has made the highest tallies of the dead, if we compare the overall conflict scenario, in the valley, in recent memory. For its dwellers, every day was a struggle to endure, both psychological, and physical. Thousands participated in funerals, post killings of these militants. Some militants were even brave enough to deliver public speeches, and raise their guns, high in the sky, amidst processions, and were not afraid to be photographed, been recorded in videos, and broadcasted on YouTube, by mobile phones.

The cries of wailing mothers, orphans, and widows, eventually became tantamount, to the conflict's repercussions. The massive protests, in south Kashmir, and the regular attendance, of thousands, at the funerals of militants, carried away by many numbers of pallbearers, made people question about Indian government's narrative, brimming on its TV channels.

Turmoil is almost synonymous, with protests, and strikes, in Kashmir. While Indian media, continued to demonise most Kashmiris, as enthusiasts of terrorism, the world looked at the conditions of this warzone, differently. Differently, because the valley, and the Jammu and Kashmir state at large, continues to be a nuclear flashpoint, and a cause of disagreement, in places such as the Organisation of Islamic Countries. The conflict became a major theme for researchers, leading human rights organisations, and the United Nations office.

However, for some Indians, the conflict also becomes a reason for indicting harassment, of common Kashmiris, trolls on social media, and other forms of unbridled hate. Quite recently, Gautam Gambhir, an Indian cricketer and BJP politician, publicly endorsed the genocide of common Kashmiris. He was the latest individual to join the tally of many Indian journalists, who turned their corporate media offices, into warmongering machines, for influencing TRPs, and nationalist whims, among the Indian masses.

After the killing of JKLF founder, Maqbool Bhatt, known among his followers, as the 'father of the community,' in the early eighties, the destiny of this war-torn valley changed drastically. Yasir Arafat's statement, about the repercussions of his hanging, became almost prophetic, as Kashmir slipped into a place of insurgency, uprisings, killings, kidnappings, and political vendetta.

This period of prolonged suffocation, of political promises, and betrayals, also became apparent, through vested, and self-serving actions of the Jammu and Kashmir Peoples Democratic Party.

Historically, it had been a political party, largely highlighting *Jammat e Islami* propaganda, even using their political slogan, of a pen and an inkpot. At a point in time, it claimed to act, as a referee, between separatist organisations, and New Delhi. In the past, it tried to mobilise the sentiment of a sustained, bilateral resolution, through Indian democratic institutions. At one point in time, Omar Abdullah, leader of Kashmir's oldest political party, Jammu and Kashmir National Conference accused JKPDP, of outright secessionism.

The result, for JKPDP, in the last state election, was not only an improvement, in electoral seats, but also a chance to fulfil the promises, it had given to Kashmiris, and the people of J&K, at large, mainly after JKNC's era of deep-seated corruption, wanton slaughter, police brutality through SOG, making pro-government gunmen culture through *Ikhwan* and *Muslim Mujahideens*, and repressing the rights of people. Yes, it was JKNC, and Omar Abdullah, who brought the pellet gun culture, to Kashmir, but it did not stop Mehbooba Mufti, in her deliberate double talk, who went ahead, in mind blogging proportions, by justifying the killing of protestors, by the security forces, at one of the press conferences, alongside India's home minister, Rajnath Singh. This was something unexpected, considering the party claimed to have caught the public imagination, for sympathising with militants, secessionists, and resolution seekers, since its inception.

She passed this questionable comment, despite visiting the homes of militants, condoling their families, and even praying at the gravesites of militants, during election campaigns, in her past. Quite recently, she joined the protestors, carrying the casket of an HM militant, Fayaz Ahmad Shah, near Bijbehara, PDP's bastion, in the past, and shedding her crocodile tears.

Despite apologising for her remarks, the political alliance with BJP, designed by Mufti Syed and Narendra Modi, had received flak inside the valley. It was dubbed as an 'unholy alliance,' and a relationship of 'strange bedfellows,' from day one.

Murtaza Shibli, in an Op-ed, for Kashmir Reader,

wrote: 'ever since its existence and more so after it assumed power in the second term, the PDP operated like a ruthless mafia gang; it carried its politics and the governmental work through a certain clandestine order that was connected via blood-links, or caste allegiances.

'Most of the inner ring of the party was either related to each other, or consisted of the *mullahs*, the traditional clergy class who, in the past, would threaten the gullible masses, with their faux command over religion, and its dishonest interpretation. In the new avatar, they would intimidate people with arrests, incarceration, and attacks through the police and other paramilitary forces. In the process, the JKPDP destroyed the Kashmir police's image and that of India's supposed commitment for peace in the region.'

He further wrote: 'Mufti's profile as a political proxy and an opportunistic chancer was impressive, but like any self-seeker, while he was sought after for his intrigues and evil plots, he had no constituency of his own; his real influence was situated within the power corridors of intrigue and not the public. He had been in politics for more than four decades and made quite a name for himself, both locally and nationally, yet he had no place that he could call his own where he could safely contest an election.'

Kashmir, also, had seen a phase of brutal crackdowns, during JKPDP's political command. It had locked Kashmir's most important mosque, *Jamia Masjid*, led by Mirwaiz Umar Farooq, for months. Islamic festivities were barred, and the spirit of the public was abused. It was something dastardly because JKPDP had started to betray the institutions, that it had claimed to represent, thereby undermining the public anger, which it eventually deserved.

The fall of JKPDP has also given JKPC, and its leader, Sajad Ghani Lone, an ex-Hurriyat man, a reason, to entice his voter base, who are looking for a third option, in the Indian democratic setup, in Jammu and Kashmir. One of Jammu and Kashmir Peoples Conference's popular leaders, Imran Reza Ansari, an ex-PDP politician, charged Mehbooba Mufti, of being severely incompetent, and transforming the party, into a family fiefdom, much like its arch-rivals, Jammu and Kashmir National Conference, in the past.

The JKPDP-BJP alliance suffered its biggest blow, in its mutual paranoias, when the killing of an eminent journalist, Shujaat Bukhari, editor of Rising Kashmir, was shot brutally, in his SUV, by unknown gunmen, just outside his office, during the Islamic month of *Ramadhan*. BJP, its quarrelsome alliance partner, claimed to have lost patience, some days after, and it told the press that it had a stronger reason to leave, due to precarious circumstances, that came after Shujaat's killing. No organisation has claimed responsibility for his assault, until now.

For separatists, of the APHC, however, nothing has changed, and the tally of the dead has become a source of their inspiration, as they still cling to their basic demand, without any concessions. However, the void for bridging perceptions, and making settlements, is still there.

In other words, it also means that Kashmir still struggles with its resolution and peace.

30 June, 2019

PART II

ELECTIONS

10

PUTIN'S OLIGARCHY

Putin's oligarchy continues to hold RUSSIA, as he has now won a fourth election term in March 2018.

There have been accusations of election rigging and forced voting, but somehow, there is very less opposition to these matters. As a precaution, he has already ordered twelve thousand police personnel to surround the cities to curb any protests.

American President, Donald Trump congratulated Putin, on his election win, just like Obama did, in 2012. This felicitation angered former Presidential candidate, John McCain, and he reprimanded Trump, as John McCain believed that it was a 'sham election win' for Putin, in the 2018 Russian election.

According to an independent election-monitoring group, *Golos*, voting papers, found in some ballot boxes, were opened. Many election observers were barred, from entering the polling stations. Some of the CCTV, at the polling booths, was covered with balloons, and it had obstructed the voting count sessions.

For a while, Russian politics has been synonymous with Vladimir Putin. He will likely remain in office, for a total of twenty-five years – a record, only kept by Joseph Stalin.

In all these years, Putin has left no stone unturned, in

increasing the military budget, mainly to gain advantages, in the conflicts, in eastern Ukraine, Chechnya, Georgia, and Syria. Although, he wants to increase the quality of Russian life.

There are various provocations, done by the Russian state, lately, which include the recent usage of nerve agents, in the United Kingdom, the expulsion of foreign diplomats, from Moscow, and the manufacturing of a new ICBM, that is believed to have the potential to strike anywhere, on the north, and south pole.

In terms of Russian military life, dissenting journalists, such as the late Anna Politkovskaya believed that serving in the Russian army is like 'living a life of a slave', in a prison. According to her writings, most of the army men give their services, at the imposing behest of the authority.

Russian politics also has made its society notorious for being a graveyard of dissenting journalists, who try to defy the government narrative. It had happened with Anna Politkovskaya, who wrote memoirs on the Chechen war, a brave journalist silenced for speaking the truth.

She had once claimed that she was poisoned on a flight to Ossetia. Three years later, after her death, her killers were all acquitted by the government: Sergej Chadzikurbanox, ex-officer with the Ministry of Internal Affairs, three Chechen brothers, Dzabrail, Ibragim Machmudov and Rustam, and Colonel Pavel Ryaguzov of the Security Forces. She was someone, who was respected, by both sides, indulging in the war.

Another journalist, Paul Klebnikov, Russian editor of *Forbes* magazine, who was known for writing against oligarchs and Russian capitalism had been murdered, in

Moscow, possibly by some hired assassin. Vladisk Listyev, a Russian TV anchor, was shot near the stairs of his apartment building as well. A Russian businessman, Boris Berezovsky had been accused of his murder, although the court believed otherwise.

In Putin's Russia: Life in a Failing Democracy (2004), the late Anna Politkovskaya wrote: 'Voting day is bureaucratic and authoritarian. The return of Soviet times during Putin's time in office is obvious. Half of the Russians support him and half do not. He has many backers who have vested interests. He does not want to debate anything with anyone and disdains any campaigning against him. He behaves exactly like Lenin's *Cheka*, or secret police, much like his KGP days. Many common Russians do not support him because they do not want the world to know that Russians are authoritarian, with a one-party system, and that Russian society is not plural.'

In this process of global domination, and the history of recent controversies, towing behind the country, Putin has faced significant pushback, on a global scale, due to his recent role, in the Syrian war. At one point in time, political commentators believed that Russian political bureaucracy interfered, in the last US presidential election. Many believe, Donald Trump, to be the most pro-Russian US president, to date.

In the past, Putin has been accused, of playing witty political games, such as, in February 2004, when he reshuffled the cabinet, just a month, before the election. His critics believed that it had further paralysed the government, riddled with corruption.

This whole scene occupied the TV channels, and it gave them some stimulus, for the presidential campaigns, later. Political commentators had called it a 'game settled for scoring political points,' and accused him of being a 'tyrant,' and a 'despot.'

Going back to the 2018 Russian election, Putin had to deal with two rivals this time around – Ksenia Sobchak, daughter of Putin's political mentor, belonging to the Civic Initiative party, and the Communist leader, Pavel Grudinin.

However, it is important to note that the main opposition leader, Alexei Navalny, had been barred from running for the election, because of corruption charges. The head of the Russian election commission believed that there were no serious violations, though.

The turnout, in the 2018 election, had been higher than the last election. The levels of poverty seem to be significantly lower, than before, despite Russia being an economic middle power. The wage had significantly grown at ten per cent, on average, despite many economic sanctions.

It is believed that a new modern culture emerged, during Putin's time, in Russia. Common Russians seem to be obsessed with cars, and high-end furniture. The car sales in Russia stand at par with Eastern European countries, such as Poland and Hungary. Russians are in love with the IKEA furniture brand. There has been tremendous growth in IKEA retail outlets – from one outlet in Moscow, in 2000, to around fourteen outlets, in 2018. There has been a popular rise in champagne culture as well. Many might shove away these things, as pro-Putin propaganda, but these things might be true.

Interestingly, this had been a unique Russian election. Despite opposition calling for a boycott, the election campaigns, it had several promotions, which were planned to mainly entice the voters, which included several selfie contests, iPhone giveaways, and even cars, as hefty prizes.

30 March, 2018

11

ITALY'S FRACTURED DEMOCRACY

IT HAS BEEN AN EVENTUAL ELECTION in Italy in March 2018. A hung parliament means that cutting deals, to form a coalition government, has become pivotal, to end the political stalemate.

However, on March 4, 2018 a month has passed, but still, there have been a series of failed negotiations, between the centre-right political parties.

The Five Star Movement – M5S has emerged as the single largest party, having a populist message, whereas the League has gained 'historic strides' in the vote share, in this election.

After the Italian election, many things have become clearer. The election reflects that many Italians favour a Eurosceptic, and strongly nationalist political base, now. Like the Brits and the Greeks, the Italians do not have positive opinions of the European Union, anymore. This is a stark difference between them, and the Germans, and the French now, who loathe, the benefits, of staying in the Eurozone.

Historically, Italy has been Europhile, with eighty per cent of people, intending to stay, in the Eurozone, but the times seem to have changed. This political mindset now shows that Italians are drifting. The result has ushered a new era, in Italian politics, which the regional political commentators call 'The Third Republic.'

Economists cite prevailing flaws, in the European common currency, and there is a dire need, for addressing the problems of the monetary system. Maybe, these reasons also reflect the fall of leftist coalition parties, in Italy, part of the previous government.

A dramatic loss of the Democratic Party, led by Matteo Renzi, has turned heads, in this election. As usual, the Italians have been demanding a stronger economy, greater job prospects, and an end to social crimes, and corruption.

The Italian economy has been in tatters, just like neighbouring Greece, which has been trying to survive on economic bailouts. In terms of fiscal competitiveness, Renzi could not do much.

The Italian youth have made the highest figures, for the unemployed. Maybe, it is due to these reasons of economic instability that has diverted the vote share, of the Italian Left.

If we look at the political career of Renzi, he had been looked at as one of the promising young political leaders, in Europe, who had emerged from the Mediterranean.

When he put forward a constitutional referendum, in 2016, aimed to reform the composition, and powers of the senate, many Italians voted against it. Its impact on Renzi was such that he resigned, as Italian prime minister, in the next ninety minutes. It put the country, into a caretaker government, until the present election.

Renzi's intention, by putting forward a constitutional

referendum, was to change the balance of power, between the central government, and the regions. He wanted to make the senate smaller, but more powerful, indirectly elected, from the regional, and municipal councils. He also favoured abolishment of the consulting organ, National Economic and Labour Council, which was an entity of Italy's corporatist past. But, due to an unpromising circumstance, the higher voter turnout did not help Renzi, in the referendum, as around fifty-nine per cent of Italians rejected the referendum.

Maybe, a change in leadership is what the Italians wanted, and it had put immense hopes, in the next election.

According to Foreign Policy Op-ed writer, Luigi Zingales: 'there is some potential in Italy's untested and young populist political leaders. If they play their cards right, they can transform the EU.'

Voting for centre-right political parties also reflects that Italians do not prefer illegal immigration, in their country. It is a collective mentality that Italians share, along with the Austrians, and the Hungarians. An increase in illegal immigration, through its vulnerable seashores, in the south, has kept the social fabric in disarray.

Not only because there has been a rise of attacks, against immigrants, but, also because there has been a significant increase, in the functions of security, and intelligence apparatus, especially against Muslims, who they believe are prone to radicalisation.

There is also a rise of fascist ideas, in Italy. Parties, such as Brothers of Italy, claim to be descendants of the Fascist Party, which is banned by the Italian Constitution, whereas party members of *Casa Pound*, including its leader Simone di Stefano, have reportedly engaged in direct action, through 'beach patrols,' where they have often harassed, and attacked immigrants, working as vendors, as well as non-Italians, peddling on the public beaches.

Economically, European Central Bank intervened in the Italian case, much later, and it also reflected their incompetence.

Also, if Italy, somehow, leaves the European Union, much of the money, inside the Italian banks will flow out. That is what the Italians do not need right now. It is because, during a Euro exit, Italians would need liquidity assistance.

The largest political party, Five Star Movement (M5S), led by 31-year-old Luigi di Maio, neither calls itself a populist party, nor a Eurosceptic party. The party has gained public support, due to the frustration, it threw against its political opponents, and promises of better welfare measures.

To make a 'government contract,' with the League, M5S leaders must make certain compromises with League's ally - Berlusconi's *Forza Italia*, who they regard as a 'corrupt, old politician.'

Salvini also has some plans, to absorb *Forza Italia* voters, in his party, and backing them down, will not be an effective game plan. Until now, any form of an alliance has been elusive.

The far-right League made significant strides, in this election for many reasons. After being accused of being xenophobic racism, and propagating secessionist ideas of 'Padanian Nationalism,' it's rising leader Matteo Salvini, dropped 'northern', from the party name, because he intended to fight elections, in the south. Salvini himself ran for an election, from the southern province of Italy, in Calabria.

April 21, 2018

12

MAHATHIR'S MOMENTOUS WIN

IN THE 2018 MALAYSIAN NATIONAL ELECTION, something historic happened. It seemed, that Malaysians wanted a change, and they wanted it badly.

The new Prime Minister, Muhammad Mahathir, will become the world's oldest leader, as he is a ninety-two-year-old nonagenarian, leading the *Pakatan Harapan,* 'Alliance of Hope.'

Mahathir, once, had been leaving prime minister Najib Razak's mentor.

After the election result, the world of Najib Razak, fell apart, in the decisive number game.

After the result, he simply went into tears, as he was unable to form the government. The government of his political party was perhaps the only government, Malaysians had ever known.

People were seen numbered in hundreds, on the streets, where they watched live televised election results.

Since 2008, the opposition managed to win state elections, and controlled two wealthiest states, but they never won a national election. In this election, the opposition changed its destiny.

The persistent democratisation of Najib Razak had suddenly turned 'authoritarian' and 'corrupt'.

Najib felled this emotional impact, simply because, for years, he was made to believe, by his supporters that there was only him, who they could look up to. The 'Barisan National' (BN), led by the 'United Malays National Organisation' (UNMO) had lost at both representative places, the federal and state levels.

Often seen playing golf, with American Presidents, and enjoying a warm relationship, with his Chinese counterparts, he finally had to bid goodbye, to his decade-old rule. His party often received financial incentives, from oil-rich oligarchs, and other social quarters, of rich businessmen.

But, this time around, Najib and the BN movement leaders blamed the Chinese, for provoking political interventions, and called the election as *'tsunami Cina'*.

At the same time, China is Malaysia's largest investor, with investments, in East Coast Railway Links Project, and other infrastructure development projects, such as Forest City, in Johor, a special economic zone, as big, as Hong Kong city.

In perceptions of Mahathir, he does not find Johor based Forest City project beneficial, for the country. He calls these projects deliberately putting their country's land for sale.

Mahathir even thinks that the investors will not share the losses if the project fails economically. His policy on foreign investments, especially those coming from China, would be a thing to watch for, perhaps due to his leftist stance. All these new economic policies, coming up, might give some fluctuations in the economy.

Regional commentators, in Malaysia, believe that holding the election, in mid-week, did not help Barisan National supporters, as most of the working-class voters, did not have time, to go to the polling booths, during office hours.

There is this sudden change of perception, among the Malaysians, who mostly were ruled, by a hybrid of Malay nationalism, economic liberalism, and conservatism.

In the past, common Malaysians used the term *'Malaysia Boleh'* or *'Malaysia Can'*, as a national slogan, that reflected their pride, where their country was bestowed with a 'developed' status.

After economic problems started developing, common Malaysians, as discontentment, from the grassroots level, used the same terms, to mock their political leaders.

This form of government, unflinching towards their ethnic nationalism, due to strategic political alliances, had been there for six decades, since the colonial British left the Malaysian peninsula. It reflected that Malays have an ugly record, for voting on racial lines.

Muhammad Mahathir pledged support from his protégé, Anwar Ibrahim, who had been jailed for quite a while. To topple Najib, both joined hands and ended their disagreements.

This political coalition, it seemed, came at the right time because nearly all Malaysians have been irate, with their public expenditure policies, the rising cost of living, and

Najib's 2015 multibillion-dollar bribery scandal, where $700 million, of the fund, went into his account.

Mahathir has promised to review foreign investment policies, and to undue certain taxes, on services, and goods. It seems that he is adamant, to act against the policies, of the previous regime, which includes reviewing the bribery scandal and bringing the funds back, into the country.

He has even promised reforms, related to human rights, freedom of religion, and belief. It is, perhaps because, for three decades, there has been a crackdown on cartoonists, journalists, and politicians.

Malaysia has been ranked as one of the most corrupt nations, in the world. In this process of reform, civic organisations are not behind either. 'Global Bersih,' an organisation of Malaysian expats, from the United States, UK, Europe, and Australia regularly protest, and call for the international government, to intervene, in their country's problems.

However, apart from Mahathir's promise of a 'multi-ethnic' nation, his plan for introducing fuel subsidies needs a careful evaluation, because it might affect the fiscal competitiveness, of the Malaysian economy. His policies, including putting an end to goods, and services tax, would be credit negative, for the Malaysian economy rating.

If we investigate the success factor of Najib Razak's regime, his vote bank had been mainly consisting of ethnic Malays, who benefited from certain government contracts, subsidised housing, and university admission guarantees.

What worked for Mahathir, had been the urban vote,

and political alliances, with ethnic Chinese and Indian communities, who have always rejected a 'second-class status', inside Malaysia.

16 May, 2018

13

IRAQIS BACK TO BALLOT BOXES

THE MAY 12, 2018 PARLIAMENTARY ELECTION in Iraq was described by Western media as a 'landmark victory of democracy' after years of instability and sectarian violence. It was the first national vote since the defeat of the Islamic State in Mosul in 2017, and the government sealed airports and land borders during polling for security reasons, according to Associated Press and Reuters. The election was contested across Iraq's fragmented political landscape, with Sunni, Shiite and Kurdish blocs vying for influence.

The Sunni vote, traditionally concentrated among parties such as The Arab Project, Mutahidoon (United Project) and the Wataniya alliance, had diminished compared to earlier elections. Analysts noted that Sunni parties no longer commanded the numbers they once did, reflecting demographic shifts and political disillusionment, as Al Jazeera and Middle East Eye reported. Meanwhile, the Nasr alliance led by Haidar al-Abadi, who had overseen the campaign against Islamic State, sought to retain power. Hadi al-Amiri's al-Fatah bloc, backed by militias with close ties to Iran, also contested strongly.

In total, alliances competed for 329 federal seats in parliament. Yet the surprise outcome was the victory of the Sairoon Alliance, led by cleric Muqtada al-Sadr, which secured the largest share of votes. Iraq's electoral commission confirmed that Sairoon won 54 seats, followed by al-Fatah with 48 and Abadi's Nasr alliance with 42, as reported by BBC and Financial Times. This result meant that Iraqis had not delivered a clear-cut mandate, leaving coalition negotiations inevitable.

Traditionally, the Iraqi prime minister must be acceptable to both the United States and Iran, reflecting the country's geopolitical balancing act. Sadr's rise was therefore striking. He had long criticised Iraqi politicians as 'pawns of Ayatollahs' and positioned himself against Iranian influence, which made his victory a shock for Tehran. In response, Iran dispatched Quds Force commander Qasim Soleimani to mobilise pro-Iranian sentiment in Iraqi constituencies before the election, but his efforts failed to prevent Sadr's bloc from emerging first, according to Reuters and Foreign Policy.

For Washington, Sadr's success was paradoxical. Once a fierce opponent of US forces, he now represented a potential partner in stabilising Iraq. The New York Times observed that Sadr's nationalist slogan 'Iraq First' resonated with the poor and working class, while his meetings with Saudi Crown Prince Mohammed bin Salman signalled a willingness to engage with regional powers beyond Iran. Sadr also hinted at alliances with Haidar al-Abadi, the British-educated former prime minister who had cultivated ties with Tehran, suggesting that Abadi still had cards to play in coalition negotiations.

Government formation required 165 seats, but negotiations were complicated by allegations of fraud. Around 176 politicians accused the electoral commission of 'bribery' and 'voter intimidation', with Human Rights Watch and Middle East Eye documenting irregularities. Some called for a re-election, but as political analyst Mustafa Saadoum explained, 'the only solution available for political blocs is to pass a law in parliament cancelling the elections before the constitutional end of their term on June 30. The government can also appeal the parliament's decision to the Federal Supreme Court of Iraq.'

Sadr's support base came largely from Iraq's poor. His past as a militia leader was notorious: black-clad death squads under his command roamed Baghdad during the sectarian conflict, cleansing Sunni neighbourhoods and attacking US forces, often with weapons supplied from Tehran, according to Washington Post and International Crisis Group. Fear dominated daily life in Baghdad during those years. Yet in 2008, Sadr disbanded his militia and redirected his followers into social and political activities. He now presented himself as a reformist, drafting his manifesto with secular intellectuals and promising to fight corruption.

This transformation was significant. Once a firebrand cleric, Sadr now embraced populism. Al-Monitor noted that he called for abolishing Iraq's ethnic and sectarian quota system, advocating instead for institutions built on 'qualification and integrity' and staffed by technocrats. His supporters had stormed Baghdad's Green Zone two years earlier to protest corruption, demonstrating his ability to mobilise mass movements. Though he did not run personally in the election and would not become prime minister, he was positioned as kingmaker in the new government.

The broader context remained volatile. Militias with independent chains of command continued to operate, believing that lawlessness could help them combat remnants of Islamic State. At the time, around 7,000 American troops were stationed in Iraq, though Pentagon figures acknowledged 5,200, mainly in advisory roles, according to CNN and New York Times. Iraq's recent history had been scarred by the rise of Islamic State, which captured Mosul in 2014 after abandoned US military equipment and $500 million from Mosul's Central Bank fell into its hands. The Iraqi army collapsed in the north, and IS fighters advanced along the Tigris Valley until Mosul was recaptured years later, as BBC and Washington Post reported.

Against this backdrop, the Sairoon Alliance represented a coalition of working-class Shiites, Sunni businessmen, liberals, communists, social democrats and even anarchists. Their shared aim was to lift Iraq out of economic crisis and confront chronic unemployment and poverty. Analysts from The Economist and Financial Times argued that nationalism was rising while sectarianism was losing ground, though the fragile coalition likely to emerge would rest on minimum conditions and remain vulnerable to instability.

Violence from Islamic State, economic stagnation and corruption were the core issues that Sadr's alliance promised to address. His populist appeal lay in pledges to reform governance, empower technocrats and reduce foreign interference. Yet the paradox remained: a former militia leader who once fought US troops now sought to associate with American-led coalitions, while simultaneously resisting Iranian influence.

The May 2018 election thus encapsulated Iraq's contradictions. It was hailed as a democratic milestone, yet marred by allegations of fraud. It produced a nationalist surge, yet left coalition politics fragile. It elevated a populist cleric with a violent past, yet offered hope of reform.

As The Guardian concluded, Sadr's victory was 'a shock to

Iran, a surprise to the United States, and a reminder that Iraq's politics remain unpredictable.'

May 25, 2018

14

LEBANON'S LONG-AWAITED ELECTION

LEBANON HELD ITS FIRST ELECTION, in nine years in 2018. Apart from native voters, Lebanese expats, living in six Arab states, put forward their votes, in this important election, which eventually paved the way, for sustained democracy, inside the Levant.

The West-backed Saad Hariri is all set to become the prime minister, yet again, although he has been weakened, in numbers. Many commentators blame this, on the waning support, from Saudi Arabia, and his decreasing wealth.

His Future Movement (FM) has largely a Sunni voter base. It was the biggest bloc, during the 2005 and 2009 elections. But there have been accusations of voter fraud.

The electoral commission recorded around seven thousand violations on voting day. Although, there had been a wider participation, of women, in this election, and a broad civil society consensus, that challenged the traditional elites.

The political space, in Lebanon, remains diverse and vibrant: Aounists, a Maronite party, also known as Free Patriotic Movement (FPM), have an alliance with Hezbollah. A Druze-dominated Progressive Socialist Party had been in the news lately, when they shifted their loyalties, from the Assad regime to the Syrian opposition. *Tashnag*, also known as Armenian Revolutionary Federation, claims to champion the cause of the Armenian Lebanese community. Lastly, the Amal Movement works for the cause of repressed and marginalised Shiite communities, living in remote areas, and to resist the Zionist aggression, of Israel.

Christian democracy also has its own space, in the country. The Kataeb party, Marada Movement, National Liberal Party, and the Lebanese Front, consisting of Arabist Christian militias, backed by the Palestinian Liberation Organisation, are significant proponents of Maronite-Lebanese nationalism.

In history, much of the Lebanese political machinery has been instituted out of the Taif Agreement, in 1989. After the infamous assassination of Rafiq Hariri in 2005, a kind of grassroots movement emerged, in the country. It was called the 'Cedar Revolution' because the people demanded an end to the military rule, that existed in the country for around twenty-nine years.

According to the writer, Zeina al Helou: 'the emergence of underground university associations of the youth inside and outside the mainstream political parties was the main reason that instigated the 2005 Cedar Revolution. They call themselves *'Beirut Madinati'* (Arabic: Beirut is my city), and aligned themselves with largely anarchist ideas, and service-based community networking.

As the result, they secured thousands of votes in the municipal election held, in 2016, although never tasted electoral success. Although, it signified the power of outsider status, and messaging outside the mainstream political spheres.'

It was the 2015 Rubbish Crises that channelled the voice of youth, with slogans such as 'YouStink!' and 'We Want Accountability'. This form of activism made worldwide headlines because of the inefficiency of the government.

After the closure of the landfill site, in Naameh, Beirut's main landfill site, there were massive protests. But the authorities closed the landfill site because it outran its capacity. The government then opened two new landfills, but it did not help the city dwellers, as waste had been scattered around every city corner.

During 2016 and 2017, some of the waste made its way into Lebanon's rivers and beaches. This prevailing problem will remain in the core agenda of the government.

The demand for electricity usage has also skyrocketed, as much of the related infrastructure was destroyed during the civil war (between 1975 to 1990), and due to several attacks, by Israel. For this reason, residents are forced to use power generators, run by several private companies, who are alleged to run 'a mafia of sorts'.

In Beirut, political belief in neighbouring Syria, which is still a grave war zone, carries much importance. The differing belief has divided the loyalties, into the pro-Syrian camp, mainly consisting of Iran-backed Hezbollah, and the anti-Syrian camp, which consists of Saudi-backed Hariri loyalists.

The refugee problem is pouring frustrations, from the common Lebanese people, as they blame the bad infrastructure, and economic woes, due to their arrival from war-torn Syrian, and Palestinian territories. The 2018 election was conducted under a newly introduced electoral law, which gave proportional representation and reduced the voting districts.

The election also saw the induction of *'sawt tafdil.'* It is a process in which each voter will cast two votes: one for their favourite candidate, and one for a list of candidates. Several commentators have expressed shock and bewilderment, at this new law. They accuse the lawmakers of introducing more complexity, in the voting process.

Currently, Lebanon faces several challenges, in its economy. The economy seems to be in tatters. It is one of the most heavily indebted countries in the world, with public debt at one hundred fifty per cent of the total GDP.

It is for this reason, Saad Hariri travelled to Paris, for an investment summit, where he pledged around $16 billion, in loans and grants, aiming to channel them, into crucial economic sectors, of Lebanon.

Hezbollah, sitting in the opposition, criticised this move and wanted Hariri to discuss this issue, in the parliament, as the public debt had reached highly alarming levels. Nevertheless, Hezbollah has improved, after winning a considerable number of seats. It means that Saad Hariri, and his ministers, will have to deal with a stronger opposition, especially when Hezbollah enjoys support, from the Christian-dominated political parties. It might give a reason for new regional tensions, and will also keep Israel on its feet.

In the past, during the Rome II Conference, Lebanon received millions of dollars, as a pledge. In an upcoming meeting, in Brussels, the issue of one million Syrian refugees will be discussed. Ever since the war in Syria has escalated, the budget deficit has increased, despite assurances of stability.

Then, it seemed that Lebanon needed heavy foreign investments. As the economy is crippling, the investment requirement continues to date, to boost the infrastructure, and quality of life.

28 May, 2018

15

OBRADOR WINS MEXICAN PRESIDENCY

THE CAMPAIGN OF THE 2018 MEXICAN PRESIDENTIAL ELECTION, in Mexico, was the bloodiest, its people have seen in decades. It is because one hundred thirty individuals have been killed, in recent times, during the campaigns.

At the same time, it had been the largest election, in Mexico's history, with about three thousand four hundred posts, up for grabs. Voting had been done, in over three thousand districts.

A grey-haired, baseball buff, Lopez Obrador won around fifty-three per cent, of the total vote. The Associated Press called it a 'landslide win.' The press wanted sensationalism, at his win, but mixed reactions have come.

Some regional analysts call him a 'populist' and 'autocrat,' who does not understand the complexity of Mexican politics, with its different economic, and political approaches, in the last thirty years. Others fear that he might eventually turn around, as the next Hugo Chavez, a protectionist, and a supporter of nationalisation.

On the other hand, Venezuelan President, Nicolas Maduro, calls Obrador's win a triumph of leftism, in Latin America, and has encouraged renewed diplomatic relations, with the country.

The regime change is mainly viewed, by people, as a stern reaction, to the country's infamous corruption crimes. He berated his party rivals, known as PRI, and PAN, for running a 'mafia of power.'

Obrador's party supporters, the MORENA, are sure enough to believe that he will make Mexico an equitable society, by investing, in infrastructure, and education. If the budget permits, the new government has plans to give $126 USD, as monthly scholarships, to university students, and school children. Also, he has vowed not to raise any form of tax, on the citizens, and will continue reviewing oil deals.

In terms of social crime, in 2017 alone, there were around twenty-nine thousand deaths, in the country. The figures reflect how notorious Mexico has become, for a high murder rate. As drug cartels offer a quick buck, many young people have been lured, into cartel operations.

The wrath of corruption, still looms, over many institutions. To access public services, around fifty per cent, of Mexicans, must pay a bribe. In a place, called Veracruz, the governor had been charged with making fake medicines.

Nicknamed 'Amlo', Obrador unsuccessfully contested, two times before. But he capitalised on his agenda, the third time around. Some call him 'Mexico's Trump', while others likened him, to British Labour Party leader, Jeremy Corbyn.

However, his views, on tackling the cartel war are controversial. He wants to give amnesty, to the proponents of the drug war. He claims to even extend his amnesty, to the kingpins, as reported by the BBC. That seems to be his solution, for the cartel war.

There are three cartel groups, intending to control supply routes, between the United States, and South America, namely Gulf Cartel, Los Zetas Cartel, and Sinaloa Cartel. While as Sinaloa Cartel is known for its high-level connections, and control of regions, in Mexico, that produce marijuana and opium, the other two Cartels are known for their brutality, past alliances, and eventual hostilities.

The turf war, since 2006, has killed around fifty thousand people. As per FBI data, the drug trade is estimated at around $29 billion, a year. The killings include torture, beheadings, and mutilation.

While Obrador seeks to establish friendlier relations, with US President Donald Trump, who congratulated him through Twitter, he, at the same time, calls Trump's strategy, of separating migrant families, at the border, 'racist and inhuman.'

It may seem hypocritical because the president elect, himself, wishes to start his border force, to stop undocumented migrants, coming from central America, into Mexico, who are then mostly enroute to the US. The new force will try to ease social crime. Mexican south still, is a porous border, vulnerable to refugees. But, it seems, everybody has a positive opinion, about trade between Mexico, and the US.

The trade between Mexico and the US totalled around $557 billion, in 2017, the highest in years. Mexico sends around eighty per cent of its exports, to the US. Therefore, redrafting the NAFTA agreement will be vital for Obrador.

With the economists and policymakers, he needs to analyse the fault lines, with the US trade.

At the same time, Obrador also has a chance to make Mexican companies, more competitive globally, by doing business, with emerging Asian markets. It speaks of the significance of the region – around eighty per cent of trade, in South America, is duty-free. These nations have signed around thirty-three agreements, with each other.

Mexicans want him to be similar, to the outgoing President Enrique Pena Nieto, in terms of regional diplomatic initiatives. His successor, irrespective of his political reputation, started the Lima group, an initiative for democratic reforms, in Venezuela. The other diplomatic effort has been the Pacific Alliance, which allows free trade between Colombia, Peru, Mexico, and Chile.

Ever since the 2010 Haiti earthquake, many Haitian refugees, in Tijuana, are living in shantytowns, made up of camps. As per ABC news, there are around three thousand of them, in Tijuana alone. For months, people have been sleeping on the floor of a church. It reflects the dismay, and uncertainty, of many people.

According to Al Jazeera, 'Nearly half of the electorate is under 40 years old. Pollsters say the youth has little faith in the government, and believe it is riddled with corruption, but their vote is pivotal. They are overwhelmingly urban, online, and more educated than their parents.'

10 July, 2018

16

IMRAN KHAN'S UNEASY CROWN

IMRAN KHAN, THE CRICKETER, WHO WON the 1992 World Cup, for Pakistan, has surprised a few, after becoming the new prime minister of Pakistan in the 2018 election.

For the ardent followers of Imran Khan, in Pakistan, and, in the diaspora, this might be the happiest day, of their lives. It is because he has come a long way, from being one of the finest all-around players, in Pakistan's cricketing history, to Pakistan's 22nd prime minister.

Imran Khan's historic win happened because Pakistanis were brimming for a change. He, in many ways, was an embodiment of a change, in the minds of many Pakistanis, with his strong, strategic, catch-all politics.

By believing that corruption is a national malaise, his cause, it seems, was helped, by the common Pakistanis. Before the election, there was a threat of around ten suicide attacks, but a transition, in the electoral process, happened smoothly. If Imran Khan sticks around for five years, to implement his political plans, he might be the first political leader, in the history of the country, to do so.

During the 2018 election, he made quite a few promises to the public, through his slogan, 'Naya Pakistan' (New Pakistan), which includes an end to corrupt institutions, bringing back wealth to Pakistan, improving tax collections, a national water policy, reforms in health and education, a billion-tree planting programme, introduction of an 'Islamic welfare state', around ten million new jobs, and five million new homes.

Imran Khan claims to have seen Pakistan, in its highs and lows, and dreams of a Pakistan, as imagined by Muhammad Ali Jinnah, and Allama Iqbal.

In terms of foreign policy, Imran Khan vows to keep good relations, with Afghanistan, a stance that earned him a quick congratulatory call, from Prime Minister Ashraf Ghani. With India, as relations have been fragile, he has made promises to improve trade relations and believes Kashmir, to be the country's biggest bone of contention. Narendra Modi also called him, after the election win. This has been a very optimistic development, after India's claimed surgical strikes, inside Pakistan's occupied Kashmir.

His tenure will be a daunting task, as Pakistan's two eminent political parties will be reviewing his actions, from the opposition. They have already made accusations of election rigging, and blame the army, for instigating the election result, in Imran's favour. He needs to be at the centre to pacify relations, between the civilian government, and the military.

Imran Khan has been around, in politics, for a while. His political career has been full of perseverance, considering the time he has spent in politics. His party, *Pakistan Tehreek-e-Insaf,* (Movement of Justice), which he found, in 1996, did not even win a single seat, in the 1997 election. During the 2002 election, he got nicknamed '*Taliban Khan*', for leading protests US drone strikes, in Pakistan. With time, he became a harsh critic of Musharaf, Zardari and Sharif. It made him a populist, in the public, claiming to represent the people, from the grassroots.

According to him, resistance from the Pashtun Taliban is happening, because they are fighting for the protection of their land, from outside forces, in Afghanistan. He boycotted the 2008 election, due to allegations of election rigging, by tearing his nomination papers apart, in public. In the last-to-last general election, he became the leader of the third-largest political party.

After the Panama Paper investigation, that indicted Nawaz Sharif, for embezzlement charges, he spectated the exit of the former prime minister, his biggest political rival, before the election. It paved the way for his brother, Shahbaz Sharif, a three-time chief minister of Punjab, to lead the rival party.

By calling supporters of Sharif, 'donkeys,' he received intense criticism, from the Election Commission, for the usage of inappropriate language. During the investigation, he often made unwarranted political attempts, which included a threat to lockdown Islamabad. In the past, Imran, and his party members, also had confrontations, with the police, during protests.

After coming to power, there are rumours that Imran Khan will be seeking a $12 billion bailout plan, from the IMF, the country's biggest to date, after discussions with the finance minister, in September 2018. However, the United States has demanded that the cash should not be used to repay Chinese loans that are used to fund major infrastructure, in the country, a blame that Pakistan has refused.

Currently, Pakistan needs about $3 billion to repay

the IMF, to avoid defaulting on loans, in the next few months. There is a balance of deficit crises in Pakistan, the Pakistani rupee has devalued, soaring inflation. There is also an acute electricity shortage, and a looming water shortage, that can likely come in 2025, with less than 500 cubic meters available, per person.

In recent times, Pakistan has been named in the list of countries, deemed, non-compliant (from 2012-2015), by the Financial Action Task Force (FATF). By being added to the list again, it will become very hard for foreign investors, and companies to do business, in Pakistan. President Trump, recently suspended about $2 billion in aid, over the country's alleged ties with Islamic militants.

Pakistan, at this moment in time, needs a leader, who is honest and accountable, to improve their image in the global scenario. Imran Khan might fit this role. His primary task, after assuming office, will most likely be making immediate reforms to the economy and ending red tape, and bureaucratic inertia.

19 August, 2018

17

BUHARI'S RESURGENCE IN NIGERIA

THE 2019 NIGERIAN ELECTION WAS UNIQUE in many ways. It was the costliest election to date in Africa, with costs going up to 242 billion *naira*. Around ninety-one political parties contested polls and 84 million visited the polling booths.

These figures themselves reflect the hope that democratic values give to the common Nigerians, as the country reemerged from military rule in 1999, after General Sani Abacha, died in 1998. Since then, Nigerians longed for a civilian to lead them. Due to a young and educated workforce, and rich oil reserves, they have high ambitions to transform the country, all along, despite greed, tribalism and corruption harming the public's collective interests. The country still faces rising conflicts in land use, and in generating oil revenues in the Delta.

Despite these growing problems, the 2019 Nigerian election, in a way, embodied the thought of change. It was also the country's biggest-ever election, even though the voter turnout has been declining since 2003. The voter turnout has been down from 44% in 2015 to 35% in 2019.

During this election, there were some important things to ponder upon, such as voting irregularities, logistical delays, and pre-election violence, which resulted in the killing of at least 58 Nigerians.

Some analysts even questioned the overall democratic credibility of the election, as the military was seen stealing election material, and harassing INEC officials, and UN and civil society observers, mostly in the state of Rivers. There were reports of cancelled ballots that affected around three million votes, signifying brazen misconduct and major electoral offences. However, the officials of the Nigerian army insisted that there were fair in doing their duties, and were betrayed by the local commission.

Tensions ran high between incumbent President Buhari and his main rival, Atiku Abu Bakr. Several electoral booths were destroyed that included electronic smart cards. As elections were delayed for a week, the stocks plummeted, and it affected the country's investors on a large scale. Election delays have been common in Africa. These delays reflect poor organisation skills. It not only caused frustration to the common people but also paranoias about politicians, who seemingly used these delays in their favour.

In the past, several national elections did not happen on time that included elections in Congo that happened two years after.

In Kenya, Kenyatta's win put the country into crisis. Voting, in general, is often a tiring process, where people wait in long queues for hours, and it makes the process not only a hassle, but it also disinterests several prospective voters.

In this tumultuous time, economic shocks were also apparent. Analysts at Vetiva Capital commented: 'the economic consequences of this decision will be felt significantly, as what was supposed to be a smooth process is now mired in lengthened uncertainty and controversy, shaking investor confidence and eroding the renewed interest from both foreign and domestic investors.'

The election also proved Buhari's resurgence, as he has a strong voter base in the north, where people call him the 'man of the people.' The voter turnout in the north was high, despite the presence of the Islamist militant group, *Boko Haram*. On the contrary, the turnout in the south was very low, where his rival, Abu Bakr had hoped for a significant increase in voter share.

Buhari secured 56 per cent of the total vote, and his rival finished at 46 per cent. The winning margin was 3.9 million votes, as per inputs by the officials.

However, many Christian dwellers in the south complain that Buhari is prejudiced towards them and that he favours Muslim support. Both politicians belong to the Fulani ethnic group that has dominated Nigerian politics since the 1960s. They believe that both leading parties, namely the All-Progressive Congress (APC) and Peoples Democratic Party, descended from the military regime of General Ibrahim Babangida, are mainly focused on winning elections, and increasing their voter base, often by spurious means. They are also mute on dissenting concerns from several activists, who vow to climate change and urbanisation.

As per reports by The Economist, politicians from both leading political parties were culpable for vote buying. In Lagos, some common people saw party workers handing cash to prospective voters. In Yola, a politician gave several sachets of spices to the wife of a prominent journalist.

Some locals believed that they needed to vote for Buhari, despite not being satisfied with his first term, because they saw a more corrupt politician in Abu Bakr.

Many Christian dwellers in the south complain that Buhari is prejudiced towards them, and favours Muslim support. Both politicians belong to the Fulani ethnic group, that has dominated Nigerian politics since the 1960s.

The Situation Room, an umbrella organisation of Nigerian civil society groups, said: 'the vote marked a step back from the 2015 general election and actions should be taken to identify what has gone wrong and what can be corrected.'

Poverty remains the most serious problem, among other problems. The economy is very slow in recovery since the 2016 recession. In the industrial hub of Kano, entrepreneurs complain of manufacturing only 10% of the total output, due to prevailing problems.

In 2018, Nigeria overtook India in terms of people living under the poverty line. In the state of Borno, Islamic insurgency is running high. Nigeria is also running short of doctors. There are only 40 thousand doctors for a population of 170 million people.

In a Guardian Op-ed, Chigozie Obioma, wrote: 'For me, the underlying problem is the lack of a coherent national value system. Currently, it is a mix of various tribal traditions and Western values cast within a Western framework, leading to a unique political system that is not democracy but one that can best be described as mitigated chaos. Since chaos breeds monsters and monstrosities, the value system has continued to degenerate, despite Nigerians wanting badly for it to improve (many voted for Buhari in 2015 in the hope that he would tackle corruption). But it is now an epidemic, with distrust infecting every sector of Nigerian society.'

21 March, 2019

18

SCHISMS OF THE EUROPEAN PARLIAMENT

IN 2019, VOTERS HAVE CHOSEN a fractured European parliament. The mandate is reflecting polarisation.

The result will trigger a flux, and more uncertain future in Europe, as Greens, populist and nationalist forces have gained ground, while centre-right and centre-left political parties are losing ground.

Despite Greens and Populists, being opposites, in their political perspectives, and actions, they still have something in common: fighting for a sustainable society. While populists are seen as opposing the elites, the Greens, popular among the urbanised middle class, are seen as sort of ecological liberals, wanting climate protection.

Going by the statistics, Eurosceptic parties have increased their share, to twenty-five per cent, which is a twenty per cent gain, since the 2019 election. The rise of populism, in countries, such as Hungary, Italy, and Poland, may trigger a referendum, in the institution itself, and open border theory, or the Schengen principle, will be questioned, in the coming years, provided, if, populist and nationalist forces, do well, again.

According to populist parties, the refugee problem is not history, and they think the crises are not monitored well, at the borders. The European Commission, now, has not yet deployed ten thousand additional Frontex officials, as a preventive action.

The European Parliament is an elected institution, with seven hundred fifty-one seats, within the twenty-eight-nation European Union. In this election, the turnout was more than fifty per cent, the highest, since 1994. The turnout has not dropped, since European elections began, in 1979.

Ralph Sina, Brussels correspondent and bureau chief for Germany's public broadcaster WDR/NDR, commented: 'This European election was decided by two questions: the refugee issue and the climate issue.'

According to Martin Selmayr, secretary general of the European Commission, the results are a 'wake-up call.' He said: 'If Donald Trump and Vladimir Putin don't engage in this European Project, the region will lose a lot.' He also went on to comment that although populist candidates, like Matteo Salvini of Italy, and Marine Le Pen, of France, went on to present a united front, their populist wave was contained, in the end. Conversely, populist parties have done well in southern Europe, but, not in northern Europe.

The election verdict stands as a litmus test, for their popularity, and they will continue, to push harder, on issues, such as controlling immigration, and the budget. They will also demand more power, for individual nations, rather than the bureaucracy, which they consider as 'elitist.'

This agenda may pose, a serious challenge, to the traditionalist, pro-Europeans. In the past, the far-right political parties were just tainted, for playing petty politics, and people simply did not want them, to govern them. They were not considered serious policymakers, but now, they are becoming a permanent feature of European politics.

As per Bulgarian analyst, Ivan Krastev: 'Of the five individual political parties with the biggest representation in the new European parliament, four are anti-European Union.'

The populist parties, that have done well, in this European Election, may have a common ideology, but they also differ on issues, such as the European budget, and Russia's role, within the EU. Steven Erlanger and Megan Specia, in a New York Times Op-ed, wrote: 'these disjointed policies, and the strong egos, involved, will make it harder, for those (populist) parties to forge effective alliances.'

In the European elections, countries, such as Britain, had voted on one issue: Brexit. It had remained a pivotal agenda, in this European election. It had divided and united numerous political politics. However, Nigel Farage's Brexit Party went on to take thirty-one per cent of the vote. This is something phenomenal because it is a political party that did not exist, four months ago.

In the European parliament, Brexit Party has more seats, more than Matteo Salvini's Lega Nord. However, Brexit Party currently holds no seats, in the regional parliament. The rival Liberal Democrats, with the slogan 'Bollocks to Brexit', scored just eighteen per cent of the vote. The Conservatives and Labour party, have had their worst European election, in a decade, with a vote share, of around eight per cent, and fourteen per cent, respectively. Nigel Farage, told the BBC: 'the vote was a reflection of the real sense of frustration out there.' He also told BBC Radio 4: 'If we don't leave on October 31, then we can expect to see the Brexit party's success continue into the next general election.'

SNP's surge, in the European election, might have major implications, for a second Scottish independence referendum. It also wants to stop Brexit. However, they have also become anti-Westminster lately, as they believe, the parliament is ignoring the wishes, of the Scots.

At present, there is a constitutional divide, between the Unionists and the Nationalists, and whether Scotland should become independent.

The Green Party, on the other hand, did very well in Nordic countries, as issues of climate change, and the anger of young people, at existing policies, seemed to help their vote. In Germany, it scored more than twenty per cent of the vote.

In Germany, centre-left Social Democrats, suffered their worst defeat, in decades, finding their alternative, in the Greens.

Christian Democratic Union, led by Angel Merkel, and her heir apparent, Annegret Kramp-Karrenbauer, had a weak electoral performance.

The present situation might soon expel Merkel, and the EU will lose an important political figure. There will be more hinders on crucial matters, including Euro, policy on China, and migration. Importantly, her party cannot claim now that Germans owe a lot to European reunification, and the cessation of wars. Both SDU and CDU, in the past, have been accused of taking over issues, of the Greens, through cutting coal, switching off nuclear power plants, transforming the energy sector, into a planned economy, and re-organisation of the automotive industry, name a few. This might have worked against their interests, in this election.

German historian Ronald G. Asch has commented that a highly fragmented European parliament will lead to more conflict, between EU member states. He also believes that German voters would regret voting, for the Greens one day, because radical climate policies, would lead to the collapse of German industrial sectors, that underpin German's economic machinery.

As per Soeren Kern, of the Gate Stone Institute, this election reflects a generational shift, and ideological clashes will continue, to dominate this institution. She commented: 'in the current time, there are two mega issues: the fight against climate change championed by the pro-EU globalists; and the opposition to mass migration and multiculturalism led by the anti-EU national populists.'

Collective European interests are on the losing side, it seems. Euro currency, now, is seen as something, which has not made a major coherence, within the countries. They are very few political parties left now that talk about European interests. The potential left-right conflict will make it difficult, to neutralise national interests.

In history, there were central political parties, in developing class and economic structures, of the ninetieth and twentieth centuries. But now, they seem to lose their relevance. Political cultures have changed. In times such as today, European voters are motivated by new issues — such as climate change, identity, and migration.

In the future, the EU will try to move forward with a

slogan: 'More Europe Now,' and try to shift more powers, to Brussels.

14 June, 2019

19

LESSONS FROM SPANISH ELECTION

THE STAGE FOR THE REVIVAL OF SOCIALISM, in Europe, seems set, as Spain's socialists, *Partido Socialista Obrero Espanol*, have gained power in April 2019.

As Spain's socialist parties have won more than 32.8 per cent of the vote, it may be the biggest vote, for the socialists, in the region, apart from the Portuguese socialists.

A government deal, is in the offing, after an inconclusive result, lingering around for a month106, or so.

After a delay, Spain's King Felipe VI tasked the elect, Pedro Sanchez, with forming a new government. His party had won one hundred twenty-three seats, out of three hundred fifty seats. The formation, of the government, will be a hard exercise, as a divisive mandate, and its reconciliation, among various political parties, will be an arduous task, in the weeks to come.

As a coalition government will most likely rule Spain, it is natural, a certain disillusionment, of Spaniards, will remain there. It is because the coalition governments, in general, are often loathed, for time-consuming decision-making, on important public matters, often prioritising regional interests, over national interests, to name a few. Neighbouring Italy, some time back, too, had voted for a regime change, but no political party had got a clear mandate, like in the Spanish general election, despite

Italians, voting for an emerging right-wing, anti-globalisation, influx.

This election has given *Partido Popular* its biggest blow, since 2014. In a Guardian article, AFP reported in Madrid, that despite all horse-trading manoeuvres, Sanchez, now, might become the new prime minister. The conservative *Partido Popular*, centre-right *Ciudadanos* (Citizens), and far-right *Vox*, have decided to stay, in the opposition.

What is working in favour of Sanchez, and his party, *Partido Socialista Obrero Espanol,* in the government formation process, is that a leftwing coalition, *Unidas Podemos*, with forty-two seats, will most likely express support, to Sanchez.

Leader of *Unidas Podemos,* Pablo Iglesias, will emerge as a kingmaker, and he knows Sanchez needs his support, especially from regions, where Sanchez's party has not done well. This scenario will also give him a chance to play his cards right, as he might pressure Sanchez, to put forward his agenda, including outmanoeuvring him, for some regionalist demands.

Madrid, for a while, has seen itself, as the voice for a pro-EU, having a left-leaning agenda. During 2008-09, Spain also felt the economic crises, and it saw the worst of austerity drives. However, at the time of Mariano Rajoy, leading the country, Catalan aspirations for independence, had reached an all-time high, and his tenure, also brought Spain, new economic woes. Perhaps, these forlorn circumstances, led to the downfall of *Partido Popular*, amongst the common Spaniards.

Catalan independence has been irking nationalist-oriented, Spaniard politicians, because of the ripples, that now have spread abroad. Ada Colau, mayor of Barcelona, is not a secessionist, but does favour a referendum, for independence. Quite lately, she was blamed for the city's many ills, from high rents, rising street crime, and street-less vendors, who have snowballed. Despite this, she got an endorsed open letter, signed by important world activists, like Noam Chomsky, Naomi Klein, New York mayor Bill de Blasio, and the economist Thomas Piketty, urging electorates, to vote for her, for the mayoralty of Barcelona, one of the most important cities in Europe.

In a Guardian article, Sam Jones and Stephen Burgen, wrote: 'for Catalan secessionists, Barcelona is both the weak link and the big prize. With about two-thirds of the population made up of either recent immigrants or people of non-Catalan Spanish ancestry, support for independence is lukewarm.'

Years before the financial crisis, the government of Jose Rodriguez Zapatero, gave a green signal, to pro-EU policies. It was a reason that Spaniards occupied the top Brussels positions, which included portfolios, such as overseeing the EU's economic policy, and foreign policy. Sanchez, after coming to power, will also try to yield his influence, in the European Union.

Sanchez's plans include advocating for a common budget, for Eurozone members, an EU-wide unemployment fund, and climate measures, such as a bloc-wide green tax, on imports, of fossils-derived electricity. He also wants a European Investment Stabilisation Fund, and more efforts to stabilise the EU's banking union, including boosting European Banking Resolution Fund. Some government sources have even said that Madrid also wants an EU fiscal union, and a European deposit insurance scheme.

There is also a chance, that all these reforms might propel some opposition, from conservative politicians, sitting in Berlin.

After the win, Sanchez went on the comment that Spain, in the future, will no more play into the hands of ring-wing politics. The emergence of *Vox,* a far-right party, had been against Catalan aspirations, from day one. Winning around twenty-four seats, they had an agenda, to ban pro-independence political parties, in Catalonia, and attacked the Spanish feminist movement, describing the move as 'politically correct.' The party has vowed to construct an 'unbreachable wall,' to keep all forms of illegal migrants, out of Spain's North African territories, of Ceuta and Melilla.

As Spain also won a high ballot vote, in the recently concluded European election, their performance in the ballots, might also propel their ambitions to target top EU jobs, in Brussels. Spanish socialists won around twenty seats, in the European parliament. At a press conference, Sanchez has even gone on to declare that he will the 'chief negotiator' for the 'social democratic family.'

It seems Madrid will most likely aim for the EU's top foreign policy job, and for a vice presidency, at the European Commission. Even Catalan separatist leaders won two seats, in the European Parliament, but the bigger question will remain, whether they could become EU lawmakers, soon.

12 June, 2019

20

NARENDRA MODI'S UPSURGE IN INDIA

NARENDRA MODI'S WALLOPPING WIN in the 2019 Indian elections, is something, the country had not seen, since Indira Gandhi's win, in 1971.

It also meant that the rival party, Indian National Congress, struggling to gain power, for ten years now, had no easy solutions, for their problems.

Modi's critics, who questioned many of his policies, and enmity against supposed minority supremacy, despite his assurances, of an inclusive, and economically stable India, cannot deny, that his win, for the prime minister's seat, is a rarity. It also shows a disturbing rise of far-right politics in India.

Before the final election verdict, Modi headed to a hermit cave, at the foot of the Himalayan glacier. He insisted cameramen snap him, at the famous Kedarnath Temple, in deep meditation, cloaked in a saffron shawl, almost like a *Sadhu*, or a *Sanyasi*.

After a resounding win, it may be perceived that Indians, who voted in this election, had no other alternative in mind. In other words, it means that the popularity of Congress, from a 'grand old party', had stooped so low, that many journalists, during Modi's election win jubilation started believing that the thought of the Indian National Congress, perceived, as a successful national party, with its appealing centrist, pro-poor, minority encompassing, and secularist credentials, would soon be in tatters.

This time around, in the elections, Congress did not even have the luxury, to cross a hundred seats. Rahul Gandhi, the second time around, failed miserably, for a distinctive, egalitarian platform. Does it also mean that Rahul Gandhi, recognised as a charismatic youth leader, in many quarters of India, did not have the mantle, to perform better, after recognising the failures, of the past? As of now, almost everyone, in Congress, is shifting the blame on Rahul Gandhi, who wanted to alleviate poverty, and initiate several reforms, in an angry, divided, and ambitious India. He lost the Amethi seat, his political backyard, to BJP's Smriti Irani.

According to an Op-ed by Zoya Hasan, in The Hindu, the win for Modi, in this election, was due to two factors, namely 'Hindutva consolidation' and 'majoritarian triumphalism'. It was not based on any commitment to economic development. The party had also fielded candidates, such as Pragya Thakur, indicted on terror charges, giving rise to new controversies. The New York Times had called Modi 'dangerously incompetent' and 'a divisive figure,' ushering in an era of dark politics, and that the voters had chosen 'a prolonged nightmare.' The British newspaper, Guardian, went further, in its criticism, as it believed that despite Modi being a charismatic campaigner, he had deployed 'terrible false claims,' and 'partisan facts,' and that the election result was bad, for multi-party democracy, in India, because BJP does lip service to reduce the 'yawning inequalities that disfigure India.'

Before the election, several thousand farmers had rallied against his policies, and failed assurances. Despite many political watchers, hailing Modi, for making India, the fastest-growing economy, in the world, the reality remains that the GDP did not cross double figures, in comparison with Manmohan Singh's tenure. In Singh's UPA tenure, the economy had once edged past ten per cent. If we take a realistic view, UPA-II scored better in eleven out of fifteen indicators in comparison with the NDA. Although, in Modi's time, FDI doubled, and global ranking for ease of doing business was also slightly up. Even if one favours Modi's tenure, for economic growth, as per average GDP growth, the fact remains that the Indian economy is just growing 0.6% faster, in comparison, to Manmohan Singh's tenure, as per the data, reflected by Business Today.

Political analysts, who favoured Modi's timeliness, and strategy, of cultural nationalism, social conservatism, and right-wing politics, believed that he had, somehow, remained thoroughly existent, in the minds of common Indians, as a *chaiwala*, or a *chowkidar*. The latter believers won, while the former lost. As he will be an incumbent prime minister, the celebrations, and sorrows, will start now.

It is also not surprising that during a 2017 poll, it was revealed that Indians have the greatest desire for autocratic rule.

Today, BJP, is the largest party in India, maybe the largest political party, in the world, in terms of membership. Its success today is palpable, in lieu of its founding fathers, and thinkers. In states, such as West Bengal, called the 'red fortress,' due to the dominance of Communism, the vote share of the BJP, had soared, up to forty per cent. It had also made significant inroads, in Odisha, and the northeast. In summary, BJP won more than fifty per cent of votes, in sixteen states, its best performance, since its inception. In this election, BJP had a ten per cent increase, in its vote share, despite the anti-incumbency element. During power, BJP managed to have control over several leading media corporates and did not have a shortage of various resources. All opinion polls, favoured the BJP, while an opinion poll, compiled by India Today, had been up to the mark.

As per audit reports and income tax reports, submitted to the Electoral Commission of India, BJP was the biggest beneficiary of electoral bonds, gaining almost ninety-five per cent, of the share, worth around two hundred twenty-two crores. The whole process had alarmed the regional parties, and other parties, including the Congress, in the opposition.

According to an article published in The Hindu, written by Shiv Visvanathan, leftism, and liberalism, in India, are distant dreams. Modi, according to him, won, due to his appeal, to urban, middle-class populations, that he managed to 'Hinduise.' This identification became the reason for BJP's empowerment, a political party, which believes India should not be called backward, or a third world. Whether one agrees, or not agrees to this thought, Modi had remained instrumental, by staying relevant, for the anxieties, and aspirations, of most Hindu voters. Some people also started believing that Modi's words were populist because they went beyond social and caste divisions, despite numerous episodes of lynching against Muslims, during his rule, and the party displaying a pompous show, that Muslims came from a generation of outsiders, and thus, were deemed, to be treated, as second class citizens.

According to Ajay Gudavarthy, in an article, published in The Wire: 'this victory is not merely about the organisational structure, and electoral calculations – this victory is more moral than political. It is more about psychological warfare than about social transformation,

The BJP managed to expose the tenuous link between social policy and electoral choices, and sold social policy in terms that actively spoke to the beneficiary's state of mind.'

As of now, Indian Muslims, after Modi's win, think that they are on a losing end, and have been disowned, by the country's new political developments. In the 16th Lok Sabha election, Muslim representation had dipped to its lowest, so far, at twenty-two seats. Indian Muslims, had their highest vote share, back in 1980, when the community had gained around forty-nine seats.

20 June, 2019

PART III

PROTESTS

21

PAKHTUN SPRING

IT HAS BEEN A WHILE since Pakhtuns have been lamenting about discriminatory policies by Punjabi-dominated politicians in Pakistan.

It seems a kind of grassroots movement has been emerging because Punjabi-dominated Pakistani politics is accusing the community of being terrorist sympathisers. But the Pakhtuns are fed up with the war and want a better world for themselves.

The area of Pakhtuns is known by other Pakistanis, as 'Illaqa e Ghair,' or 'no man's land,' in English. Believing Pakistani ISI as a troublemaker in the region, Pakhtuns think that the nationalist leaders are willing to keep the political chaos relentless in Afghanistan, just because they could keep the American dollars flowing into Pakistan.

'Free Karachi Campaign' spokesperson Nadeem Nusrat believes that ISI is mobilising Taliban as counterinsurgents (renegades), to subdue the aspirations in the region. According to PTM itself, there is the good and bad Taliban existing in Pakistan. The good ones are supposed to be closer to the establishment.

As many 'bad' Taliban militias have been killed, by the Pakistani army, the events have internally displaced thousands of Pakhtuns, to major cities in Pakistan. These displaced Pakhtuns mostly come from remote villages in the tribal belt.

Since February 2018, the reasons for protests are clear, as much as they can be. Locals are having resentment against the repressive system, freedom of speech and widespread corruption. That is why PTM is propagating a truth and reconciliation commission for all extrajudicial killings that happened in the Pakhtun belt.

There had been a ten-day sit-in protest regarding seeded landmines, that often kill civilians and children, removal of security checkpoints and a plea to release several individuals from detention by the security agencies.

The so-called 'Pakhtun Spring' started in 2015, when a human rights activist named Manzoor Pashteen, a man claiming to have seen all the cruel realities of war, along with 25 comrades from the tribal areas, launched first protests regarding planted landmines in their region.

When Arab Spring started, Pashteen founded the Mehsud Tahafuz Movement, in 2013, to secure the rights of the tribesmen. His party had been formulating to make a list of enforced disappearances.

PTM was formed in Dera Ismail Khan as an initiative for removing landmines from Waziristan and other parts of the former Federally Administered Tribal Areas, affected by the war in North-West Pakistan. It initially began as a justice movement for Naqeebullah Mehsud, who was extrajudicially killed in a fake encounter. Initially trying to fight for the rights of the Mahsud tribe, PTM eventually started propagating for rights for the whole Pakhtun tribe.

The displacement of many Pakhtuns, however, has also resulted in a blessing in disguise, as they now have greater access to healthcare, education, jobs, and other amenities in Pakistani metropolitans.

However, the influence of al-Qaeda and Pakistani Taliban in FATA areas piqued the Pakhtuns to the point of sustained political change through activism. They want an end to the political disorder.

Under Frontier Crimes Regulation (FCR), an agency that comes under the federal government, and traces its origin to colonial times, they can arrest many people in the family and a clan, along with an alleged convict, committing a social crime.

Swat region, in recent times, has seen Islamic puritanism at its absolute worst, when a hardline Taliban preacher, Mullah Fazlullah, raised his army and started giving sermons on the radio. He beat his fellow associates ruthlessly and beheaded them and challenged the Pakistani federal government at the same time.

When on February 18, 2018 Swat civilians organised a rally in Islamabad, a media blackout happened. The police filed cases of sedition and accused them of terrorism, although the rally had been peaceful.

Some days later, another protest happened in a place known as Bajaur, where the Pakistani military had conducted many operations against the Taliban, since 2007 onwards. The Pakistani media did not cover this event and censored it.

The Urdu media, specifically, has been very biased against the Pakhtun population. They are ridiculed in local soap operas, humour-based shows, and morning shows. The stigmatisation is a routine occurrence on Pakistani TV channels and newspapers. Also, massive stage shows and rallies of PTM are largely ignored by mainstream media channels, leaving social media the only tool to disseminate their issues with the rest of Pakistan. That is why many Pashtuns feel that they are strangers in their own country.

Dawn Oped writer, Ghulam Qadir Khan, believes Britishers, in their past, feared two things – the Russian invasion and the second was Paktun rebellion. The Britishers always had a cold relationship with the tribals, in one way or the other. They stereotyped them as savages and illiterates. Thousands of Paktuns are still under surveillance and get killed in fake encounters.

According to a PTM member, out of 4000 missing Paktuns, only 239 had been recovered. A tribal elder Malik Sher Aziz recently commented: 'the UN and the US-led international community should work together to bring an end to Pakhtun genocide, end the ongoing human rights violations, enforced disappearances, landmines plotting and toy bombs planted by Pakistan's security forces in Waziristan.'

Pashtun labourers, traders, students, and professionals face harassment in a mundane manner. There have been attempts to Arabise them, as many Pakhtun symbols have been attacked including jirgas, dance music rituals and shrines of saints revered by Pakhtuns. They claim to have lost their houses, grazing lands that they owned and their cattle.

Mohsin Dawar, chairman of the National Youth Organisation, and a senior leader of the Pakhtun Tahafuz

Movement has believed lately, that there is specific racial profiling going on across Pakistan, as of now.

In places, such as Okara, family members search for their missing ones. Most of the farmers earn a living by growing wheat in winter and corn in summer.

At this point, many tribal elders known as 'Malaks' have been succeeding their power to the youth, who are tech-savvy, aware and active on social media.

23 March, 2018

22

IMBROGLIO IN ORBAN'S HUNGARY

Budapest hasn't seen hundred thousand people, marching together, in front of the national parliament, for years. This massive crowd had huddled together, to demand the cancellation, of Viktor Orban's re-election in April 2018.

Protestors were seen wearing EU and Hungarian flags, which reflected their unease, against the recent election win.

Viktor Orban won a presidential term, as his anti-immigrant message, resonated strongly. His right-wing *Fidesz* party took two-thirds of the overall parliament seats.

During the election rallies, he talked of crushing the refugee wave, on the borders, and a crackdown, on civil society groups. Many common Hungarians think that his re-election will jeopardise democratic freedom, in the country.

It is amazing to see Orban's transformation, if one looks, at his political career. In 1989, in a public speech at Budapest's Hero Square, he won the hearts of two hundred fifty thousand listeners, by calling for free elections, and telling the Soviets, to withdraw the occupation.

Now, years later, after being Hungary's prime minister, he talked of crushing the refugee wave, on the borders, and a crackdown, on civil society groups, during election rallies.

Opposition parties alleged election result irregularities, while organisers believed that the current ballot box system favoured the current leader.

Orban has been charged with nepotism, for installing allies in the court, and extending influence, in the media institutions.

The Organisation for Security and Cooperation, in Europe, criticised the election, for 'intimidating and xenophobic rhetoric, media bias, and opaque campaign financing.'

Pro-government media machines labelled this event, as propaganda, by the 'Soros Empire'. Jewish billionaire, George Soros, has been popular, in promoting liberal democracy, around the world, with his philanthropy initiatives.

During the election rallies, as well, Orban spoke against Soros, for being a threat, to Hungary's Christian identity, and for his support, to asylum seekers. The orphaned lives of asylum seekers, and people fleeing war, and prosecution, mean very little to him.

In May 2015, when the European Commission proposed compulsory quotas, to redistribute asylum seekers, his answer was a fence, and construction of a one hundred seventy-five km (one hundred ten miles) barrier, along the southern border, with Serbia. The barrier had been built, by a combination of soldiers, prison inmates, and unemployed Hungarians, on community work schemes.

By mid-October, a forty km extension was added, along

the border, with Croatia. It was topped with coils of razor wire, and then reinforced with a second fence, with a live nine-hundred-volt electric current, night-vision cameras, and a service road, in the middle. This barrier was guarded, by personnel, of ten thousand police, and paramilitaries.

The message from Orban, despite the EU's policy, on welcoming the refugees, was loud and clear: Hungary had closed its borders, to non-Europeans.

Orban even passed a law to criminalise migrants, especially those, who tried to cross the fence.

Quite lately, he accused the opposition, of being a pawn, of his global investment initiatives. A pro-government weekly, *Figyelo* accused several academicians, journalists, and NGOs -including the Hungarian Civil Liberties Union, Amnesty International Hungary section, and the Hungarian Helsinki Committee. But the groups have pledged to carry, on their activities. This recent publication by *Figyelo* has been criticised by the US Government.

The magazine made a written tirade against many individuals and called them 'mercenaries. The magazine had used the Magyar term *'spekulans'*-speculator.

An English news site, and an opposition-leaning newspaper, were also shut down, before the start of the election. During his rule, Orban wants to penalise organisations, that support asylum seekers, through a new ordinance.

Hungarian political commentators believe that the country is 'slipping into illiberalism.'

Viktor Orban, it seems, is transforming Hungary, into an

authoritarian state, like regimes in Turkey and Syria.

Being a watcher of political events, in Hungary, the European Parliament is debating to suspend Hungary's voting rights, in the trading bloc. A full seven hundred fifty-one-member bloc is scheduled to vote, on this issue, in September 2018.

Judith Sargentini, an EU spokesperson said: 'the government in Budapest poses 'a clear risk of serious breach' to EU's democratic values that warrant a serious penalty.'

To ponder on Viktor Orban's political intentions, it is important to reflect on Hungary's history – which had been rife with foreign invasions, of being invaded and ruled by Turks, Austrians, and Russians.

Hungary lost seventy-two per cent, of her territory, during the Treaty of Trianon. The result was that thirty-one per cent of ethnic Hungarians, found themselves, outside its borders, as a minority community, in Romania, Czechoslovakia, and Yugoslavia.

In World War Two, most of Hungary's Jewish population was exterminated, in death camps. During post-war deportations, Hungary lost many of the Germans, and other ethnicities, that had settled in the country, since the 18th Century. Hungary had been emptied of her people. This laments with Viktor Orban, now and then, as Orban is known to bring up these facts of history, during his public talks, most notably, in September 2015, at a monastery, in Banz, in Bavaria.

During the talk, at the monastery, he had reflected on a parable, of a Christian Europe, to be adamant, against a Muslim World. For this reason, Orban wants every Hungarian school child, to read Geza Gardonyi's novel, *'The Eclipse of the Cresent Moon,'* where a central character, Gergely Bornemissza, plays an explosive soldier, defending a fortress, from a Turk invasion, in northern Hungary, at the Castle of Eger.

In February, the UN human rights chief, Zeid Ra'ad al-Hussein, accused Orban, of being a 'racist,' and a 'xenophobe.'

The Hungarian Foreign Minister, Peter Szijjarto, rejected the criticism, as 'unacceptable,' and insisted the human rights chief resigns.

For a strong regionalist, nationalist, anti-immigration, and Eurosceptic political approach, Viktor Orban has won the third election, in Hungary. But it is keeping his opponents talking.

20 April, 2018

23

POLITICAL TUMULTS IN ORTEGA'S NICARAGUA

ONE OF THE LARGEST CIVIL UNREST has happened in Nicaragua, in April 2018, ever since the civil war, of the 1990s.

The demonstrators are calling for President Ortega's resignation. Lately, the crowds that assembled, in front of Managua's cathedral, have been massive.

To curb, the ongoing violence, several TV channels, were shut down, as protesters threw rocks, at the police. There has been looting, both at public offices, and private shops.

As police retaliated, with tear gas shells, and rubber bullets, around fifty-eight people, have died, in the ongoing violence.

Many students have died, including one police officer, and a regional journalist, who tried, to broadcast his footage, live on Facebook. It appeared that the journalist ran a small media outlet, called '*El Meridiano.*'

In an interview with Univision, the journalist's sister said: 'I never imagined that he would film his own death.'

In response to the killings, many civilians have been injured, in the clashes. In the northern city of Leon, pro-government thugs burned a university campus area and a radio station.

Diplomatic relations with Costa Rica have worsened, as the country wants the Nicaraguan government, to reconsider the decision, to close media offices.

As per The New Yorker staff writer, Jon Lee Anderson: '*La Prensa*, a Chamorro family initiative, is the only newspaper, in Nicaragua, that resists the government narrative, in the country. Its website had been taken down sometime during the citizen protests.'

Lately, the two countries have locked horns with each other, on issues, mediated by the International Court of Justice, at The Hague.
The situation has prompted the Nicaraguan Attorney General, to pass an ordinance, for a formal enquiry, into the deaths.

In comparison to neighbouring countries, such as Honduras and El Salvador, the gang violence, and street protests, are much less.

Due to this reason, Ortega's economic plans were productive and increased growth.

However, since 2014, a series of protests have happened, against the president. It reflected certain oppressive tendencies, of his rule.

It started with the *Campesino* protestors, near El Chipote Prison, being beaten by policemen.

In 2015, Omepete residents greeted a government-affiliated medical team, with banners, against the regime. In June of that year, around thirty thousand people, demonstrated against government policies, in Juigalpa, mostly consisting of peasant workers. It was followed by Managua protests, in July.

In 2016, hundreds of farmers gathered, in La Fonseca, where they demanded dissatisfaction, against the construction of a water canal, with a collection of signatures.

In April 2017, around twenty protestors were arrested, in Juigalpa.

The civil unrest again started, in 2018, because President Daniel Ortega tried to change the country's social security system, known as the *Instituto Nicaraguense de Seguridad Social (INSS)*.

A controversial pension plan had been drafted, by the president, which reduced the allowances, retired servicemen received, to reduce the budget deficit, in the country.

If we investigate the leadership record of Ortega, in the country, he has won the national election three times, back-to-back.

After serving the Sandinista Revolution, from 1979-1990, he again came into power, in 2006. Currently, he enjoys support from Venezuelan president, Nicolas Maduro.

During his tenure at the office, he instituted a series of anti-poverty programmes, partially funded by Venezuelan petrodollars. The welfare initiatives won support, from poorer communities.

Many Nicaraguans considered Ortega, as the one, from the Nicaraguan revolutionary tradition.

Although, in times such as today, the people call him a worse political figure, than Samoza himself, as he has been in office, for more than ten years.

It is nothing, but ironic.

The protests, happening, now and then, for four years, reflect a kind of political rot and dismay, of the common people.

The Sandinista regime had been inspired, by the ideas of Carlo Fonseca, who likened himself, to the Cuban Revolution leaders. He particularly laid emphasis, on the emancipation, of Nicaraguan peasantry. This important event proceeded, with the ousting of the Samoza monarchy, in 1979.

Around that time, forty thousand Nicaraguans were killed.

Samoza had been one of those tyrants, who believed: 'I want more oxen and fewer people in my country.'

Ortega was part of the Sandinista junta, and in later years, acted as the regime's coordinator, after the collapse of the monarchy.

Aligning himself, with the Catholic Church, he has been charged, with nepotism, and partisanship, by his opponents, as he had installed his family members, and close friends, in the military, and several government posts.

As per his prevailing norms, Ortega has installed his wife as vice president, the space for the opposition is largely diminished and terms limits are also abolished. It seems that Nicaragua is slipped into a dictatorship.

His wife, the vice president, made loathsome comments lately, calling the protestors 'bloodsuckers,' 'vampires' and 'criminals.'

In Nicaragua, the political situation seems like a powder keg. That is why the government will try to hold talks, with several public stakeholders, involved, in the coming time.

Many commentators think, that the United States could play a constructive role, to end the rising political tensions. It is considering legislation, that will freeze loans, from international financial markets. The bill, drafted in 2017, is called the Nicaraguan Investment Conditionality Act.

In its history, the Sandinistas, aligned themselves, with the Soviet Union, so that they could help Marxist guerrillas, come into power, in El Salvador, Guatemala, and other countries. This 'collective red stance,' made the United States, think of the Nicaraguan regime, as a prime adversary, of American foreign policy.

However, this ordinance will not ease the sufferings, but will further deteriorate, the already volatile situation.

May 2, 2018

24

STREET ANGER OF JORDANIANS

JORDAN HAS WITNESSED ITS WORST political
unrest, in five years, since May 2018. The public anger
sums it all up, which reflects, a prolonged frustration.

There were chantings of local folklore and slogans, like
what was heard, during the 2011 Arab Spring, such as:
'the people want the fall of the government', and 'I strike
today to live tomorrow'.

This fury, of protestors, has prompted King Abdullah II,
to oust the current prime minister, Hani Mulki, through a
decree, from the royal palace.

The main difference, between the 2018 protests, and
the protests, in 2011, is that during the Arab Spring,
the far-flung tribes, were at the centre stage, in holding
the protests. In these protests, city dwellers, coming
from Irbid, Aqaba, Al-Zarqa, and Salt, in addition to the
capital, have recorded high participation.

Omar Razzaz will replace Mulki, a Harvard-educated
former World Bank Official, previously based in Lebanon,
who formerly taught, at the Massachusetts Institute of
Technology, for four years.

Al-Rai, a Jordanian newspaper, was one of the first to
disseminate the news, of leadership change, in the country.

The protests had spread, and continued massively, for five days, after Mulki announced new austerity measures, and tax increases (from 4.5 per cent to 10 per cent).

Critics argue that it has increased the price of bread, fuel, electricity, and other commodities.

Jordanian Government, however, argues that the new tax law will affect the wealthy, and will leave the poor, unscathed.

The protests were called, by a political group, known as '*Hirak Shababi*' (Youth Movement in Arabic), as well as thirty-three other civil society groups, and associations, including the Jordanian Engineer's Association, and Jordanian Teachers Syndicate – both groups have a combined membership, of three hundred thousand.

The monarch called, for an extensive review, of the tax system. He has urged the government to produce a new tax bill, in coordination with parliament, unions, and other stakeholder groups.

Since the last eight years, the income tax law, in Jordan, has been changed around four times, and the rancour about it, reflects, in the minds, of the people. It is because they believe there has been no genuine answerability, from the government.

Now and then, they accuse the government, of frittering away the national exchequer, in corruption.

In Jordan, the King has a final say, on all issues. He also has the discretion to review any political, or economic changes, made by the government. It also reflects a cold shoulder, of the monarchy, against a grassroots movement. The protestors, in turn, have been demanding the dissolution, of the parliament.

Common Jordanians have long complained, of paying burdening taxes, for poor services, offered by the government. The new tax proposal, it seems, is unfair towards the middle class, and the poor, living, in the country. For quite a while, watchers in the country, have complained, of poor welfare measures, in the education, and healthcare sectors. The salaries have failed, to keep up, as well.

Jordanian political analyst, Helmi Asmar, who writes for the regional newspaper, *Ad Dustour* believes: 'We have no reasons to be optimistic right now. Will Razzaz be able to hold the country together with the old system and the old machinery? It remains to be seen.'

A one-day strike had been called, after thousands of people gathered, near the prime minister's office, for the seventh consecutive street protest. The police have detained around sixty people, so far. Around forty-two policemen were injured, mostly, by fireworks.

Jordan is a major Western ally. Its economy depends on foreign aid. But, in recent years, aid and foreign investment have declined. In 2016, Jordan received seven hundred twenty-three million in aid, from International Monetary Fund. Economists argue that it has been the main reason for the price hike, in food, and other services. The state debt remains constant, at around thirty-seven million American dollars.

In Amman's old central market, the cart sellers, and small vendors, line up to sell their fruit stocks, on makeshift tables. The market is known for cheaper rates, than the supermarkets. The demand of consumers remains always high. But, on the other hand, Jordanians have been unhappy, making a living, in one of the Arab world's most expensive cities. The worry, of a price rise, always afflicts them, because salaries are either low or diminishing.

An Israeli newspaper, *Yedioth Ahronoth*, claims that the US, and its allies, in the region, such as Israel, Saudi Arabia, Egypt, United Arab Emirates, have escalated the protests, in Jordan, because the kingdom has refused to let down its Palestinian cause, for a while.

According to Middle East Eye: 'eyewitnesses saw most shops, and businesses, shut in downtown. Central markets did not receive the usual fruit and vegetable deliveries, and butchers and supermarkets were not supplied with fresh meat and poultry, as farmers and food catering traders joined the strike.

Final exams were still administered despite the participation of the 140,000-strong Teachers Association, whose members joined pharmacists, garment traders, and contractors among others.

Due to prolonged conflict, in Syria and Iraq, a large influx of refugees has entered Jordanian territory.

The unemployment rate has swelled up, to eighteen per cent. The jobless youth make the highest tally.

For Jordanian workers, it seems to be a redundant affair.

7 June, 2018

25

AGRARIAN DISTRESS IN INDIA

INDIA IS NOT ONLY A COUNTRY THAT now has the world's tallest statue, but it is also a country of debt-ridden, anguished farmers, malnourished children, and where millions of people still sleep on the road pavements, and cannot have ample meals, for a day.

A protest march called '*Dilli Chalo*' (Delhi March), by a hundred thousand farmers, mainly an amalgam of two hundred seven organisations, called All India Kisan Sangharsh Coordination Committee (AIKSCC), in November 2018, just before the next Indian prime ministerial election in 2019, reflects that Narendra Modi's slogan '*Sab ka Saath, Sab ka Vikas*' (everybody's support, and everybody's development) hasn't resonated well, with every citizen, in the country.

For these dissenting farmers, hoping for a better future, for their children, the protest march, to New Delhi, has involved a great amount of sacrifice, because people have been travelling, in trains, and tractors, taking long journeys, and leaving back their homes, during the lucrative harvest season.

As per the charter drafted by Nation for Farmers, on *Kisan Mukti March*, 'credit crises and exploding rural indebtedness', were discussed.

Some protesters carried skulls and bones, of farmers,

who had killed themselves, in desperation. Some farmers stripped themselves naked, and laid themselves down, in front of TV cameras, to draw attention, to their protest, demanding loan waivers, and remunerative/minimum prices, for their produce.

It seems that the left-leaning political institutions have remained crucial, in their mobilisation, as thousands of protestors, marched towards Ramlila Maidan, from five different locations.

The whole scenario also reflects a lack of redressal policies. Farmer suicide has remained a core social issue, in states, such as Rajasthan, Uttar Pradesh, Maharashtra, Telangana and Odisha. Farmers fetched about thirty-six thousand crores less, in the last crop season, due to lower market prices, of commodities.

Agriculture remains the leading occupation, in India, where it provides livelihood, to fifty-eight per cent, of the population, but agriculture only contributes fifteen per cent, of the total GDP. This reflects a huge, glaring imbalance. Also, the mafia of commissioning agents, who control the supply chain distribution network, and marketing element, of the produce, end up charging the consumer, higher prices. In the end, the farmer is neglected, as he sells his produce, for meagre amounts, to the agents.

A lower rate of inflation, during Modi's tenure, has, unfortunately, resulted in dwindling agricultural incomes. Loans offered, at higher interest rates, have become another issue, for Indian farmers, lately. Add to that, increased input costs, such as fertilisers, pesticides, diesel, and the higher cost of tractors, have also added to their grief.

As farmer incomes are becoming lesser, it seems that farmers have been put, to a knife's edge, because small and marginal farmers are turning towards daily wage labour.

As per Sukhpal Gill, of Punjab Agricultural University, there were some solutions finalised, by the erstwhile Planning Commission – such as farmer cooperatives, self-help groups, and farmer producer organisations (FPOs), to help marginal farmers.

As per research data, compiled by Gill, Mahatma Gandhi National Rural Employment Guarantee Act (MGNREGA) can provide work, to distressed farmers. FPOs are in their infancy, in places, such as Punjab and Haryana, where the National Bank of Agriculture and Rural Development (NABARD) have been its main promoter. In India, there seems a need for public investment, in agriculture, including research and development, technology and infrastructure.

If we go back to history, around fifty years ago, when Lal Bahadur Shastri was incumbent, as prime minister, India faced a terrible famine, but he urged soldiers, and farmers, to unite, and collectively squabble the crises.

Politically, Shashri's words became a symbolic gesture, in the coming time, but no such mantle has been experienced, by people, during Narendra Modi's tenure. His government has produced no report, of farmer suicides, committed in India, since 2015. Nor has his government shown a clear blueprint, regarding climate science, and climate change, a discourse that is taking place, globally. These issues have not been conceived, as important political questions, in India, until now.

In current times, a lot of agricultural research is blaming

neoliberal economics, climate change, and environmental degradation, developed through WTO, World Bank, and IMF.

Under WTO guidelines, the interest of international markets, and rich farmers takes precedence. That is why, under the recommendation of the M.S Swaminathan Committee, an opportunity was provided to quit WTO's Agreement on Agriculture (AoA) and to draft an independent policy.

Roshan Kishore, wrote in Hindustan Times, that the present government has targeted inflation, and it has not proved, the right policy because it has directly worsened the trade of farmers. It is because non-farm prices have increased, more than farm prices. This scenario is bothering policymakers, deciding on structural reforms. Add to that, unfavourable weather conditions, such as skewed rainfall, have added to the agrarian distress, for Indian farmers. As per Kishore, this crisis might also propel caste wars, in the coming future.

Despite *Hindutva* becoming a favoured political idea, in urban, and small cities, mainly among the youth, it seems that Modi's government is favouring a hegemonic discourse, of cultural and religious aggression, over the welfare of its people. The events that happened during Modi's tenure, vouch for them, – it includes a ban on beef trade, and the Ram Mandir issue. It has appeased his Hindu nationalist voter base but has divided the country, on other social, and economic issues.

In a multi-ethnic, multi-cultural and multilingual country, such as India, democracy has shown its flaws, by not representing everyone. Lately, Modi's demonetisation drive, an initiative that demonetised around fifteen lakh crores, to mainly tackle corruption, was also received with mixed reactions, especially by poor people, living in far-flung areas, with no functioning financial institutions, around them.

During that time, India's poor struggled with the overall guidelines, dictated by the central government.

In a cacophony around them, people were getting killed, in ATM queues. About twenty-five died, in the first week of the demonetisation drive. Modi's demonetisation decision, earlier, had put the country in the doldrums, reflecting similar tales of desperation, and hopelessness around.

Modi had promised to double farmer income, during rallies, but, seeing the eventual aftermaths, of the collective anger, that reverberates, it seems, he has failed miserably, to win the hearts, of Indian farmers.

2 December 2018

26

YELLOW VEST PROTESTS

WHEN MACRON BECAME THE PRESIDENT of France, he vowed to keep the pride of its democratic traditions, intact, by bringing a new revolution.

He wanted to make French democracy, a role model, for the modern world.

His supporters loved his Euro-centrism, his balance of political charisma, and his intellect, amidst difficult times, in Europe. Some called him a younger version, of de Gaulle, if not Napoleon. British columnists likened this ex-banker, Hollande's protege, to the 'next Blair,' and wanted their version of Macron, in their country.

Although Macron started on a positive note, very few predicted the protest-stricken streets, of Paris, nineteen months after.

As France's new president, who won an election, as an independent candidate, mostly because the other political opponents destroyed each other, in rebuking, and blame games, he gave promises of a renewed, and stronger welfare system, but, ordinary people, in France, have expressed unhappiness.

As the result, some of his admirers, praising his international cooperation, and for instituting good labour laws, in the past, have already gone quiet.

Wearing yellow fluorescent vests, as their revolutionary symbol, these protestors, mostly old, unemployed, and living outside the suburbs, of Paris, are called *gilets jaunes*. They are leaderless, anti-political, and reflect a form of angry anarchism.

By calling him deaf and dumb, to their grievances, they taint Macron, as an arrogant president, who was mainly pleasing the rich, with his ineffective neoliberal agenda. *Gilets jaunes* compare him, to a cruel despot, of similar times, when *Sansculottes*, a militant republican class of leaders, that represented common people, during the French Revolution, besieged Bastille, in 1789, due to a popular uprising, against the government.

French people have been culturally sensitive, whenever democratic institutions isolate them. Similar kinds of protests have happened, in the country, during 2005 riots, and in May 1968, that toppled Charles de Gaulle. These weekly protests have targeted both the businesses, and the state. At roundabouts, in several places, protesters were wanting the attention of driving cars.

It was in 2008, when a law suggested that all French drivers should carry a yellow French vest, in their cars. It is from this law, from where this new rebellion in France, derives its name.

The yellow vest movement, aiming to overthrow Macron, has been mainly caused by increasing fuel taxes, including a carbon tax, austerity measures, the digitisation of administration, repeal of 2017 wealth tax, and removal of traffic enforcement cameras. These protests are directly targeting the strong France-Germany partnership, that has vowed to keep the far right, anti-EU opponents, away, in 2022 elections. For centrists, and rational minded, social democrats, if Macron fails, Europe will fail, too.

As tax waivers seem central, to this revolt, in other words, it means that even a small tax increase, that was deemed insignificant, in the past, sanctions a rebellion now, in France.

The protests also gained momentum, and popularity, when people, protesting on rising diesel, and gasoline prices, started a petition, on Facebook, that had gathered around nine hundred eighty-six thousand signatures.

Never since the early 19th century, when revolutions were common, in France, has a movement tried to overthrow a legitimate, democratically elected government. There are bands of violent youth, called *casseurs*, and Black Bloc militants, who have camouflaged themselves, in protest crowds, and smashed whatever they found, on the streets.

In 17th century France, working-class people organised similar protests, against the monarchy, who felt that they were betrayed by the upper-class ideologues, and fought over issues of representation.

As the protests have spread, it has concerned democrats, who value its tradition, all around the world, and not only in Europe. Its ripple effects are already showing up, in countries, such as Canada, a former French colony.

As per the French construction group Vinci, the damage caused by the yellow vest protests has resulted in the loss of several tens of millions of euros. Nearly two hundred fifty sites were affected daily, by the actions of protesters, and there had been considerable damage, to equipment, and infrastructure, as well. About thirty-two emergency vehicles were destroyed. The consumer industry, on the other hand, had a loss of around two billion Euros. The city of Paris has estimated damage, of around three to four million Euros.

For quite some time, the standard of living in France has been declining. There are many households, in French cities, that do survival jobs, that fetch low salaries, that barely fill their car tanks, and refrigeration stock, after the end of every month. Although, they do not mostly file cases, of government assistance.

Sarah Maza, wrote, in the Washington Post: 'the rebels' pain is sharp and all too real, but the available evidence suggests that long-dismal economic conditions for those at the bottom have not gotten significantly worse under Macron. France's young president has not made the poor noticeably poorer, but his aloofness has made them a whole lot angrier.'

Many commentators, in the country, believe that far-right supporters of Marine Le Pen, have fuelled this rebellion, as the movement is slowly picking up, the rancour of anti-Semitism, racism, and anti-immigration rhetoric. During the protest days, banners appeared, where Macron was accused of being a puppet of Jewish moneyed interests.

Whether Le Pen, an antagonist to the ideals of the French Revolution, appeasing blood and soil voters, like her father, who often evoked the memory of Vendee, a region, which opposed the French Revolution, has fuelled these protests or not, the fact remains that she will enjoy political leverage out of this rebellion, that erupted, in mid-November, 2018.

After yellow vest protests, a police union, called *les gilet bleus*, had been also demanding higher wages, and better conditions, by starting their protests, against the government, as budgets sanctioned, for them lately, have become lesser, over time.

To curb the yellow vest protests, Macron had finalised new minimum wage guidelines, with an increase of hundred Euros, and tax waivers, for overtime workers, and pensioners.

December 19, 2018

27

CIVIL UNREST IN HAITI

THE STREETS OF HAITI ARE IN MAYHEM, after several Haitian protestors, demanded the resignation, of President Jovenel Moise, over allegations of misuse, of around four billion American dollars, unaccounted public funds, and soaring inflation, affecting common households.

These protests erupted in February 2019 and have forced the closure of schools, shops, government offices, and public transport.

As cars have been set ablaze, and people have clashed, on the streets, with the police, several demonstrators have been killed since then.

At the fences of Haiti's state TV offices, fire extinguishers were seen thwarting the burning cars. Roads were blocked, with burning tyres. Some youths were seen carrying stolen cooking stoves, amidst protests, near Port-au-Prince, reflecting serious economic problems.

During the unrest, UN forces from Senegal were seen patrolling the streets, of the country's capital. As per initial reports of CNN, these protests had begun on the second anniversary of Jovenel Moise's election. It is because the protestors have been unhappy with Moise. After all, he did not initiate any probe, into corruption cases, against the former President, over issues with *Petrocaribe*, an oil cartel of various Caribbean states with Venezuela, that provides subsidised petroleum products, with an option of financing over a twenty-five-year period.

The amalgam offered a down payment, of just sixty per cent, which eventually led to Haiti's burdening debt crises. It seemed that Hugo Chavez signed the deal to win more allies, in the region. During Maduro's time, the deal slowly began to wind down, and its aftermaths have now been reflected on the streets.

In the skirmishes, around four people were declared dead, as protestors were seen dragging blood-stained dead bodies, on the streets. Some protestors even blocked roads that lead to Moise's house, and some even stoned his property. To reconcile with the protestors, President Moise, a member of *Pitit Dessalines* party, was seen standing, on a motorcycle, and gesturing, as a sign of solidarity. But, in a recent statement, he said that he will not step down, as his resignation will pave the way, for drug traffickers, to dominate the country, and this radical step, if taken, will also instigate a civil war.

Soon after, the opposition leaders demanded that people should pour onto the streets again. The protestors used the slogan *Kot kòb Petrocaribe a?*' meaning, 'Where is the *Petrocaribe* money?' During the weekend, around two hundred people burned American flags, calling on Russia, for assistance. They shouted: 'Down Americans, Long Live Putin.'

In July 2018, there were similar protests, when the prices of gasoline, kerosene, and diesel had a double-digit increase. There have been also reports of food shortages. It was part of the policy of the International Monetary Fund, to eliminate fuel subsidies, and increase government revenue. It also led to the resignation of former Prime Minister,

Jack Guy, after a no-confidence vote was passed, on him, in the parliament,

In a prison, near Aquin, several prisoners escaped, after leaving their cells, for a scheduled shower, as prison guards, became busy, curbing nearby demonstrations.

In its economic woes, Haiti owes billions, in debt, to Venezuela. However, the president has assured that the recent scandal, of alleged misuse of public funds, will be investigated. To curb the recent public discontent, the prime minister announced a remedial measure that will include a reduction in the prices, of basic commodities.

Prime Minister, Jean Henry Ceant, has announced a thirty per cent reduction, in his budget allocation. He is suggesting the president, and the Senate, follow the same policy. By addressing the nation in the media, he said that there will be an audit, of all autonomous state enterprises, to ensure any diverted funds, are recovered.

A direct programme, with food producers, will come up, that will investigate cutting down prices, of staple foods, such as rice – from fifty to thirty-five *gourdes*.

Prime Minister Ceant said in an interview: 'There would be the abolition of all the unnecessary privileges of senior state officials' such as fuel costs, phone cards, travel abroad, number of consultants on files and reconsideration of providing them with a second residence. These savings will, for example, strengthen the judiciary by giving it additional resources to facilitate the completion of the *Petrocaribe* trial.'

Quite recently, Haiti suffered from natural disasters, such as Hurricane Matthew, which struck, the southwestern part of the country, near Les Anglais, in 2016. In 2010, thousands of people died, in a massive earthquake. In its rising social problems, the Haitian government loses an estimated sixty billion *gourdes,* annually, at borders and customs, due to the smuggling of goods. In 2017, a Haitian special Commission accused twelve government officials, and several heads of private firms of embezzlement.

As per World Bank figures, Haiti is the poorest country, in the Americas, with fifty-nine per cent, of people, living below the poverty line. Around twenty per cent of people, live in extreme poverty.

In this unrest, more than a hundred tourists were stranded, and they were sent back, to their home country, in a rescue flight, with the help of the Canadian government. Among these tourists, there were missionaries, from Southern Alberta, and nurses, who were trapped in a compound, in Grand Goave, some fifty kilometres, from the capital.

Many Canadian tourists, came into the country, through purchased vacation packages, by Canadian Airliner, *Air Transat.* As the result, the Canadian government has advised its citizens, not to travel to the country. It also called for US citizens to leave the country, till commercial flights remain operational. Some five hundred Filipino tourists were also advised, by the Department of Foreign Affairs, to make security arrangements, for themselves, during the political turmoil. They were asked to register online, at the Philippine Embassy, in Washington DC.

In this tumultuous time, Haitian authorities have confirmed the arrest of five US citizens, who were found with illegal weapons.

Jacqueline Charles, wrote in the Miami Herald, that they

were on some 'US Government Mission,' and were also found with a telescope, satellite machine, and drones, besides some automatic rifles.

US Government, on the other hand, has called, for a greater investment climate, job opportunities, and 'genuine dialogue and compromise,' in the Caribbean country.

February 2, 2019

28

ALGERIAN CIVIL DISORDER

ALGERIA HAS BEGUN TO EXPLODE, in anarchy, to the extent that it is on the verge of an Arab Spring movement. The North African country is witnessing a flurry of massive protests, across Algiers.

The people are demanding an end to the current president's rule, Abdel Aziz Boutefilka, after his campaign manager, filed his nomination papers, to rerun for the president.

The country witnessed its largest rally, on March 1st, 2019 when tens of thousands, of people, poured onto the streets. The angry protestors were huddling the boulevards, in the country's capital. One of the placards, during the protests, sarcastically remarked: 'Respect the dead. Bury him, do not elect him.' The police had even fired tear gas, near the presidential office.

They have even rejected Prime Minister Noureddine Bedoui's technocratic offer, to include young Algerians, in the parliamentary process, who constitute more than seventy per cent, of the total Algerian population. Several Algerian youths believe that they would not have made graffitis, on the walls, if they were happy, with the system.

For them, Bouteflika symbolises gerontocracy. Article one hundred-two gives the discretion, to impeach the president.

The protests have received support, from civil society,

including judges, teachers, and the veterans, of the independence struggle.

These mass protests sparked off, when in central Algiers, on February 24th, 2019 a recently instituted *Mouwatana* ('Citizens Democracy'), called for some action. They have also expressed resentment, over the recent trend, of mass migrations, to Europe, by many Algerians. The families, of disappeared migrants, have marched as well, and have called the *harragas* (migrants), 'martyrs.'

According to The Guardian: 'Despite a heavy police presence, crowds gathered at Algiers' Grande Poste square hours before the scheduled start of a demonstration calling on Bouteflika to step down after two decades in power.'
It has been a while, since 2013, the 83-year-old Abdel Aziz Boutefilka, using a wheelchair, was shifted to a Swiss hospital, and since then, he has not been actively involved, in the politics, of the country.

He can hardly talk or even walk. He does not even remember his fourth term, due to gradual memory loss.

As per The Economist: 'the president has been seen on the television, looking confused, while his close aides fawn over him. Algeria is, in desperate need of renewal. But, the ruling clique of generals, businessmen, and politicians, have proved incapable of reform, unable even to pick a successor, to the cadaverous Mr Bouteflika. It is time it handed power, to a new generation, which might unlock Algeria's vast potential.'

For many years, Algeria has been ruled by a secretive *cabal* known, as *'le pouvier,'* from where the people, in power, are believed to have minted money and dictated their politics. While the *cabal* calls itself stable, and generous to people, its critics call these men, with power, instruments of stagnation. These critics want the power, to be handed over, to the next generation, from these so-called 'authoritarians', who mostly have channelled their wealth, through various state-funded projects.

However, the cabal argues that they know the pulse, of the country, and that it was due to Boutefilka's leadership, that the country did not see any unrest, during the 2011 Arab Spring. It had largely avoided any unrest, in the country, by giving low-interest loans, and housing to common people.

But, as the country's budget relies largely on oil, the *cabal* also believes that they can no longer keep many people happy, on subsidies, and secure government jobs. It is because unemployment has spiked to eleven per cent, many of the youth, are largely jobless, and there has been an increase, in corruption, and red tape. Gone are the days, of the 1990s, when the GDP, in the country, was high. The global decline, of oil, in the recent past, has also added, to Algeria's economic woes.

As per data, compiled by The Economist, the debt now equals the country's nine per cent, of GDP. The foreign reserves have shrunk by fifty per cent, since 2013.

Having said that, the powerful Senate, in Algeria, discourages any form of dissent, against these leaders. It muzzles the press and often locks up journalists, and other people, for any criticism, and harassment, drawn against them. To be more precise, the stature of Boutefilka, is such, amongst the *cabal*, that he is likened, to *El Cid*, an 11th-century Spanish nobleman, whose dead body was, supposedly, put on a horse, and sent back to war, to inspire the remaining troops, engaged, in a battle.

Algeria had its last free, and fair election, in 1991. After that, the army generals cancelled the rest. This also led to a civil war, in the 1990s, called the 'black decade', which killed over two hundred thousand people.

General Ahmad Gaid Shah believes that there are various existing political quarters, which want to bring the chaos, of the past, back into Algeria.

All this division represents a dismal scenario. Currently, the common Algerians, hate the populism, of the *cabal*. Most of the Algerians think of Boutefilka, as an ailing, broken-down man, and look down upon him, with scorn. Although his party, National Liberation Front (FLN), fought the war, with the French, the people have no memories of French colonialism, in their country, anymore.

In the upcoming election, the opposition bloc does not want to participate. Ali Benflis, the former presidential candidate, who just got twelve per cent, of the votes, does not intend to run for the office. The independents have been blocked.

As per several regional analysts, in Algeria, a retired army general, Ali Ghadiri will most likely run, for office. But there is also an auto mechanic, a cousin of a French Algerian businessman, named Rachid Nekkaz, who unsuccessfully, ran for an election, in 2007.

According to reports by Reuters, talks might be held, under UN diplomat, Lakhdar Brahimi, to ease the already chaotic situation. It might decide, on the country's new constitution, and set the date, for new elections.

16 March, 2019

29

SUDAN UPRISING

THE PROTESTS IN SUDAN which started in December 2018 have not subsided even after three months. However, this mass revolution, in the country, has not been broadcasted well, on the global media, besides the regional African media, at large.

Trade unions, professional associations, and opposition groups have largely supported this new Sudan uprising. It is because there is profound street anger on the streets.

In 2013, Sudan dodged the Arab Spring, but the people can no longer hold themselves now. The protests initially started as a demonstration against rising bread and fuel prices. Currently, there are also low limits on ATM withdrawals. Since 2018, Sudan's inflation was the third highest in the world. Now, thoroughly upset over his rule, protestors are demanding that he should stop ruling them. They are vying with him for a Hosni Mubarak-style resignation.

Football ultras, associated with Hilal Team, have blocked bridges. Sudanese Professional Association (SPA), a grassroots movement, has made a strong dissent against the monarchy. In realpolitik terms, it is called a 'fluid political landscape.'

Local media and international media have called these protests 'peaceful demonstrations' that have happened in 14 out of 18 provinces in the Sudan region. Some protestors even tried to enter the parliament, including the presidential palace in Khartoum.

Sudanese British Billionaire Mohammed Ibrahim said: 'People are hungry, and they see the looting of the country's resources by the ruling clique. But, when they are pushed against the wall, they just have nothing to lose.'

Various media sources have cited that around 31 people have died in the ten-week-old uprising, while several opposition groups and human rights groups, put the number to around 51, and there have been over 2600 arrests. Assorted police and army vehicles were seen shooting into the crowds, detaining and assaulting journalists, activists, and opposition figures.

The political slogan, *'just fall, that is all'* (*tasqut bas*), was first used on Twitter, and Facebook pages, in December 2018. In a Foreign Policy Op-ed, Nesrine Malik calls the protests fuelled by 'organisational planning' and 'spontaneous emotion.' He further writes: 'Bashir's government, which came to power via a military coup in 1989, has grounded Sudanese society to a nub. The country's basic institutions—Sudan's civil service, its economy, its education system, its military, its very culture—were degraded to better maintain the government's grip on power, and to ensure its monopoly on the means of economic extraction.'

Sudan's economy has been in tatters since it broke away from South Sudan in 2011. After the division, it controlled 70 per cent of the oil wells, which gave the country, a significant source of foreign currency. However, the Sudanese Pound, saw a significant drop in its value against the US dollar, since the protests began. In the recent past, people were also unhappy about the scrapping of the Gezira Irrigation Scheme, a massive agricultural project, between the banks of the Blue and White Nile, near Khartoum. As the result, farmers, herders and several unemployed workers, moved to Khartoum to make out a living for themselves. The fortunate ones, with networks and money, moved to other places in the Gulf region.

Analysts at Khartoum believe that these economic woes stem from various IMF-led structural changes that were mainly instituted, since 2017. But government officials are also firm on the belief that these protests are instigated by 'foreign agents and traitors,' intending to harm the national interests of the country.

Despite these ongoing protests, the regime of President Omar al Bashir, known as *'Inqaz'* (salvation), is in no mood to step down. Since the 1980s, Sudan saw a civil war that spread from the Nuba Mountains to the south of Darfur. He seized power again in 1989, with a cohort of military officers, which declared the 'national salvation revolution.'

As of now, Bashir has promised an increase in the salaries for civil servants, and increased health insurance, too. In January 2019, the Sudanese government passed a budget that aimed to reduce inflation, from 70 per cent to 27 per cent. He also announced new regulations for trading and transporting gold and foreign currency. But, none of these measures has stopped the protests, as they have entered the third month.

That is why the Sudanese president declared a state of emergency in February 2019. He dissolved the national government as well as the regional government and replaced them with senior military officials. He also fired his longtime ally General Bakri Hasan Salih as vice president, and replaced him with General Awad Ibn Awof, a hardline minister, who has been criticised, due to his role in the Darfur conflict, and he has several American sanctions against him.

As per a regional analyst, working for Africa Confidential: 'Riyadh and Abu Dhabi, as well as Doha, have regarded Bashir as a fickle friend because he tended to play both ends against the middle. He has pledged allegiance in the past in return for subsidies and then gone his own way.'

Bashir also is known to have differences with United Nations Secretary-General, Antonio Guterres, after the recently concluded African Summit in Ethiopia. International Criminal Court also wants him for war crimes in Darfur.

Since the political unrest escalated, there have been around twenty deflections by various parties, who abandoned the reconciliatory dialogue initiated by National Party Council (NPC) and supported the opposition.

Political upheavals are not new in Sudan. In 2013, amidst the succession of South Sudan, the government violently cracked down on protestors, resulting in the death of 185 people, according to Amnesty International. There were protests in 2018 as well, where slogans such as 'Freedom, Peace, Justice' and 'Revolution' were chanted on the streets. To quell the situation, he declared a one-year state of emergency. Of this move, there was an outbreak of protests in the northern town of Atbara, in 2018.

Several political commentators, such as Abdinor Dahir, are of an opinion that this regional instability might propel further unrest in neighbouring Egypt, Chad, Libya, and South Sudan. He further notes that these continuing protests would also prove detrimental to international trade, especially navigation from the Red Sea, which is already affected due to the war in Yemen, and pirate operations in the Gulf of Aden. Sudan is one of the largest refugee-hosting countries, in Africa (currently holding 2.2 million IDPs and 695,000 refugees from South Sudan, Syria, Yemen and Eritrea). Any kind of major regional instability would mean that it could propel a new wave of refugees, towards the shores of Europe.

In March 2019, a senior military source dispelled some breaking information to Middle East Eye, where Salah Gosh, head of Sudanese intelligence, was accused of having the support of the UAE, Saudi Arabia, and Egypt to oust al-Bashir as president. The unknown source also cited his private talks with Yossi Cohen at the Munich Security Conference between 15-17 February 2019. Gosh was also believed to have attended meetings with several European intelligence chiefs, and the head of the common media centre. It has been called a 'plot hatched by Israel's Arab allies.'

Gosh has been known, as the CIA's man in Khartoum, and American intelligence wants this man in place, replacing Omar al Bashir's 30-year rule. He was also their spy chief, during the 2000s, in their war on terror against al-Qaeda, even visiting the US in 2005, when Sudan was on their list of state-sponsored terrorism.

As of now, the uprising is also inspiring Sudanese American teens, who have been drawing parallels between the American civil rights movement and the Sudan uprising.

The older Sudanese American generation had fled

the country to escape Bashir's flagrant human rights violations and flagrant corruption. The people of their older generation have revolted before, during 1964 and 1985. It seems that the bad old times of anarchy and misrule are back in their home country.

29 March, 2019

30

ANTI-GOVERNMENT PROTESTS IN ALBANIA

THERE HAS BEEN MOUNTING PRESSURE, on Albanian socialists, in charge of the government, by opposition protestors, who demand an end, to their democratic tenure.

The opposition calls the government of the Socialist Party of Albania, an illegitimate government, of thieves and criminals. These protests got active, in February 2019, in the Balkan country.

During mid-May 2019, more protests were held, at the Martyrs of the Nation Boulevard, in Tirana, before moving to other sites.

Protestors, holding umbrellas, on a rainy day, threw various kinds of flares, gasoline grenades, and Molotov cocktails, and attempted to barge, into the main government building, at the boulevard. As a reaction, security personnel, in return, fired tear gas, injuring many people.

Several observers saw threatening words, written at the building, where the OSCE ambassador, in Tirana lives. The Italian Embassy, in Albania, has condemned this threat posed, to his office, and called for protests, within the legal framework. However, the protestors have vowed to reunite, in full determination, and have promised a response, to this incident.

The crowd, having men, wearing masks, also condemned the arrest of a Democratic Party leader. The number of casualties, remains unclear in the media, although, around fifty people have been taken, into custody, for 'hitting someone, while on duty,' 'disturbing public order,' 'destroying property through arson,' and 'breach of rules' regarding explosives. Ambulances were seen taking the injured, to the hospital. Interior Minister, Sander Lleshaj said that thirteen Tirana policemen were injured.

Earlier, in 2017, the protestors had alleged fraud, in the last parliamentary election. They want an early election, and want a temporary, caretaking government, until then. Prime Minister Edi Rama has retorted, to their claims, as false allegations, and threats, to democracy. However, the opposition accuses Rama's cabinet, of having links, to organised crime. They had blocked national highways, earlier, and several of the leaders, from the opposition, have resigned, to put more pressure, on the ruling government.

The new wave of protests has come, at a time, when European Union is deciding on opening accession talks, with Albania, and neighbouring North Macedonia. The EU, and United States, have given support, to the government, and have urged the opposition to take part in the local elections, on June 30.

Conservative leaders, such as Basha, and Prime Minister Rama, have backed the moves, to join the EU, but the opposition leaders believe that as corruption, is reigning high, in the country, it could prevent Albania, from achieving its membership plan.

Under Rama's first administration, Albania secured European Union candidate country status, and the prime minister vowed to tackle fraud and reform the energy sector. However, accusations of links, to the drugs trade, continue to distress, the ruling government.

The protestors were seen chanting the same slogan that they used, during the downfall of Communism, in the country, during the 1990s. In a raging statement, conservative politician, Lulzim Basha told the public: 'We are here with a mission, to liberate Albania from crime and corruption, to make Albania like the rest of Europe.'

A year earlier, in 2018, there were student protests, in Albania, held at different universities, to oppose high tuition rates, better living conditions, dormitories, and greater voting rights, for students, in the Senate, to name a few. These protests were started, by the faculty of the Polytechnic University of Tirana, and they spread, as the youth marched towards the Ministry of Education, Youth and Sports.

This anti-system protest was one of the biggest, Albania had seen, in recent years. Memes were presented, during the protests, and the discontent, also spread through social media. Students left a broken steering wheel, and the constitution at Rama's office, after being unimpressed, by the changes. These student protests hurt the image of the government.

In the recent past, there were also significant protests, against house demolitions, in Tirana, for the extension of a new boulevard, although the government had promised compensation, in several phases, for the dwellers. The residents, as a reaction, had blocked the bulldozers, to protect their homes, but were fired tear gas, in advance, and had gotten arrested. The new law on legalisation was first implemented, on the New Boulevard project.

The pending decisions, of the European Court of Human Rights, amounted to hundreds of thousands, of Euros, in compensation, for expropriations. The Albanian government had blackmailed, an Albanian judge at ECHR, over these pending cases. The construction, of the new project, was also stopped, in 2014, by the prime minister, because compensation to dwellers, was thought to be below market prices, then.

After that, Rama, eventually, not only used the compensation fund, for new construction but also excluded some buildings, for the compensation. The buildings awaiting demolition, without compensation violates, international conventions, the Constitute and Law on Social Housings, as it had been argued for Outer Ring Road, and the Lana River project, in Shkoza.

These growing protests, for different political reasons, inside European countries, including Albania, as a recent example, do indicate that Europeans are unhappy with the clientelism, partocracy, and authoritarianism, of political leaders. But the self-evident question arises, regarding when will the real change come, through democratic institutions. The masses only hope that it is not a utopian dream.

During this time, the ruling government, often use these episodes to their favour, mostly, by hoping that the street energy through protests, calms down. The anger, on the streets of Tirana, continues to hamper its regional and foreign policy, at large.

20 May, 2019

31

SERBIA TURNS AGAINST VUCIC

SERBS PARTICIPATED IN WEEKLY protest rituals, in January 2019, that involved resistance against President Aleksandar Vucic, who came into power in 2012, after twelve years, in the opposition.

Every Saturday, since then, Serbs gathered, at Republic Square, at Belgrade, to counter ongoing assault, on media freedoms, participative democracy, and political violence.

With neighbouring Albania, and Montenegro, also volatile, Serbia's protests have been called, the beginning of a 'Balkan Spring.' These protests escalated, in December 2018, and it might give emergence, to a new global movement, from Europe.

In March 2019, protests escalated, as riots spread to several neighbouring cities, including the second-largest city, Novi Sad. However, protests outside Belgrade, are smaller, in comparison. This crescendo has helped several angry people, and opposition leaders, to barge, into the headquarters, of Radio Television Serbia.

Several thousand protesters remained, in front of the building, as activists chanted 'Vucic thief,' in the corridors of the building. The state police eventually controlled these riots, by using pepper sprays and bringing a truck, near the building.

Many in the crowds, of around seven thousand five

hundred people, also whistled 'He's finished.' It was a similar slogan, used, during the ousting of Slobodan Milosevic, in October 2000. Bosko Obradovic, leader of a far-right political party, *Dveri*, has even gone further ahead, and accused Vucic, of being ready to accept Kosovo's independence.

As per an Op-ed written by Elis Gjevori: 'In the Balkans, politics operates much like a revolving door where politicians go out one end and come back in from the other generating a crisis of credibility. There is widespread cynicism towards politicians who promise change but once in power they often emulate their predecessors is difficult to overcome.'

According to Associated Press, Vucic rejected to bow down, to their demands – even if there were 'five million people', on the streets. He labelled the opposition leaders, as 'fascists', 'hooligans' and 'thieves', and vowed to take a response, within Serbia's democratic framework. His current plan seems to end the conflict, with Kosovo, finding ways to comply, with IMF's austerity demands, and devising a strategy, to enter European Union.

In November 2018, there was a beating of Borko Stefanovic, a member of the Serbian Left Party, in the opposition, in the southern city of Krusevac, where he was left injured, and hospitalised, after being hit, by some blunt objects, by angry rioters.

Despite claiming to be an honest leftist, he had his share of wanton controversies. It included the mediation, behind the 2008 sale of the state petroleum company, *Naftna Industrija Srbije* (NIS), to Russia's Gazprom Neft. The deal had caused outrage, for its tendering process, and the final sale price. The deal was seen, in the category of such privatisations, which led to the eventual economic downfall, of former Yugoslavia. Vucic launched an investigation, into this deal, in 2014.

After the assault, Stefanovic believes that he was attacked because he had publicly spoken, against connections, between political servants, and criminal networks, and he also alleged that there was corruption, in awarding state contracts, and in dispersing state money.

The next day, his associate, Dragan Djilas told the reporters that Vucic was, himself, behind the assault. The first demonstration, held in Krusevac, went under the banner, 'Stop the Bloody Shirts,' which had been organised, by the Alliance for Serbia, an amalgam of political parties, including the Serbian Left, spanning the country's political spectrum.

The protestors had also demanded a probe, into the politically motivated murder, of Oliver Ivanovic, a Kosovo Serb politician, in 2018, an outspoken Vucic critic, who had been fiercely anti-government, particularly, when it came to reprimanding organised crime.

The Belgrade protests happened, shortly after, and were mostly organised, by the students, enrolled, at the University of Political Sciences. These recent protests are not the real testimony, of Vucic's authoritarian rule, which is being mocked by many observers.

When in 2017 Vucic became the president, citizens took to the streets daily, for over two months, but in May, the protests eventually died out. It also signifies that these protests lacked grassroots initiatives, and a certain aimlessness meant that there was no clearer path, set for a victory against the state. That is why, he has been likened, to an autocratic president, seen in Russia, and Turkey before.

Many Serbs also voted for Vucic because they could not find a good alternative. The list of candidates included leaders, including former ombudsman Sasa Jankovic, who promised to build Serbia a coastline.

Despite being an ally of Russia, Serbia also wants to be a member of the European Union, under the current geopolitical context. However, in an evaluation, of April 2017, presidential election, the Organisation for Security and Cooperation in Europe said: 'biased media coverage, an undue advantage of incumbency and a blurred distinction between campaign and official activities undermined the level playing field for contestants.'

Also, in a 2017 report, by Transparency Serbia and the Centre for Investigative Journalism, there is political control, over security forces, and the rule of law is undermined.

In the past, Vucic was Slobodan Milosevic's minister of information, in the final days, of the Yugoslav wars. He was given powers, to fine journalists, who criticised the regime and banned unfriendly TV networks.

His ruling centre-right Serbian Progressive Party, enjoys a complete grip, over Serbia's government, judiciary, and security services. He has imposed restrictions, on the Serbian media, to such an extent, that only a few media agencies have been brave enough to write about allegations, of corruption, cronyism, and voter intimidation, that have plagued governmental functions.

Foreign Policy Op-ed writer, Aleks Eror, wrote that the entirety of the anti-Vucic ideological spectrum was being represented—from student Marxists to Bosko Obradovic, the ultranationalist leader of Dveri, a far-right opposition party of religious conservatives—sometimes causing scuffles among the protesters. This highlights the fragmented and impotent nature of the Serbian opposition, which is united by its opposition to Vucic but unable to agree on much else.

The president has blamed these protests on Kosovo, possibly for a land swap, to resolve the dispute, with ethnic Albanians, and Muslims, as animosities, have risen twenty years, after both countries, fought a war.

If we go back into history, much of the current far-right extremism, spreading globally, was given birth, during the Balkan conflicts, of the 1990s, especially during the Bosnian War.

It also created a generation of Christian extremists, and nobody stopped them, from doing all sorts of bad things, in their home country.

May 28, 2019

32

TENSIONS IN MONTENEGRO

PROTESTS IN MONTENEGRO HAVE TURNED
ugly, after its citizens, took onto the streets in February
2019, triggering yet another unrest, in the Balkans.

Montenegrins want President Milo Đukanovic, to resign,
over alleged corruption, and abuse of office.

Several protestors, not having any affiliation, with political
parties, marched through the Montenegrin capital,
Podgorica, chanting slogans, such as *'Milo Theif.'*

The protestors are also demanding the resignations, of
their Prime Minister, Dusko Markovic, the Supreme
State Prosecutor Ivica Stankovic, and the Montenegrin
chief prosecutor for organised crime, Milivoje Katnic.

A local journalist and activist told Antonela Rajcevic:
'they want to turn this place into the next Monte Carlo.
It is great if you are a billionaire or a millionaire, but it is
not a good place for the common citizens of Montenegro.'

To continue, being part of the government, the political
leaders have rejected these protests, which included
opposition leaders, although they had initially supported
these demonstrations.

In March 2019, around ten thousand demonstrators
marched the streets. It was one among many such protests
happening, since the beginning of the year. At the peak,

an attendance of around twenty-five thousand protests has been recorded.

The rallies started after Dusko Knezevic, a former ally of Dukanovic, accused him, and his ruling Democratic Party of Socialists (DPS), of fraud and misconduct, mainly involving questionable financial deals. He has now fled the country, and is now in Britain, as Dukanovic accused him of money laundering and fraud.

In December 2018, Montenegro's central bank placed the small Atlas Banka, governed by Knezevic, under temporary administration, as the bank's capital, which flunked in providing minimum risk requirements. In January 2019, Atlas Banka tried to increase its capital again, after hiking it in October 2018 by 1.37 million euros ($1.56 million), to 32.03 million euros.

According to Reuters, both Dukanovic and the DPS, have denied the allegations, from Dusko Knezevic.

In the public, these demonstrations are seen under legal norms, unless, and until, they turn violent. Marija Backovic, a teacher from Podgorica, amidst the demonstrations, said: 'We are not the danger for this country, those that are destroying it for 30 years are the real danger.'

Dukanovic has been associated with Montenegrin politics, for over thirty years, either serving as a prime minister, or president, since the country's independence, in 1991.

He might be Europe's longest-standing leader. He also defied Russian perspectives, and joined NATO, in 2007. In 2016, Dukanovic survived an assassination attempt, and a coup, that was designed, to bring a pro-Russian party, into power. Two Russian intelligence officers, and two opposition politicians, among thirteen people, were eventually convicted, by the country's federal court, over a 2016 election day plot, aimed at toppling Montenegro's government. At that time, countries such as the United Kingdom had expressed solidarity, during post-plot Montenegro.

However, his critics say that he has effectively turned Montenegro, into a one-party state, almost like a fiefdom, insisting on having complete control. He is also believed to have undermined the rule of law, and given more power, to himself, and his scions.

In 1996, Dukanovic turned against Serbian leader Slobodan Milosevic, as he was favouring an independent Montenegro. He was the man, who oversaw the division, of Yugoslavia, into Serbia, and Montenegro. Montenegro eventually started to have heightening separation, from Serbia, under his leadership. He emerged victorious, in the May 2006, independence referendum.

The populist reaction, coming from Balkan countries, including Montenegro, is that the governments have failed, to provide an adequate roadmap, particularly a composite European future.

Earlier, Berlin Summit had happened, where Angela Merkel, and Emmanuel Macron, tried to find a consensus, between Balkan leaders, ahead of the sixth annual Western Balkans Summit, in Poland. All this is happening, at a difficult time, because of an existing trade row, between Kosovo, and Serbia. At the same time, EU countries loathe the ties of Balkan countries, with China and Russia. However, they fail to realise that it is due to their isolation, that Balkan countries want an economic, or political alliance, with China and Russia.

In 2018, a Chinese bank funded Montenegro eighty-five per cent, of the cost, of a one hundred eighty km highway, the country's biggest infrastructure, to date, linking its south port, Bar, with northern Serbia.

Montenegro is seeking to join the European Union, but to gain membership, it requires to deracinate organised crime, corruption, and nepotism, and reduce the red tape, of bureaucracy, before it can become a member of the bloc. Joining NATO has also deeply divided Montenegro.

In a 2017 report, the US state department criticised Montenegro's lack of judicial independence, and police corruption, and recognised a threat, to press freedom.

Johannes Hahn, one of the EU's most senior figures, had recently made a statement about countries, in the Balkans that accepted Chinese aid. He called these Balkan countries, as 'Trojan horses,' within the bloc. This is an odious statement, to say, about European nations, willing to join the European Union.

Statements, like these, make the people of these countries, seem like 'lesser Europeans.' As of now, the reactionary measures, coming from the EU bloc, is that they are cutting funding, to western Balkan countries, from the World Bank, and IMF, leaving China, and Russia, to fill that gap.

It was pro-European leader Dukanovic, who once said, in an interview, to Reuters: 'Moscow, through politics, and Beijing, via loans, aims to prevent NATO and EU expansion in the Balkans. Unless the EU realises that, I am afraid its future might be in jeopardy.'

2 June, 2019

33

POLITICAL AGITATIONS IN HONG KONG

HONG KONG HAS BECOME A POWDER KEG, and a city on the edge. Anger has been brimming, from all quarters of society, as over a million protestors, about fifteen per cent, of the population, mostly young, in black-clad uniforms, belonging from myriad political camps, and social groups, marched the streets, to protest a new law, that would allow people, accused of crimes, from Hong Kong, to be extradited, to China. The movement started in March 2019 but went big scale in June 2019.

The law says that convicted people would be subjected to China's 'opaque justice system.' It is also a move that would make Hong Kong, a haven, for many Chinese bureaucrats, and leaders.

The protestors also seemed to have paranoias, of political manoeuvring, from the Chinese, that included spying. They also want the release of previous protestors, held accountable, in the past. Hongkongers believe that the Chinese government also has several local gangs, at their disposal, and several other several teams, including intelligence.

For several weeks, protestors had blocked all-important roads, leading to the city centre, and huddled near police headquarters, creating a political storm. It is because one of the privileges, Hong Kong has, had since the late 1990s, is a semi-autonomy system, that consists of an independent judicial branch. In June 2019, police used pepper spray, rubber bullets, and tear gas. All the mayhem, resulting, from the situation, has led the executive Carrie Lam, a Chinese agent, to publicly apologise, and suspend the law. The protestors want him to resign, despite Lam giving a public apology. In this raging time, a girl, in a deep meditative pose, sitting on the road, has become iconic, in these protests. Called as the 'Shield Girl', she was recently highlighted, in an artwork, from China's leading dissident artist, Badicua. But, the opposition fears, that once the protests die down, they might re-implement the law, causing new tensions.

The British newspaper, The Independent, reported that one hundred eighty thousand citizens attended a vigil, in the city's Victoria Park. This place symbolises, to many, a place of commemoration, of the 1989 Tiananmen Massacre, where Chinese Communists, once upon a time, commanded to disperse the crowds, to nullify the call, for a democratic China. This place, still, is a popular visiting spot, for locals, and foreign visitors, even after three decades. Historically, during the 2005 World Trade Organisation ministerial meeting, in the city, riots happened, again, and the local people received beatings.

As a reaction, the rioting of Hongkongers has also resulted, in some convictions. At least five protestors have been jailed, and they might get heavy prison sentences, based on the country's law. Unlike the 2014 umbrella movement, it is largely perceived, as a leaderless movement, and deployed modern use of technology, such as social media apps, like Telegram, that was eventually taken down, by the government.

They also used airdrop, a file-sharing application, on Apple devices, to share messages and memes. Protestors also used cash to buy tickets, rather than travel cards, that would allow them to be tracked, as some protestors also hurled metal barriers, at the police. Their response had been ferocious.

Isaac Cheng, the vice chairperson of the pro-democracy group, *Demosisto*, vouches for this fact. Five years back, it was Joshua Wong, Demosisto's co-founder, who started the umbrella movement.

Student's Union of Higher Institutions had reiterated four demands from Lam, which included withdrawing extradition law, completely, and permanently, dropping all charges laid down against protestors, and establishing an independent probe, into the claims of 'police brutality.'

The union gave a strong statement lately: 'Hongkongers do not need crocodile tears from a murderous regime, nor will we accept a mere suspension' of the bill.' The agitating scenes, which created a controversy, suggest that China is willing to have more control, over the city, on its southern coast. This law is been seen, as a threat, to its autonomy, as Hongkongers, saw in it, the collapse of Hong Kong's economic prosperity, and the betrayal of promises, assured, in the 1980s. Hong Kong, reverted, to China, in 1997. The autonomy is set to last for fifty years, till 2047. Culturally, there is also a desire for a British way of life, and the return of British-era institutions. That is why Hong Kong, almost looks like an ungovernable city, now in time.

To Reuters, in an interview, Robert Chung, the director of the Public Opinion Programme at The University of Hong Kong (HKUPOP) commented that the headcounts of protestors carry little importance, and it is more about the reality of regional politics, that he is concerned about, even though there are techniques, such as Jacob's method, that can measure the capacity to hold protests, at any place, for analysts. 'We are still caught between the unnecessary tension between science and democracy,' he said.

Around five years ago, the Communist Party of China, rejected the chance, of democratic reform, leading to the 2014 Umbrella Movement. It was a three-month occupation on the streets, and many young people were politicised by it. The movement was crushed, when many pro-independence lawyers, self-determination-seeking, frontline activists, were imprisoned

In The Independent Op-ed, Joshua Wong, and Alex Chow wrote: 'once upon a time, the people of Hong Kong were proud of creating a robust, export-oriented industrial city, one of the four Asian tiger economies, later turning into a global financial city with booming tourism.'

As turmoil, and anarchy spread, business tycoons, started moving assets, out of the city, and backed away, from major business deals.

Hongkongers believe, that under the current global scenario, the world is seeing their city, as an unliveable place, with a high influx of industrial activities, cowing press behaviour, lack of fairness in social and land policies, and high housing costs, in a concrete jungle. This deterioration also reflects the arrogance, and ineptitude of Hong Kong officials, and Chinese officials. Hongkongers, in this living age, have high ambitions, that include co-existence, vibrancy, equality, and various other value systems.

All these protests, do indicate, Hong Kong's relentless pursuit, of a sustainable democracy, a system, that is continuously deteriorating, by external political factors. In history, its sovereignty was handed down, from Britain to

China, in 1997, under the Sino-British Joint Declaration, in 1984. It now seems inevitable that Hongkongers want power, to be devolved, to the local people.

June 21, 2019

PART IV

POLITICS

34

KOSOVO TURNS TEN YEARS OLD

THE LANDLOCKED COUNTRY OF KOSOVO, on 17th February, 2018, will celebrate its tenth anniversary, but it faces myriad challenges in the future. Since its independence, in 2008, it has been a partially recognised state.

It seems that Kosovo's six main ethnicities (Albanians, Serbs, Turks, Gorani, Romani, and Bosnians), stand close, in terms of collective national conscience, but, in real life, they carry burdens, of their war-torn past.

Out of one-nighty three UN member states, only one hundred and thirteen have voted, in favour of Kosovo's sovereignty. Countries, such as Russia, and China, do not recognise it. Kosovo is yet to receive membership, in the UN, and the EU.

During the winter, and spring of 1999, a NATO intervention, in a seventy-eight - day airstrike, began, in favour of ethnic Albanians, against the Serbian forces, led by Slobodan Milosevic.

As NATO bombs fell, millions of Kosovar Albanians, predominantly Muslims, were expelled, from their villages, in an unfortunate event, of ethnic cleansing. As a barbaric event, it filled the pages of Europe's modern history.

Kosovo had spent nine years, under the control of the

United Nations. Later, Serbia tried to normalise relations, under the Brussels Agreement, but no constructive political settlement was devised, with the Government of Kosovo.

In the fieldwork, war correspondents, who have witnessed the country's war, have often written about military checkpoints, thousands of buildings that were destroyed, lines of refugees, displaced Kosovars, looking for safe zones, and the distant black smoke, coming from the burning villages.

In an Op-ed for New York Times, Andrew Testa wrote on February 15, 2018: 'the people seemed weighed down by resignation, as well as widespread disgust at perceived government corruption. Before the war, Kosovars had a better life and more opportunities. The country is crippled by low wages, unemployment, and a stagnant economy.'

According to a 2017 report, by International Committee for Missing Persons, four thousand five hundred people went missing, during the war. For Kosovars, where seventy per cent population are under thirty-five, it is almost impossible, to travel, due to stern restrictions, and neglect.

In 2005, a mass grave of ethnic Albanians was found, near Belgrade, the Serbian capital. Kosovars have also made a memorial, to victims in Meja, where Serb police executed around three hundred seventy-two Albanian men and boys. It had been the largest massacre, in the Kosovo War.

In the post-war period, it is believed that depleted uranium weapons, used during the 1999 war, have caused the contamination, in the surroundings, including drinking water, animals and air (as researched by Dr Jasmina Vujic from the Department of Nuclear Engineering, at Berkeley

University of California, who believes in this notion). More than a hundred locations, in Kosovo, including borders, rivers, village roads, and forest paths, are seeded by landmines.

In an interview with Radio Sputnik, Marko Gasic, a London-based Balkans expert said: 'this is not really a state; this is a territory, almost like an atoll occupied by a superpower, in which the natives are told what to do, and they don't know anything different other than what they're told'.

It seems that the Serbians are only surviving, in the northern part of Kosovo, in the Mitrovica area, where they also retain control. Whenever the Kosovo Liberation Army, has established its control, the Serbs, residing, in the occupied areas, have been cleansed.

In terms of geostrategic politics, the US has created the biggest military presence, in Kosovo, since Vietnam. This military presence, as a foreign policy, starting from Camp Bondsteel, in eastern Kosovo, will help the US, to keep the Russians out.

The political history, of this region, in the Balkans, has continuously evolved. In 1389, at the Battle of Kosovo, Polje, Serbs, fighting alongside Albanian allies, lost to the Ottoman Empire. It was not until 1912 when Albanian forces took it back. But Serb forces soon took control, and in 1918, the city became part of the Kingdom of Serbs, Croats and Slovenes, a predecessor to Yugoslavia. In 1947, the capital was moved, from Prizren, to Pristina. At that time, Pristina was a small city, of only twenty thousand inhabitants, who spoke Turkish. In the process, most of the Ottoman architecture was destroyed and replaced by communist structures.

Presently, Pristina struggles with pollution problems and corruption. Forty per cent of Kosovars remain unemployed. There is Islamic extremism, which exists in several geographical quarters, even if Kosovars are largely gender-neutral. Organised crime is rife, which includes the cocaine trade, and sex rackets, outside its borders. In schools, however, most children attend mono-ethnic classes, where teachers also belong to the same ethnic group – walls separate Albanian, and Serbian students.

It is a city that has been built twice; first during the part of Yugoslavia, as a socialist city, and second after the 1998-99 conflict with Serbia. Around forty thousand illegally constructed buildings, exist in Pristina, without permits, or through fraudulent permits.

In 2014, the Pristina mayor, Shpend Ahmeti, started receiving death threats, as soon as after five months, after being in office. It is because he wanted to bring clean, and rational governance, cheap heating, to public schools, and an end to waste crises, in the most corrupt city, in Europe.

In terms of culture, Kosovo-born artists, such as Rita Ora, Dua Lipa, and Era Istrefi, are regulars, on the international music charts. Pristina's clubs, bars, and live music venues have very few ethnic boundaries. Fortunately, these local artists have thrived. Petrit Halilaj, a young artist, was awarded a special jury prize, at the 'Venice Biennale,' in 2017.

February 2, 2018

35

STATE EMERGENCY IN MALDIVES

THE GOVERNMENT OF MALDIVES EXTENDED the state emergency, by thirty days in February 2018.

The nation, surrounded by ninety-nine per cent water, has been increasingly looked, at as a strategic island, by neighbouring countries.

President Abdulla Yameen believes that there is a threat, to national security, in the country. He had refused a Supreme Court order of freeing imprisoned, opposition leaders, including ex-President Mohammad Nasheed. The families, of these imprisoned leaders, have also been harassed.

There can be a new start, of a cold war, in the Indian Ocean, between China and India. The Maldives International Airport, and the major highway, connecting the airport, fall under China's 'One Road, One Belt Plan.' The Chinese state has plans, to make islands, out of the water, in the Maldives.

As per inputs, China has acquired rights, to over seventeen islands, of the Maldives. Many of them, are believed to be converted, into working stations, with sophisticated naval airbases and communication facilities. This is a stance, which is similar, to what the Chinese are planning, in the South China Sea, shortly.

Prime Minister, Narendra Modi, has been looked upon, as India's Reagan – the ex-US President, had sent troops to Grenada, in the Caribbean, to oust a communist regime, in a similar political scenario. But, will the BJP-led government send its troops, to the Maldives? That remains to be seen, as of now.

The political crises, in the Republic of Maldives, deepened, when police used excessive force, to curb protests, by the opposition, who continued to hold anti-government protests.

Dr David Brewster, an Australian senior analyst, believes that both powers, such as China and India, are willing to expand their roles, and presence, in the Indian Ocean Region (IOR), as strategic rivalries, have heightened in recent times.

Brewster has reaffirmed India's ambitions, about deepening ties, in ASEAN, and EAS, to counter Chinese diplomacy. The plan includes building bases, in the Andaman and Nicobar region, as well as in Mauritius, and Seychelles.

Since Abdullah Yameen had become the incumbent president, there have been stories, where it is believed that radicalisation has increased, among the Muslim youth, living in the Maldives. Many have joined the ISIS ranks, lending themselves, to the sectarian Islamic war, in Syria and Iraq.

Yameen has also been regarded as a military threat, to India, because of his allegiance to China, Pakistan, and Saudi Arabia. The Saudi kingdom may open a new naval base, in the Maldives, in the future.

Brewster also believes that powers, such as the United

States, and Australia, will expect India to take the lead, and might support India's military actions.

Coming back to the strategic importance of Maldives, the designated sea lines of communication (SLOC), from where Middle Eastern oil transits, to countries, such as Japan and China, fall, via the Maldives. The busier northern SLOC, passes between India's Minicoy Island, and the northernmost Maldivian coral atoll.

Back in time, Maldives had been the last South Asian Island, to be decolonised, in 1965.

The British maintained bases, in its Gan and Hittadu islands, until they were shut down, in 1978. Its culture has been largely affiliated with Dravidian origin, with links of Tamil and Malayalam, in its language.

Looking at the recent political history, of this largely Muslim-dominated island, its former President Mohammad Nasheed, had been in jail, for around thirty years, and was an Amnesty International Prisoner of Conscience, in 1991. His predecessor, Gayoom arrested him, around twenty times.

Unlike, incumbent President Yameen, Nasheed was not interested, in having close ties with the Chinese state. On December 8, 2017, Yameen signed a Free Trade Agreement (FTA), with China, which surprised New Delhi. As of now, the Doklam standoff, on the Bhutan-Tibet border, has fractured relations, between China and India. In addition to this pact, Yameen had endorsed Chinese investments, for promoting tourism, healthcare, and tackling climate change issues, in the Maldives.

Mohan Gurusamy, wrote, in an Op-ed, in 2012, in Deccan

Chronicle: 'in 2012, Mr Nasheed's successor President Mohammed Waheed cancelled the previous government's decision to award the $500 million contract to manage Male international airport to an Indian company, GMR Group.'

In the past, and the present, India has also followed a policy, to contain any form of Chinese aggression, in international waters.

Mohan Gurusamy, an analyst studying political issues, further believes that there have been reports of eleven Chinese ships, at least one Chinese frigate, a thirty thousand tonne amphibious transport dock, and three support tankers entering the Indian Ocean region, from the Sundra Strait, between Java, and Sumatra.

When the Americans, occupy Diego Garcia Island, with its state-of-the-art, high-tech military types of equipment, control rooms, terminals, and military arsenal, including B-52 bomber planes, and naval vessels, it is probable that any form of Chinese-sponsored obstruction, in the region, will ring alarm bells.

Diego Garcia, which lies just to the south of Maldives, eighteen thousand km, from the southern tip of India, is a pivotal spot for the American defence strategies, to exhibit control in the area.

February 26, 2018

36

PLIGHT OF SRI LANKAN MUSLIMS

COMMUNAL VIOLENCE BETWEEN BUDDHIST Sinhalese and Muslims escalated sharply in Sri Lanka in March 2018, forcing the government to impose a nationwide state of emergency on 6 March. International outlets such as Reuters and Al Jazeera reported that the immediate trigger was the killing of a 41-year-old Sinhalese man in Kandy district after an altercation with Muslim youths. His death sparked retaliatory attacks, with Sinhalese mobs ransacking Muslim businesses and setting fire to mosques. Human Rights Watch noted that police struggled to contain the unrest, and at least two people were killed while dozens were injured.

The violence had already been brewing. In late February 2018, riots broke out in Ampara after false rumours spread that a Muslim-owned restaurant had laced food with sterilisation pills. This baseless claim inflamed tensions and led to attacks on Muslim property. By early March, the unrest spread to Kandy, where mobs destroyed homes, shops, and mosques. Al Jazeera confirmed that 24 suspects were arrested for arson, while the government used emergency powers to detain dozens more.

Muslims make up around 9 per cent of Sri Lanka's population, behind the Tamil minority. Reuters reported that Sinhalese nationalists accused Muslims of vandalising Buddhist sites and attempting forced conversions, though these allegations were often based on rumours. The

Associated Press described how hundreds of Muslim residents in Mullegama barricaded themselves inside a mosque after mobs attacked their homes, accusing them of stealing a temple donation box. At least 20 homes were badly damaged, and witnesses said police did little to stop the attackers.

Radical Sinhalese Buddhist groups such as Bodu Bala Sena and Ravana Balaya have played a role in stoking ethnocentric nationalism, promoting the slogan 'Sri Lanka for Sinhalese Buddhists.' Their rhetoric amplified fears that Muslim practices such as polygamy or alleged attempts to alter demographics threatened the majority. In Ampara, mobs spread rumours that Muslim traders were mixing pills into food to make Sinhalese men impotent, a claim later debunked but which fuelled violence.

The government responded by banning social media platforms temporarily, citing the spread of hate speech and incitement. The Guardian reported that Facebook and WhatsApp were used to circulate inflammatory messages, worsening tensions. Hundreds of Buddhist monks later rallied in Colombo, demanding stronger action against minorities.

The paradox of violence in Buddhist-majority states such as Myanmar and Sri Lanka has drawn international attention. Buddhism is often associated with peace, yet nationalist movements have weaponised it. In Myanmar, Buddhist militias were implicated in attacks on Rohingya Muslims, while in Sri Lanka, Sinhalese mobs targeted Muslim communities. Analysts have noted that this contradiction undermines Buddhism's global image as a non-violent faith.

Sri Lanka's history of communal violence is long. The

1915 Sinhalese–Muslim riots created deep divisions, and more recently, Aluthgama on the western coast saw anti-Muslim violence in 2014. The civil war between the Sinhalese-dominated state and Tamil Tigers also left scars. Human Rights Watch documented how the final phase of the war in 2008–2009 at Mullivaikkal involved mass civilian deaths, with thousands of Tamils killed by the army. Survivors continue to search for missing relatives.

The decline of Sufi Islam and the rise of Wahhabi-influenced practices, often funded by Saudi institutions, has unsettled many Sinhalese Buddhists. Some compare Sri Lankan Muslims to Israeli Jews, portraying them as wealthy and self-centred, a stereotype that feeds resentment. Political divisions have also played a role: Muslims largely voted against Mahinda Rajapaksa in the 2015 election, which further entrenched perceptions of disloyalty among Sinhalese nationalists.

International actors urged restraint. UN Under-Secretary-General Jeffrey Feltman called for 'swift and full implementation of the government's commitment to bring the perpetrators of the violence and hate speech to justice, to take measures to prevent a recurrence, and to enforce non-discriminatory rule of law.' Human Rights Watch stressed that minorities must be protected and that impunity for communal violence would only deepen mistrust.

The Sri Lankan diaspora also reacted. In Dubai, the Sri Lankan embassy hosted community meetings where expatriates called for peace and emphasised pluralism, rejecting divisions of religion or caste.

The events of March 2018 revealed how fragile Sri Lanka's social fabric remains. Despite the end of the civil war in 2009, ethnic and religious tensions persist. The riots in Ampara and Kandy showed how rumours and nationalist rhetoric can quickly escalate into violence. The government's reliance on emergency powers, rather than long-term reconciliation, highlighted the absence of structural reforms. As Al Jazeera observed, the violence was triggered by a single death but fuelled by deeper grievances and mistrust.

Sri Lanka calls itself a socialist country, yet Buddhism is the official religion, and segregation is evident in education, with Tamils, Muslims and Sinhalese often studying in separate schools. This institutional separation reinforces communal identities rather than bridging them. Unless Sri Lanka addresses these divisions, majoritarianism will continue to deepen fissures.

The paradox remains striking: a country that promotes Buddhism as its state religion has repeatedly witnessed Buddhist mobs attacking minorities. As Reuters and Associated Press coverage showed, the violence in 2018 was not isolated but part of a longer pattern of communal unrest. Without accountability and reconciliation, Sri Lanka risks repeating the cycle of violence that has haunted its modern history.

13 March, 2018

37

IRELAND AFTER THE GOOD FRIDAY
AGREEMENT

WHEN THE GOOD FRIDAY AGREEMENT was signed in April 1998, it rekindled something that had long seemed unattainable in Northern Ireland: faith in political dialogue. For decades, the region had been trapped in a cycle of violence so entrenched that many ordinary people believed resolution was impossible. Yet, against expectations shaped by years of bloodshed, a negotiated settlement emerged. It did not erase the past, but it transformed the future by replacing armed conflict with constitutional politics and by drawing deeply divided communities into a shared, if uneasy, framework.

Northern Ireland's conflict is often narrated as a struggle between Catholics and Protestants, but this simplification obscures a more layered reality. While sectarian identities played a central role, there has always existed a significant section of society that resisted being reduced to religious or political binaries. Even today, many citizens seek a third space—one that does not define their lives solely by unionist or nationalist loyalties. This quiet rejection of rigid identity categories is among the least acknowledged yet most consequential legacies of the peace process.

The roots of the conflict stretch back centuries. Ireland's earliest settlers, the Gaels, were pagans who embraced Christianity in the fifth century, establishing a largely unified religious culture. The introduction of Protestantism did not occur organically but through English political intervention beginning in the sixteenth century. During the Tudor and Stuart periods, vast tracts of land—predominantly owned by Catholics—were confiscated and redistributed to Protestant settlers as part of plantation policies. These changes reshaped the demographic and political landscape, particularly in the north-east, where Protestants gradually became dominant, while Catholics remained the majority across much of the island.

Partition in 1921 formalised these divisions. Northern Ireland remained part of the United Kingdom, governed by a Protestant-majority administration that systematically marginalised the Catholic minority. Discrimination in housing allocation, employment and voting rights became structural features of the state. As historians and journalists writing for The Irish Times have documented, these inequalities persisted for decades, creating a sense of permanent exclusion among Catholics that eventually erupted into organised protest.

Inspired by global civil rights movements, Catholic communities began mobilising in the late 1960s. Their peaceful demonstrations were frequently met with force, prompting riots and unrest that spiralled beyond the control of local authorities. British troops were deployed in 1969, initially welcomed by some Catholic neighbourhoods as protection, but soon viewed as an occupying force. What followed was a thirty-year conflict known as the Troubles, marked by bombings, assassinations, internment without trial and the pervasive militarisation of daily life.

The prison protests of the late 1970s and early 1980s represented a critical turning point. Republican inmates in Belfast's Maze Prison demanded recognition as political prisoners, refusing to wear uniforms and later engaging in hunger strikes. In 1981, ten prisoners died, including Bobby Sands, whose death while serving as a Member of Parliament intensified international attention. Journalists such as Peter Taylor of the BBC later observed that while the hunger strikes radicalised communities, they also exposed the moral and political dead ends of violence, reinforcing the need for a negotiated settlement.

By the early 1990s, exhaustion with conflict was widespread. Secret talks, ceasefires and sustained diplomatic engagement gradually paved the way for inclusive negotiations. The Good Friday Agreement emerged from these efforts as a complex compromise rather than a definitive solution. It established a devolved Assembly and a power-sharing Executive, ensuring that governance could not be monopolised by one community. It affirmed that Northern Ireland would remain part of the United Kingdom unless a majority voted otherwise, while recognising the legitimacy of Irish nationalist aspirations. Crucially, it guaranteed the right of individuals to identify as British, Irish or both.

The agreement's success lay not in reconciliation— an ambition perhaps too grand—but in its ability to dramatically reduce violence. Armed checkpoints disappeared, border installations were dismantled, and paramilitary groups began decommissioning weapons. While dissident attacks occurred, the scale of conflict never returned to that of the Troubles. Writing years later, correspondents for The Guardian described the post-agreement period as an imperfect peace, but one that allowed a new generation to grow up without the normalisation of fear.

Women played a vital yet often under-recognised role in this process. Prior to the agreement, the 1996 elections brought women from Catholic and Protestant backgrounds into a political alliance that prioritised dialogue over dogma. The Northern Ireland Women's Coalition, supported by grassroots activists and women within Sinn Fein, introduced perspectives that challenged the dominance of militarised masculinity in negotiations. Their emphasis on social issues, reconciliation and inclusivity influenced both the tone and substance of the agreement.

International mediation proved equally decisive. Former US President Bill Clinton and Senator George Mitchell provided diplomatic momentum and credibility at moments when talks appeared on the verge of collapse. Their contributions were later acknowledged when Belfast City Council conferred the Freedom of the City upon them, a symbolic gesture reflecting the agreement's deep emotional significance for many residents.

However, peace did not translate into stability. The institutions created by the Good Friday Agreement have repeatedly collapsed due to political deadlock.

As analysts writing in The Financial Times have noted, power-sharing often produced paralysis rather than partnership, with disputes over symbols, language, and legacy derailing governance. Northern Ireland remained economically dependent on London, and Belfast struggled to reclaim its former status as a major commercial centre.

The Brexit referendum of 2016 exposed these vulnerabilities with unprecedented force. While the UK voted to leave the European Union, a majority in Northern Ireland voted to remain. This divergence revived fears surrounding the Irish border, which had become largely invisible under the peace settlement.

American journalist Kevin Cullen, who spent decades reporting from Ireland, warned that the return of customs infrastructure could disrupt the fragile normalcy achieved since 1998, reigniting political and psychological divisions.

Although British leaders, including Theresa May, repeatedly assured that Brexit would not undermine the Good Friday Agreement, events proved more complicated. The Northern Ireland Executive collapsed following the 2017 UK general election and remained suspended amid disputes exacerbated by Brexit. Proposals for direct rule from London resurfaced, unsettling communities that had come to view local governance as a symbol of peace.

Public sentiment, meanwhile, has evolved. As Grainne Long has observed in interviews cited by Irish newspapers, many citizens are increasingly disengaged from constitutional debates. They care more about healthcare, education, and economic security than nationalist rhetoric. Rugby matches, not referendums, dominate conversation.

Yet this pragmatic outlook exists alongside a resurgence of identity politics, driven partly by demographic change and economic uncertainty.

Controversies surrounding paramilitary influence have further complicated the landscape. Investigative reports in local and British press have alleged that remnants of the Provisional IRA retained control over illicit fuel operations, including diesel laundering. Such revelations, alongside reports of internal intimidation, have eroded support for militant republicanism among ordinary people, particularly as economic survival eclipses ideological loyalty.

Commentators such as Fintan O'Toole have argued that the Good Friday Agreement, while ending war, institutionalised sectarian categories by embedding them within governance structures. Politics became less violent but remained divided. This paradox lies at the heart of Northern Ireland's post-conflict condition: peace without full integration, stability without consensus.

The Good Friday Agreement did not resolve Ireland's historical grievances, nor did it erase the trauma of the past. What it achieved was more restrained and more enduring. It replaced guns with ballots, prisons with parliaments, and silence with dialogue. Its survival depends not on nostalgia for 1998, but on the capacity of society to adapt its principles to new realities. Northern Ireland today stands not at the end of history, but at a crossroads where peace must be continually re-negotiated, defended, and re-imagined.

15 April, 2018

38

US-IRAN NUCLEAR STANDOFF

PRESIDENT TRUMP'S DECISION TO withdraw the United States from the Iran nuclear agreement was one of the most significant reversals in recent foreign policy. The agreement, formally known as the Joint Comprehensive Plan of Action (JCPOA), was signed in 2015 between Iran and six major powers — the US, Britain, France, Germany, Russia, and China — under President Barack Obama. Its purpose was straightforward but strategic: to limit Iran's nuclear programme in exchange for sanctions relief, allowing the country to reconnect with the global economy.

Under the deal, Iran agreed to strict limits on uranium enrichment, dismantled thousands of centrifuges, and restricted heavy-water production. The International Atomic Energy Agency (IAEA) was given broad powers to inspect facilities and verify compliance. The restrictions were designed to extend Iran's 'breakout time' — the period needed to produce enough material for a nuclear weapon — to at least a year, reducing the immediate risk of proliferation.

Supporters praised the JCPOA as one of the most rigorous verification regimes ever applied to a nuclear programme. Critics, however, pointed to weaknesses. Chief among these were the sunset clauses — provisions under which some restrictions would expire after 10–15 years. Opponents argued that once these clauses took effect, Iran could legally expand its nuclear capacity, potentially shortening its breakout time. Others complained that the deal ignored Iran's ballistic missile programme and its support for militias across the Middle East.

Regional rivals echoed these concerns. Israel argued that the agreement overlooked Iran's wider ambitions. In 2018, Prime Minister Benjamin Netanyahu presented what he claimed were Iranian nuclear archives, suggesting a long-standing weapons programme. Yet the IAEA continued to report that Iran was complying with the deal's technical limits. Intelligence assessments also confirmed that Iran was abiding by the accord, even as scepticism persisted about its long-term effectiveness.

For Trump, the issue was broader than nuclear restrictions. He repeatedly described the deal as 'defective', claiming it strengthened Iran rather than restraining it. Having campaigned on a promise to abandon the agreement, he announced in May 2018 that the US would withdraw and reimpose sweeping sanctions.

The move carried strong political symbolism. The JCPOA was widely seen as Obama's signature diplomatic achievement. By discarding it, Trump not only reshaped US policy towards Iran but also repudiated his predecessor's foreign-policy legacy. As journalist Peter Baker noted, it marked 'a dramatic break with the internationalist diplomacy of the Obama years.'

Secretary of State Mike Pompeo outlined the new framework: twelve demands Iran would have to meet before sanctions could be lifted. These went far beyond nuclear issues, requiring Tehran to end support for groups such as Hezbollah and Hamas, halt missile development and withdraw from regional conflicts.

In effect, the Trump administration sought to turn a narrowly focused nuclear deal into a sweeping geopolitical resettlement.

Economically, the strategy was equally forceful. Washington reinstated sanctions on Iran's oil exports, banking sector, and shipping industry, while threatening penalties for foreign firms trading with Tehran. As Robin Wright observed, this amounted to 'a sweeping attempt to isolate Iran economically and diplomatically in the hope of forcing a renegotiation.'

Meanwhile, investigative reporting raised questions about Trump Organisation business ties. Journalist Adam Davidson in The New Yorker examined a property development in Azerbaijan linked to partners of the Trump brand. He reported that one company involved had connections to Azarpassillo, an Iranian firm suspected of acting as a front for the Revolutionary Guard. Davidson argued that such networks showed how political power and commercial interests often overlap globally. He criticised the Trump Organisation for failing to scrutinise its partners, though the company maintained it had only licensed its brand.

Other world powers responded differently. European governments — particularly Germany, France, and Britain — tried to preserve the JCPOA despite US withdrawal. They created a financial mechanism, INSTEX, to facilitate trade with Iran while avoiding American sanctions. European leaders argued that the deal remained the best available way to restrain Iran's nuclear programme. Russia and China also supported the agreement, while even close US allies such as Canada backed its continuation.

Inside Iran, the consequences were severe. President Hassan Rouhani had championed the deal as a path to economic recovery and improved relations with the West. The US withdrawal weakened his position and emboldened hardliners, who argued it proved America was an unreliable partner. Gradually, Iran reduced its compliance, enriching uranium beyond JCPOA limits. Tensions escalated in the Gulf, with incidents involving oil tankers, drone strikes and increased US military deployments.

The collapse of the JCPOA was therefore more than a technical dispute. It reflected a clash between two visions of diplomacy. Obama's administration had pursued engagement, hoping economic integration would encourage moderation. Trump's administration rejected this, opting instead for coercive pressure to force broader concessions.

Whether the withdrawal restrained Iran or accelerated its nuclear ambitions remains debated. What is clear is that it reshaped the Middle East's diplomatic landscape: weakening moderates in Iran, straining relations among Western allies and reviving a confrontation the JCPOA had been designed to contain.

11 May, 2018

39

RESOURCE WARS IN NIGERIAN FARMLANDS

IN THE FERTILE MIDDLE BELT OF NIGERIA,
Benue State has long been celebrated as the nation's
food basket, yet it has also become the epicentre of one
of Africa's most troubling internal conflicts. Within the
village of Aya Mbalom, Christian farmers and Muslim
Fulani herdsmen once lived in relative harmony, their
livelihoods tied to the land and its rhythms. That fragile
coexistence has unravelled in recent years, replaced by
violence, displacement, and destruction. The April 2018
attack on St Ignatius Catholic Church, where gunmen
killed two priests and at least seventeen worshippers,
marked a grim turning point. Reuters and Premium
Times reported the incident as part of a wider wave of
assaults across Benue, underscoring the vulnerability
of rural communities. Joe Parkinson of the Wall Street
Journal later described Nigeria's farmer–herder clashes as
cumulatively more lethal than Boko Haram's insurgency,
a reminder that dispersed communal violence can produce
staggering death tolls over time.

Since then, Benue has witnessed repeated atrocities.
Amnesty International documented in July 2025 that
more than half a million people had been displaced across
the state, with camps in Guma and Makurdi hosting tens
of thousands in dire conditions. Human Rights Watch
noted that in June 2025, over a hundred people were killed
in Yelewata, an attack that epitomised the state's failure
to protect civilians. Al Jazeera reported at least fifty-six
deaths in twin assaults in April 2025, stressing that official

figures often underestimate the true toll. These accounts converge on the same conclusion: the crisis is systemic, eroding the social fabric of Benue and leaving families trapped in cycles of flight, rebuilding, and renewed attacks.

The roots of the conflict lie in overlapping pressures. Benue's fertile soils have long attracted farmers, while Fulani herders traditionally moved cattle southward during dry seasons. International Crisis Group has repeatedly warned that desertification in northern Nigeria and the Sahel is forcing pastoralists into settled farming zones, intensifying disputes. While claims that '75% of land' in states such as Sokoto and Katsina has become desert are contested, the trend of land degradation is undeniable. Longer dry seasons, erratic rainfall, and shrinking grazing corridors push herders into areas where farmers are expanding cultivation to feed growing populations. Nigeria's population, projected by the United Nations to surpass that of the United States by 2050, places immense strain on land and water. In Benue, average farm sizes shrink as families grow, intensifying competition. Journalists from the Investigative Journalism Centre in 2025 documented families in Ukum and Guma repeatedly displaced, rebuilding homes only to face renewed attacks.

Policy choices have sharpened tensions. In 2017, Benue enacted an anti-open-grazing law, intended to protect farms and encourage ranching. Premium Times and Vanguard reported that while farmers welcomed the measure, pastoralists saw it as punitive, lacking viable alternatives. Enforcement often triggered confrontations, and without investment in ranching infrastructure or compensation schemes, the law became a flashpoint rather than a solution. The human toll is staggering. Amnesty International described 'squalid' conditions in IDP camps, with inadequate water, sanitation, and healthcare. UNICEF's situation reports in 2025 highlighted severe needs among children and pregnant women in Guma. Journalists from Channels TV reported protests in Makurdi after attacks, with residents alleging that warnings had been ignored and security forces arrived too late. Agricultural output has collapsed. Cassava, maize, and soy production in Makurdi and surrounding areas has been repeatedly disrupted, threatening national food security. Schools, clinics, boreholes, and reservoirs have been destroyed or abandoned, compounding the humanitarian emergency. Camps formed in repurposed primary schools, with thousands sharing a handful of toilets, have become semi-permanent features, a stark indictment of prolonged insecurity.

At the same time, political responses have often been inadequate. President Muhammadu Buhari urged dialogue and attributed the conflict partly to poverty and unemployment, controversially downplaying the prevalence of firearms among herders. Nigerian newspapers criticised these remarks, noting that survivors consistently reported attackers armed with rifles. The White House, under successive administrations, expressed concern over communal killings, with State Department statements urging accountability. Nigerian editorialists interpreted this as a clash of perspectives between Abuja and Washington, though it reflected standard human rights diplomacy. Nobel laureate Wole Soyinka visited Makurdi in 2018 and warned that the killings resembled 'ethnic cleansing,' invoking parallels with Yugoslavia in the 1990s. His remarks, carried by Pulse Nigeria, underscored the gravity of the crisis but also risked oversimplifying its complex drivers. Analysts such as Crisis Group stress that Fulani civilians are themselves victims of violence and cattle rustling, and that armed actors claiming to represent communities rarely speak for them. Grey

Dynamics in 2023 similarly cautioned against treating 'Fulani herdsmen' as a monolith, noting that identity militias often invoke communal labels without legitimacy.

Rumours abound also claim that Boko Haram militants have been hired to attack Christian villages circulate widely, but investigative outlets and rights groups have not substantiated systemic coordination. Journalists like Joe Parkinson emphasise the need to distinguish between insurgency in the northeast and communal conflict in the Middle Belt, while acknowledging overlaps in weapon flows and criminality. On the herder side, leaders of the Miyetti Allah Cattle Breeders Association have blamed cattle rustling for reprisals, with statements carried by Nigerian media. Usman Ngelzerma, head of a Fulani advocacy group, has accused regional media of bias and documented slain Fulani civilians. These grievances are real, but they cannot justify attacks on non-combatants.

The crisis in Benue is part of a wider Sahelian pattern. Pastoral mobility has long been an adaptive strategy, with herders moving cattle across thousands of miles from Senegal eastwards. As climate stress sharpens, pastoralists extend movements southward, colliding with farmers expanding cultivation. Reuters and Al Jazeera have chronicled similar clashes in Plateau, Kaduna, and Nasarawa, and International Crisis Group warns that without investment in grazing corridors and dispute resolution, 'resource wars' could spread across West Africa.

Three commitments are essential for responsible analysis and policy. Evidence discipline requires reliance on multiple independent sources for casualty estimates and perpetrator attribution. Where figures diverge, analysts must explain why—access limits, duplication, or politicisation—rather than sensationalise. Structural diagnosis demands focus on land governance, climate adaptation, and security provisioning. Anti-open-grazing laws without ranching investment invite confrontation. Conversely, properly funded ranching pilots, mapped transhumance corridors, and drought-resilient fodder schemes reduce friction. Accountability and protection are non-negotiable. Attacks on civilians, churches, schools, and clinics are serious crimes. Human Rights Watch and Amnesty International call for investigations and prosecutions. Nigerian authorities should prioritise mobile courts for rural crimes, integrate vigilante structures under lawful oversight, and deploy rapid response units to flashpoints. This is not a call to arm civilians—a step that risks civil war—but to restore public security through professional policing.

Practical steps include expanding early-warning systems linking village councils, religious leaders, and security agencies; funding boreholes and buffer zones with fair compensation; convening mediation forums between herders' associations, farmers' unions, and church councils; prosecuting perpetrators transparently; and scaling humanitarian support to IDPs. Aya Mbalom's tragedy is not only about inter-communal grievance but about the state's responsibility to secure lives and livelihoods amid climate stress and demographic pressure. Journalism—from Reuters' casualty reports to ICIR's field narratives—shows how survival wars engulf families when governance fails. Human rights documentation—from Amnesty and Human Rights Watch—provides the record. Analysis—from Crisis Group—frames the path out. The task now is to turn evidence into policy: demilitarise identities, secure rural spaces, and restore the pastoral–agrarian coexistence that once defined Benue's heartland.

3 June, 2018

40

UNFREEDOM IN THAILAND

WHENEVER THERE HAS BEEN A MILITARY JUNTA, ruling a country, and making amendments to the constitution, repression, is almost probable, or inevitable. The regime, in Thailand, seems one of those brutish examples: the Thai regime attained power, in May 2014. Before this, the 2006 military coup, made news headlines.

A year later, in March 2015, Prime Minister Prayut Chan-Ocha, replaced the Martial Law Act, of 1914, with Section 44, which made him enjoy full impunity, without any accountability, from the judiciary, administration, and legislature.

The Thai government, in their official narratives, argues about the freedom, they have given to their people, through the constitution, most notably, in the 1997 amendment, of the Constitution, which guarantees, an addition of forty rights, as compared, to fewer rights, that were drafted, in the 1932 Constitution. However, many countries, including the United States, Japan, the European Union, and others think otherwise. They ought to re-normalise their relations, only after civil rights, are enshrined in the public.

It is believed that the Thai coup leader, Prime Minister Gen. Prayut Chan –Ocha has routinely curbed dissent, in the public sphere. He is known to put a restraint, on public debates. As of now, hundreds of activists, have been jailed for computer-related crimes, sedition, and *lese majeste* (insulting the monarchy). The military can detain people, for up to seven days, without the consent of lawyers.

Prime Minister Chan-Ocha, who heads the National Council for Peace, and Order (NCPO) has promised to hold an election, in February 2019. Even if the election is held, it will be a broken promise. If the election was conducted, anyhow, it would probably not be free, and fair.

The NCPO had summoned, around seven hundred fifty-one people, belonging mostly, from the previous regime, that includes former Prime Minister Yingluck's Pheu Thai Party, and the United Front, for Democracy against Dictatorship (UDD), known as the 'Red Shirts.' Other individuals, who were summoned, were politicians, activists, and journalists, accused by the military, of anti-coup activities, and *lese majeste*, a common law for indicting people. T

he military had prosecuted, around twenty-two people, and refused to provide information, about them, who were, most probably, in secret detention.

The NCPO also ordered print media, not to be critical, of the military. TV, and radio programs, were instructed, not to invite commentators, critical of the situation, in Thailand. In April 2015, the Thai junta suspended the broadcasting, of Peace TV, and TV 24, two satellite TV stations.

Military units, in Bangkok, and other provinces cancelled, at least thirty political events, and academic debates, lately. The military also banned at least twelve seminars, and public forums, on issues related to land, and community rights. At least twenty-two other public gatherings were also blocked, by the military.

Recently, the NCPO banned political gatherings that involved more than five people. The junta subjected them, to a year, in prison, and fined them, twenty thousand *baht* (approximately US$600). At least sixty-three activists have been arrested, since the junta, came into power, for organising, and taking part, in public gatherings.

In World Report 2018, Human Rights Watch alleged that the Thai military junta had done nothing, to augment the functions, of democratic institutions, which include, holding elections, through the ballot boxes.

HRW Asia Director, Brad Adams believes: 'instead of restoring basic rights as promised, the junta prosecuted critics and dissenters, banned peaceful protests, and censored the media.'

In November 2017, the military junta disapproved a petition, in which the locals demanded the abolition, of a coal plant construction, in the Songkhla Province.

The Thai government, in an uncouth manner, suspended a law called the Suppression of Torture, and Enforced Disappearance Bill that makes torture, and enforced disappearance, a criminal offence. It seems that the government would not reintroduce the bill, at the current time.

To the watchers, it seems to be a chaotic affair, as there is no justice given, to the 2003 War on Drugs victims, and the 2010 street protestors.

In the current times, Thai society is facing innumerable problems. According to the US Government's Bureau of

International Labour Affairs, a list of one hundred thirty-six goods is been produced by child labour. As per this report, child labour, in fishing, agriculture, and forestry, is most common, followed by manufacturing, mining, quarrying, and pornography.

In the south, an ongoing insurgency is raging, since 2004, in the former 'Sultanate of Pattani', also known as 'Three Southern Border Provinces' (SBP), along with Songkhla Province, and the northeastern part of Malaysia (Kelatan).

In the past, Pattani Sultanate traded, with China, Japan, and Europe, in its days of triumph, and glory.

During the eighteenth century, the Malay population, in an ethnically dominated Thai, and Buddhist population, was met with cruelty, by the Thai military generals, who would order men, women, and children, to be tied together, only to be trampled, by an elephant.

Over six thousand five hundred people have died, and over twelve thousand people, have been injured, in the conflict, between 2004, and 2015.

The insurgency, currently, is led by hardcore *jihadists,* who pit themselves, against the Thai-speaking, Buddhist community. They have attacked, not only police, and army men, but also schoolteachers, civil servants, and Buddhist monks. Basically, anyone, who they thought of as agents of right-wing Thai imperialism. Car bombs, too, have become common, in parking areas, in the region.

In a gruesome incident, in 2004, the Thai army arrested hundreds of young men, for protesting other arrests. They were huddled together, into trucks, and taken away, to an army base, where seventy-eight of the prisoners, were believed to have been suffocated.

In 2004, it had been believed, regional analysts, that foreign militants had penetrated the area, with the help of foreign funding. The regional economy largely sustains rubber plantations.

The headcount strength of militants, ranges, from around ten thousand, to thirty thousand. Only feeble attempts, at political dialogue, have been initiated.

The government has also refused the recognition of the Malay language, in the region. It seems that the struggle is basically against the political centre, to attain greater autonomy, within the region.

12 June, 2018

41

US KOREA DENUCLEARISATION SUMMIT

At ONE POINT IN TIME, THE WAR OF WORDS, between North Korea, and the United States, gave looming dangers, of a possible armed escalation, between the two countries. The development, of a nuclear arsenal, in North Korea, was met with several diplomatic challenges, before.

Trump, at one point in time, believed that his nuclear button was 'more powerful.' The US, is already, in the arms race, for acquiring supersonic missiles, notorious for travelling faster, than the speed of sound, that could hit their target, faster than ICBM missiles.

Trump once called Kim Jong Un 'a madman', while Kim ensured of destroying any United States aircraft, such as B1-B Lancer, before they entered North Korean airspace. The war of words had put millions, of lives, at stake. At one point in time, it seemed almost inevitable that North Korea would hit the US territory, first. The US did not have the 'first to attack policy,' anyway.

It did take a while, for Trump, to change his judgment, about Kim Jong Un. He now calls him 'funny,' 'very talented,' 'someone who loves his people,' and 'whom his country loves with fervour.' Perhaps, it may have been necessary, to win favours. It was something, contentious because according to an enquiry by the UN commission, Kim Jong Un is accused, of crimes, against humanity.

The latest statements, at the summit in November 2018, meant that former statements, made by both leaders, were just ill-thought hyperboles, for various reasons.

One of the notable propagandas, by a North Korean website, was a doctored picture, which showed a North Korean nuke, hitting a US-nuclear-powered aircraft carrier, USS Carl Vinson.

After a series of failed negotiations, and strategic defence strategies, exhibited by the US, in the troubled seawaters, of the Korean Peninsula, a historic denuclearisation summit, in Singapore, was finally concluded. Interestingly, Trump thinks that he has built a 'special bond' with Kim. The news of this peace accord is a respite, to ASEAN countries. A nuclear war, in this region, could have been unthinkable, in terms of human catastrophe, and the destruction of nature. As per inputs from US authorities, Kim Jong Un had built an arsenal, of around twenty to sixty nuclear warheads.

Trump has ensured that he would meet Kim Jong Un 'many times', in future, for North Korea's denuclearisation program. The United States is vying for verification, for complete denuclearisation.

As per Stanford University nuclear scientist Siegfried Hecker, the whole denuclearisation process could take, at least fifteen years.

To increase diplomatic ties, the American president wants several US officials, and other international personnel, inside the North Korean territory.

The best that the US government can hope for is a sustained, and phased denuclearisation process, in the years to come. It is mainly because North Korea has been a closed country, in terms of diplomatic relations, with its six-decade isolation, from the world.

The country had high aims, to produce ballistic missiles, and nuclear weapons, with its state-funded government programs.

The IAEA has had no access, for inspection to North Korean nuclear facilities, since 2009. The country also expelled nuclear inspectors, in the past.

Despite this, North Korea had shut down, its Punggye-ri nuclear site, and has also vowed, to destroy its nuclear testing site. Now, by every means, North Korea must give access, to IAEA, to affirm a sort of western alliance, which seemed highly unlikely, in the past. In that perception, it is a very significant diplomatic summit.

As per Panmunjom Declaration, 2018, DPRK will commit to complete denuclearisation and will ensure long-lasting peace, in the region. In return, the US will lift the heavy sanctions, and its diplomatic freeze, with the international community. It is believed that after the summit was over, Kim Jong Un alleviated, some financial burdens, upon his country. Perhaps, the country can trade more, in textiles, seafood, and other natural resources.

In the regional media, post-summit, he was projected as a world leader, and the only source of authority, in North Korea. But, having said that, it is believed that the old generation leaders, who saw their predecessors, ruling the country, will not accept this change if their power is threatened.

It seems that loyalism is almost required, for Kim's rule,

in the country.

A report by the Crises Group explained: 'coordination between allies and other interested actors was essential. Seoul desires to diminish the risk of war and fulfil the Moon Jae-in administration's promise of rapprochement with the North, impelling it to help draw Pyongyang and Washington together. Beijing wants to maintain the prevailing strategic balance or shift it in Chinese favour and to guard against a turnaround that could see Pyongyang cosy up to Washington. Tokyo, a staunch US ally with a lot at stake but no independent ability to influence developments, is keen to protect its strategic interests, including reducing its vulnerability to North Korean shorter-range missiles and nuclear, chemical, and biological weapons.'

This policy, that Trump is pursuing, with North Korea, is the complete opposite, of what he intends, to do with Iran. He wants no diplomatic contract, with Iran, at any level, perhaps due to their pertaining rancour, against Israelis.

Trump has extended this priority, even to American corporates, who do business, with the country.

If we compare, Iran and North Korea, the latter is more powerful, in terms of a nuclear arsenal, and the aftermaths of war, in the region, will be much higher, than its other Asian counterpart. Seoul is just thirty miles away, from North Korea.

20 June, 2018

42

AN AFGHAN CEASEFIRE THAT WAS BROKEN

THE HISTORIC CEASEFIRE IN AFGHANISTAN in June 2018 was a respite for men with arms, from both sides. It allowed them to visit their homes and family.

Since this brief interlude of peace, people hoped for a longer ceasefire, so that both parties involved, could think of peace, and reconciliation, in the longer term.

The calm of Eid-ul-Fitr gave an impression, of the peace that Afghanistan, could have, in the future. The three-day truce was something historical because it happened nearly after a decade.

Since the US invasion of Afghanistan, despite the highs, and lows, of Taliban insurgency, it finally seems that the Taliban is dominant, in the country, exerting its rebel, and political influence.

The US, on the other hand, cannot think of wiping out the Taliban, eventually. The only way out right now is a sustained political dialogue.

Compromises must be made, by either of the parties involved. But the Taliban does not want to negotiate, with Ashraf Ghani's government, because they think that he is an 'American puppet.' They do not want to give up their arms, to a regime, which is hell-bent, on keeping 'occupiers', in their country.

In a New York Times Op-ed on June 27th, 2018, Prime Minister Ashraf Ghani wrote: 'I will negotiate with Taliban anywhere. For 38 years now, peace in my country has remained a dream, a prayer on my lips. During the ceasefire, the Taliban entered our cities to join the celebration. Afghans belonging to the countryside returned to their homes, for the first time in years. For three days, it made no difference whether you were a Taliban or an Afghan soldier; a woman or a man; a Tajik, a Pashtun or a Hazara. For three days, Afghans were united and elated by the possibility of peace. We rediscovered tolerance and acceptance within us.'

The intentions, of the US government, with their perpetual drone strikes, and bombings, are clear. They have been around, for seventeen years, but they have not thought, of the continual collateral damage. It is because of a lack of unity of command, and using old strategies, such as excessive use of airpower, failed counterinsurgency attempts, and catch-and-kill operations. The war is killing, and terrorising common Afghans. Nothing much has changed, in that scenario. But, the US claims, in its attempts at hard-nosed diplomacy, that it wants to work, with the Taliban, the Afghan government, and common people, for a resolution.

As per UN data, published, in February 2017, there was a rise in indiscriminate attacks, by the US forces, that contributed, to at least, ten thousand civilian injuries. Around three thousand five hundred were killed. Most of the common Afghanis blame it, on the continuous support, of the US-led government, in Afghanistan – Ashraf Ghani's National Unity Government.

According to inputs, by The Hill, Taliban fighters, government officials, and security forces were seen mingling, breaking the fast, and clicking selfies together. Laurel Miller, The Hill's Opinion Editor wrote: 'the Afghan people on both sides are tired of war and that even fighters would like to find a way out of perpetual fighting.' These events do indicate some sort of potential, for prolonged peace, in the troubled country, but ironically it did not last long.

After the ceasefire ended, around thirty Afghan soldiers were killed in Bagdis, west of the country. It appears that the Taliban is now relying, on targeted killings. International Crises Group has predicted more violence, in the cities. In Kabul, alone, ninety-four per cent of killings, have been done, by suicide bombings, lately.

Donald Bolduc, wrote in an article, in Daily Beast, that the Taliban controls 14.5 per cent of the districts in the countryside. In 2016, the Taliban's influence was only nine per cent.

'In 2017, there was a sixty-three per cent increase in land cultivation for opium poppies and an 88 per cent increase in raw opium production. All this happened in a matter of one year,' Bolduc claims, according to an official US Govt. report.

The Taliban, have even attacked schools, and other facilities, since 2016. They often beat the guards, and set the chairs, books, and classes ablaze, despite the government's safe school' slogan.' There are children in the country, who work for a living, while also attending school.

Accords' latest publication, in Afghanistan, produced by Conciliation Resources, recommends a new approach, to dealing, with the situation. The contributors, in this publication, include the Taliban Political Office, in

Qatar, senior representatives of five Taliban factions, and the Chair of the High Peace Council. It also includes perceptions of common people, men, and women, from academia, military, political, and civil society.

The publication's peace approach insists that a 'lack of confidence', between two parties, is the sole reason, for failed negotiations. The main reason, is corruption, in the national institutions. There are stark differences, in the idea, that a civilian government should run main cities, with significant populations, and that the Taliban, control the countryside.

The publication reflects that there is 'pervasive violence', affecting the country, because of a 'glaring gap', between 'words' and 'actions.'

The international reactions, to the Afghan Peace Process, have come, from Pakistan, too. Ambassador Lodhi believes that a Quadrilateral Coordination Group (QCG), consisting of Pakistan, Afghanistan, China, and the US, remains a useful platform, to pursue a resolution.

Many political analysts believe that it is the inefficient strategy, of a NATO-led coalition, that helped, in the resurgence, of the Taliban. As the conflict has remained, over time, it has given the Taliban a chance, to propagate their ideology, maintain active relations, with local chieftains, and spread its influence, in the local, and international media machines.

The world calls Taliban 'combatant civilians', where guns, and war, are a part of their lives. As of now, the Taliban are recruiting local poppy farmers, to join their ranks, and the income earned, has also gone, into their operations. Farmers have been reliant, on growing this notorious crop, to sustain a living, for their families.

As of now, it seems poppy eradication, and finding alternatives (commercialising the poppy industry into the pharmaceutical industry), will remain, a conciliation measure, among the peacemakers.

28 June, 2018

43

STRING OF PEARLS

FOR QUITE SOMETIME CHINA HAS been, in the quest, for political, military, and economic espionage. This has been done through a network of installations, known as the 'String of Pearls.'

It is aimed, to project, a dominating presence, in littoral South Asia. One such aim, exhibited by the 'String of Pearls' strategy, is maritime dominance.

By embarking on this approach, China wants to counter other superpowers, such as the United States. Some support China's geopolitical rise, against American hegemony, for a needful balance of power. What China wants to do, has been already done, in the past, by the British, Portuguese, Dutch, and Spaniards, during colonial times.

Indian strategists fear that Chinese economic buildup, due to the advent of ports, in Colombo, Sri Lanka (Sri Lankan government leased Hambantota port, for a ninety-nine-year lease, to the Chinese, where the latter agreed to pay $1.2 billion, as a fee), or Gwadar in Pakistan, are makings of a string of pearls.

Factually, it was a report 'Energy Futures in Asia: Final Report,' drafted in 2004, that made this model popular.

The String of Pearls strategy, refers to control, in the Strait of Malacca, Sri Lanka, Pakistan, Maldives, the Strait of Hormuz, Somalia, Bangladesh, and Myanmar.

An American consultancy firm, Booz Allen Hamilton, published a report, 'Energy Futures in Asia', where it predicted that China would expand its naval base, throughout Indian Ocean Region (IOR), by building civilian maritime infrastructure, soon.

Many observers have pointed out that Chinese activities have intensified, in the Arabian Sea, lately. China seems to have a plan, to outstretch from the Southern part to East Africa. In the South China Sea itself, it is operating, with several of its military installations, and naval ships.

Apart from 'String of Pearls' strategic model, China uses the 'Pit Stop model,' 'Lean Colonial model,' 'Dual Use Logistics Facility,' 'Warehouse Model,' and 'Model USA.' Whereas 'Dual Use Logistics Facility' model, and 'String of Pearls' model are strategically similar, the other models, allow the placing of military troops, in other countries.

Jack Detsch, wrote in The Diplomat that the rivalry between China, and India, in the Indian Ocean, threatens peace in the region, with large investments, in ports, docks, and trans-shipment facilities, along the basin. It is a route, through which seventy per cent of the world's oil travels.

For certain political, and economic advantages, China has developed ties, with Bangladesh, through investments, in Chittagong Basin, and Cox's Bazaar. Having ports, in Bangladesh, means that China has strategic access, to the Bay of Bengal, India's backyard. The Chinese also opened a port, in Djibouti, in 2017, which can host around ten thousand troops.

To counter this move, India has requested access, to French ports, in Djibouti, in the past. India signed an agreement, for a new base, in Seychelles, and requested access, to the ports, of Oman. A pact on it was signed, in Singapore, in 2017.

Furthermore, India wants to further expand its bases, in the Andaman and Nicobar Islands, at the end of Malacca Strait, for its fight for survival, in the waters of Southeast Asia. This policy is called Act East, by improving ties, with Vietnam and Japan. Act East policy has been received with praise, from Washington DC. In return – Washington calls for a 'Free and Open Indo Pacific,' and it reflects a sort of competitive turbulence, in these troubled waters of trade.

Through its Belt and Road initiative, China wants to make inroads, in the Indian Ocean. The Chinese also might be interested, in securing more routes, in the Persian Gulf, and the Strait of Malacca, although none of these two ideas has been drafted on paper, yet. Although, as per the 'China 2015 Defence White Paper', the plan seems to move, from 'offshore waters defence', to 'open seas protection'.

These aggressive stances are prompting India, to buy more submarines. It spent $8.1 billion to purchase six diesel-electric submarines. Sittwe, Myanmar's busiest port, received $100 million in aid, from the Indian Government. It is part of the larger Kaladan Multi-Modal Transit project. Currently, India claims to control maritime, in the Strait of Malacca. As a result, India is planning to make its own 'String of Pearls,' from Madagascar, via Djibouti, Oman, and Seychelles, all the way to Singapore.

However, there are several analysts, who argue that 'Dual Use Logistics Facility' is more appropriate, for the Chinese, to pursue, at this moment in time. It will help

China to operate, in a 'restrictive political and economic environment.'

It will include provisions of medical support, ship, and equipment repair, communications support, and ammunition storage.

Political analysts believe that Karachi would be a base, for such operations. In addition to that, the Chinese state can conduct combatant evacuation operations, for Chinese citizens, including humanitarian assistance, relief operations, and other economic interests.

Dr Christopher D Yung, a research fellow at Institute for National Strategic Studies (INSS) believes that 'Dual Use Logistics Facility' seems palatable, to the Chinese, because this model will work, without imposing a threat to the United States, which mainly pursues global military dominance.

Having said that, China cannot pursue the 'String of Pearls' approach, in the Indian Ocean, if it builds a more robust logistical infrastructure, to support a military force, as there is a need for a large naval and air force, focusing on military combat operations.

23 July, 2018

44

DISCRIMINATION AGAINST UYGHUR MUSLIMS

THE UN BELIEVES THAT THERE ARE ABOUT one million Uyghur Muslims, in internment camps, in secrecy. The entity has recently put sanctions, against Chinese officials.

The Chinese government denies such claims, and interprets the internment, as a place, only for criminals, with registered offences, who are being sent, to 'vocational, educational, and employment centres. The Chinese call these centres, 'schools,' and even 'hospitals.'

In January 2011, Radio Free Asia alleged that around one hundred twenty thousand Uyghurs were deemed to be held, as political opponents, at re-education camps, in Kashgar, in the Republic of China. China Human Rights Defenders (CHRD) put a figure of two hundred two eight thousand, in 2017.

According to an Op-ed, by Sigal Samuel, in The Atlantic, this indoctrination process lasts for several months, during which they were forced, to renounce their faith, and are forced, to recite Communist propaganda songs, every day.

There are similar reports, where the inmates were forced to eat pork, drink alcohol, forbidden by Islam, and there are also reports, of torture, and death, as punishments. Chinese officials, on the other hand, claim that the convicts are ensured, a fair trial. But there are stories, reflected in the media, where it is alleged that Uyghurs, in detention, are not given enough food, are housed, in small, overcrowded rooms, and are made to watch films, by a state-appointed *imam*, who explains the 'legal religious practices,' and 'correct interpretations of Islam.'

China fears separatism, in the Xinjiang region. Uyghurs believe that the region is part of the Second East Turkestan Republic, a short-lived, Soviet-backed republic. They fear, that this kind of separatist movement, could spill over, to other places, such as Tibet, and Taiwan. It is one of the remotest, and most heavily policed regions, of China, which makes it harder, to report human rights violations there. Neighbouring Russia has encouraged Kazaks, and Uyghurs, to immigrate there so that they could attack Chinese territory. The government employees, working for the Communist government, in Xinjiang, are not allowed, to fast in Ramadhan, and public schools, and are discouraged, from participating, in religious activities.

Muslims likely immigrated, to China, a few generations, after the Islamic Prophet, as part of Arab diplomacy, through embassies, and trade, who settled along the Silk Road. For Muslims, Kashgar and Hotan remain historic central cities, for Islamic culture, in Xinjiang. The citizens of Kashgar have been angry, at the demolition of houses, in their city, by the Chinese authorities. The official reasons were that the housing colonies were unhygienic and prone to earthquakes, but Uyghurs see it as a strategy, to reduce their power and influence, in the city.

Historically, there were serious disturbances, in the northwestern city, of Ghulja. Thousands were convicted, and detained, in 1995. The political matter escalated, in 2009, when large-scale ethnic rioting happened, in the capital, Urumqi. Some two hundred people were killed, mostly Han Chinese. Before this chaotic event, a rigorous crackdown named the 'Strike Hard 'campaign, provoked demonstrations, in the city, in 1997, that were vehemently suppressed. In June 2012, six Uyghur militants made a failed attempt, in hijacking a plane, from Hotan to Urumqi. There was bloodshed, in April 2013, when seventy-seven people, were killed, after police opened fire, on men, armed with knives, attacking government buildings, in Shanshan County. There was bloodshed, in October 2013 again, some months later, when a car stormed, into a crowd, and blew up in flames, in Beijing's Tiananmen Square. In March 2014, there was an attack, on Kunming Train Station. Two months later, in May 2014, car bombs killed thirty-one people, in a crowded Urumqi market, and explosives were also hurled, into the crowd. Two months after, in July, a knife attack killed around ninety-six people, in Yarkant. An *imam* of the mosque was stabbed to death, a few days later. About fifty died, in Luntai county blasts, in September 2014.

China has blamed ETIM, founded by Hasan Mahsum, for attacks inside Xinjiang, and outside the territory. Although, some analysts blame the group's incapacity, to launch frequent, and big-scale attacks. This scenario has prompted the Chinese President, Xi Jinping, to a 'strike first' policy, against any form of Islamic extremism. He, along with his official peers, want superpowers, such as the United States, not to mingle, in their internal affairs.

One of the communist party newspapers has argued that the onslaught, in the region, is to prevent Xinjiang, from becoming the next Syria. They simply cannot think of letting it go, because the region is three times bigger than France, and it is also a territory with huge resources, of oil, gas, and coal. It is a source of logistical connectivity, with Europe, and Central Asia. The region sells its cotton fabrics, to famous corporations, such as Gucci, and Chanel. Politically, it may be the most militarised zone, in China, with one, in every three Chinese, working for the army.

The Uyghur Muslims call the region, East Turkestan, and have cultural ties, with Mongolia, Kazakhstan, Tajikistan, and Kyrgyzstan. Although some communities, such as Hui Muslims, speaking the Turkic language, are politically neutral, and they are allowed to fast, in Ramadhan. Since 1949, the conflict escalated, since the Communist government, encouraged mass migrations, of the Han Chinese, until the 1970s. Due to regional autonomy, some Han Chinese, have also complained, of second-class treatment.

The US Congressional-Executive Commission, on China, has described the recent aggression, 'as the largest mass incarnation, of a minority population, in the world history'. According to the World Uyghur Congress, every family has around three, or four people, being taken away. It is believed that there are villages, with no men, on the streets, where only children and women live. Families are losing contact, with their loved ones.

China is playing the card of economic development, but Uyghurs believe that they are in conflict, with the larger Communist State, on cultural, and religious grounds. Having an upper hand, China has launched a calculated onslaught, against Uyghur extremism, to prevent terrorism, and to bring the supposed peace, to the country.

Long beards are also banned, for younger men, and so are the women's veils, and families cannot have Koran, in their homes. Even Kazakhs, and Kyrgyz Muslims, have been sent to the camps.

As per The Independent newspaper, prisoners have suffered thoughts of suicide. Others suffer from insomnia, depression, anxiety, and paranoia. Ironically, this cultural, and religious persecution has not been condemned, by any of the Muslim countries, including Indonesia, Pakistan, Saudi Arabia, Malaysia, and Turkey.

All these countries enjoy an economic relationship, with China. It also seems that the Muslim world, is largely unaware, of the situation, in Xinjiang.

In this scenario, there are many political leverages, that are ending up in China's favour. One of them is a major donor of financial aid, to many Muslim countries.

31 September, 2018

45

ASSAM'S CITIZENSHIP ROW

OVER FOUR MILLION PEOPLE HAVE BEEN stripped of their citizenship, in July 2018 by the Indian state of Assam, by India's National Register of Citizens. This exercise had been, in the making, for the last three years, and was monitored, by the Supreme Court of India.

Around four hundred thousand data entry operators, and government officials, have been involved, in this exercise. Many bogus, and fake submissions, have been detected, by India's National Register of Citizens.

Thousands of troops were deployed before the first draft was made public. The idea to update the register was to mainly identify illegal immigrants, from Bangladesh. This has happened for the first time, since 1951.

From 1985 to February 2018, a total of twenty-nine thousand, seven hundred thirty-eight foreigners were expelled.

This exercise had been a psychological despair, to thousands of people, when they were suddenly declared illegal immigrants.

Hundreds of thousands, of people, from Bangladesh, fled to India, during the Bangladesh war of independence, from erstwhile East Pakistan, between March and December

1971. Most of them settled in Assam.

Historically, since the beginning of the twentieth century, there has been an influx of people, from East Bengal (now Bangladesh), due to an oppressive feudal system (*Zamindari*). The British colonists had encouraged immigration, to Assam, as well.

The Muslim league wanted Assam, to become a part, of erstwhile East Pakistan, however, Assam's only Sylhet district became part of erstwhile East Pakistan. During the partition, the borders were porous, and not protected, so people continued to come.

These migrants now make up a chunk of the population, in Assam's fifteen districts, out of thirty-three districts. In 1983, more than two thousand suspected migrants were massacred, by a mob, in the village of Nellie. Assam has had a history of ethnic tensions, between indigenous Assamese communities, and Bengali Muslims.

Most of them, are engaged in agriculture, and work as farmers. Some have claimed that they had been detained, in the camp, for a mere spelling error. There were also quite a few people, who shared their space, with convicts, accused of murder, and rape. The powerful All Assam Student's Union (AASU) has been spearheading the anti-immigrant movement.

According to Indian Express, many people found their names, with spelling errors. Sometimes a man's photo appeared, against a woman's name, or some different surnames popped up. At times, only the middle, and last names have been published.

Initially, many workers, who worked, in small shops, in

many regions of Assam, continued to work, in their small shops, and declared it, as a rumour. Others feared, that they might be killed, when hundreds of people, were taken in cars, in some places. Many hundreds continue to be detained, in a camp, in Silchar, one of the six detention centres, in Assam. Around thirty-five people ate, and slept, in one room, and shared one toilet, with no locks, in the camp. Some people had declared all their necessary documents, but complained that their names are not on the list. There were also quite a few cases, who had supposedly paid agents, to procure voter cards, and PAN cards.

The demand for the update of the National Register has been there for some time. The first agitation happened, in 1979, and the first decision to update the register was taken by the central Government, in 1999, but the work did not begin. In July 2009, Assam Public Works – an NGO – filed a petition, in Supreme Court, demanding an enquiry, into NRC. It was, in 2010, when the government decided to inquire, into the citizen register, in two districts, but the work was halted, by public violence, in Barpeta district.

One of Assam's foremost intellectuals, Hiren Gohain believes: 'The danger is now from Hindu rightist forces who want to encourage Bangladeshi Hindus to come to Assam, settle down here and in their own words 'save Assam from the Muslim menace.' They mean by India as a Hindu India. That is their solution to the problem. Their (the BJP) idea of citizenship is like that of Israel. As in Israel, every Jew, wherever he is born, is considered entitled to citizenship. India is mentioned as the home of Hindus.'

The supreme court decided that anyone, who came to Assam, after 1971, would be stripped of their citizenship, and would be called a 'foreigner'. According to *The Telegraph*, 'people whose names appear on the 1951 NRC, and those who appear on any voter list in Assam up to midnight of 24 March 1971, and the descendants of the above are eligible to register for the NRC. People who came to Assam from Bangladesh between 1 January 1966 and 24 March 1971, registered themselves with the Foreigner Regional Registration Office, and were declared by the Foreigner Tribunal as Indian citizens are also eligible.'

In an article by Taslima Yasmin, in The Daily Star, Bangladesh's position has been that there has been no unauthorised migration to Assam, since 1971. She emphasised that out of many issues, between India and Bangladesh, illegal migration, from Assam, has never been brought up, by the Indian government.

There has been no humane approach, implemented by the Indian government, considering the sensitive regional dynamics, in the region. Some political analysts blame the politicians, inside Assam, who did not act against illegal immigration, because of the vote bank.

When an eminent perfume businessman launched his party, All India Union Democratic Front (AIUDF), in 2005, the party was seen banking, on Muslims, of Bangladesh, or East Indian origin.

Ever since the BJP came into power, in Assam, the opposition, both, at the regional level, and central level, have accused the party, of targeting Muslims.

BJP, the party in power, believes that the Congress party, led by Rajiv Gandhi, did not have the mantle, to act against illegal immigrants, back then.

During the election campaigns, it had vowed to act against outsiders and has kept its word on that, post elections. People, however, can file petitions, between August 30, to September 28.

6 September, 2018

46

MEXICAN POLICE UNEARTH MASS GRAVES

AN UNMARKED MASS GRAVE HAS BEEN FOUND, in the region of Veracruz, in Mexico, in September 2018. It is believed that the site could contain the remains, of around five hundred victims, according to an advocacy group, *Solecito*.

Other investigators believe that the figure could be up to one hundred seventy-four. It is one of the largest mass graves, found, in Mexico. According to local inputs, there have been around thirty-two burial pits, on the site, and the bodies may have been buried, at the site, two years ago, since 2018.

The site is on a narrow isthmus, between the Gulf of Mexico, and the Alvarado Lagoon, about an hour southeast of Veracruz. Arbolillo, a small fishing village, is the nearest inhabited point.

A criminal group had sent a map to *Solecito*, where they indicated that the current mass burial site, contained remains, of more than five hundred bodies. It has marked a national crisis, as many families rushed to a morgue, for clues, that could help them, find their missing children, relatives, and siblings.

During the investigation, around two hundred identity cards, and one hundred fourteen pieces, of clothing, were found, as well as different accessories, and personal items.

According to TeleSur TV channel, another mass grave was found here, possibly containing the remains of three hundred victims, of gang warfare. There are possibly other pits, at the site, where the investigators are not working right now. Mexican Human Rights Commission believes that the existence, of such burial sites, shows a lack of concern, for law enforcement. As per their data, around three thousand two hundred thirty human remains were found, in mass graves, between 2007, and 2016.

According to a BBC report, drones, and ground penetrating radar, are helping the locals, and forensic experts, in the investigation, at the scene. Photographs clicked, by journalists, showed investigators probing the thick fertile soil, wearing white protective suits, and gloves, setting the remains on white sheets, and then putting them, in red plastic bags. Access to investigators required a twenty-minute walk, through mangroves, and thick tropical vegetation. The dead bodies were presumably carried by boat and were spread out, under palm trees.

Although the federal government verified, this development, the local Veracruz Governor Miguel Angel Yunes Linares, had initially refused, to provide necessary heavy machinery, digging utensils, or federal, and forensic analysts, to assist the scene.

Violent crime has long plagued Veracruz, an oil-rich state, in the Gulf of Mexico. The area is notorious for extortion, and kidnapping. It is home to one of the oldest ports, in Mexico, and drug gangs, such as Jalisco New Generation Cartel, and Zetas have waged war, against each other, for power dominance in the territory. The territory's former governor, Javier Duarte was charged with involvement, in disappearances, diversion of state funds, through phantom companies, and embezzlement. In his tenure, the state debt had doubled, and there was an increase, in gang violence, and kidnapping. Over time, Veracruz has also become dangerous, for fieldwork, and journalists. Duarte was also questioned, for the killing of a photojournalist.

In 2016 and 2017, around two hundred fifty-three skulls were discovered, in Veracruz. The victims often include people, who refuse to get recruited, into cartels, and their rivals. Relatives of people, who are missing, in Mexico, have been campaigning, to help find their loved ones, for a long period.

Hundreds of human remains have also been found, in states, including Tamaulipas, Durango, and Morelos, during a decade-long war, led by the Mexican military, to battle the cartels, that resulted in turf wars. Around, twenty-nine thousand murders, happened, in 2017 alone, according to a US Congressional Research Centre report. More than thirty-five thousand people have disappeared, in Mexico, including nine thousand women, and six thousand three hundred minors, according to the National Registry of Data on Missing and Disappeared Persons. It is possibly the worst record, in two decades.

In January 2018, earlier this year remains of at least twenty-three people were found, including skeletons, and four without heads, in an area, beside a stream that was difficult to access. They were found, in the community, of Pantanal, in the state of Nayarit, on the Pacific coast, an area notorious, for turf wars, between Sinaloa, and Jalisco narco-trafficking empires. The town, Xalisco, situated in Mexico, remains a vulnerable route, for heroin trafficking, supplied towards the US west Coast. United Families was formed, in 2017, alone, in Nayarit, in response to a surge, in homicides.

Solecito spokesperson, Rosalia Castro Toss, believes that the state does not have enough staff, to handle cases, of thirty-seven thousand missing persons.

With aims to battle impunity, in Mexico, an innovative legal experiment has been started, by a coalition of Mexican human rights organisations, known as a GIEI, granted by Inter American Commission on Human Rights (IACHR), with strong links to the federal government, and social movements.

Al-Jazeera's John Holman, reporting from Mexico City, said: 'the 114 identification cards were like "gold for families" searching for their loved ones because it provides clues for their possible resting place. It comes now to the incoming administration of Andres Manuel Lopez Obrador to show the political will that has been lacking throughout this government to try and get grips with this problem, to try and help people to find their lost relatives and investigate this sort of mass grave.'

Drug-related violence, in Mexico, has escalated, since the army was deployed, to fight the powerful cartels.

Since then, more than two hundred thousand people have been killed, in total, in the conflict.

12 September, 2018

47

AUSTRALIA'S ERRATIC LEADERSHIP
CHANGES

AUSTRALIAN POLITICS HAS SEEN a turbulent decade. Three prime ministers have led the country, since 2007, but no one has served a full term. Before 2007, John Howard assumed the PM office, for eleven years. Since then, Australian democracy has been in shambles.

What does it notify? Incredibility of democracy, or leadership failures? As per Associated Press, 'Australians hate revolving prime ministers.'

Australia is now called the 'coup capital of the Pacific.' Aussies complain that their leaders insist upon 'Game of Thrones-like political institutions' than actual governance.

First, Kevin Rudd was replaced, by his deputy, Julia Gillard, back then, in 2010. When she lost a general election, after losing popularity, in the public, Tony Abbot replaced her, in 2013. But Abbot lasted only until 2015, before Malcolm Turnbull succeeded him. When Turnbull assumed charge, he was accused of leading a 'party room coup.'

In August 2018, The Economist reported that there was another coup, in which the rightist, conservative bloc, of Mr Abbot, was instrumental, in toppling Mr Turnbull. Other sources say, that ex-police officer and right-winger, Peter Dutton, was instrumental in unseating him.

Now, as Turnbull has left the prime ministerial office, it has paved the way for Scott Morrison, nicknamed 'ScoMo,' the former public treasurer, to lead the federal government. In his position as a treasurer, he preferred raising taxes and cutting spending.

As an observant Pentecostal Christian, he also oversaw many of the faith's tourism campaigns.

With the result, Turnbull's loss has triggered a by-election of his Sydney seat.

Australia keeps on losing its prime ministers, mainly because of a 'leadership spill.' These spills are dangerous, because they require only fifty per cent of approval, from the total votes.

The political parties, representing Australian politics, often approve, of these leadership changes, because they believe it will benefit them, in the next elections, and even in the opinion polls. But the frequent leadership changes mean that leadership, at the federal level, has become weak, and inconsistent.

'Labour spills,' what they were called, had started between Rudd, and Gillard. After that, spills also happened between the conservatives Mr Turnbull, and Mr Abbott, as early as 2009. Australia, until now, has not seen a prime minister, who can break through this internal problem.

Opinion polls, that reflect the public mood, are against these spills. According to these polls, the left-leaning opposition, Labour National Front was leading, from fifty-one to forty-nine per cent, to a fifty-six lead. The ruling coalition's primary vote fell to thirty-five, while Labour went up to thirty-nine.

Turnbull, a wealthy former investment banker, and lawyer has been mocked, by his party cadre, as 'Mr Harbourside Mansion,' because he owned his home, in the most expensive suburb, of the country. He had won support, because of his support, for same-sex marriage, action on climate change, and Paris emission targets. Pre- election in 2018, he became the largest donor, for the election, with a contribution of $1.75 million.

Energy wars had escalated, in his tenure, after he introduced a bill, intended to reduce electricity prices, that was criticised, by the opposition, as there were also some limits, on greenhouse emissions, which were in line, with the Paris climate change agreement. It led to his eventual demise when his party members opposed him.

Scott Morrison, his successor, in his past, implemented the 'stop the boats' asylum seeker policy. He oversaw policies that withheld refugees, in offshore detention camps. This tactic has been condemned, by the United Nations, and human rights groups.

Morrison will likely stay in office, until the next election, which will happen, in May 2019. It means that he will be Australia's sixth prime minister, and fourth from his party in eleven years. He won after enough signatures were collected, from the rebel party members that called for a 'spill,' or 'leadership contest.' It included four people – Malcolm Turnbull, Scott Morrison, Julie Bishop, and Peter Dutton. While Bishop was eliminated in the first round, Morrison eventually beat Dutton with a lead of forty-five to forty votes. This reflects a deep fracture within the party cadre. Turnbull called this leadership contest, an 'internal insurgency.'

On his Twitter, a ruling Nationals MP Darren Chester

went on to apologise to the Australian public and commented that the public deserved a much better rule, by the federal government, in these ten years.

Defence Industry Minister Christopher Pyne, a Turnbull ally, commented: 'I think some people should have considered the greater good of the people of Australia, and the government, rather than their own self-interest and ambition.'

It is believed that Morrison will restructure the cabinet. More than ten frontbenchers have resigned, since Turnbull lost the leadership contest, signifying a sort of fragmented scenario.

According to an article, written in the Guardian, the first task for Morrison will be to promote rapprochement, between the rival wings, of his party. He will also foresee the drought situation, that has struck the region, of New South Wales.

'A relationship has grown increasingly toxic, as Turnbull gave ground, to conservative insurgents, especially over climate change, and energy policy, only to be rewarded, with more and more demands,' the report claimed.

18 September, 2018

48

DANISH GHETTO LAWS

IN THE QUEST FOR NATIONAL ASSIMILATION, in Denmark, the minority liberal government has passed a law, called the 'ghetto deal' in March 2018, targeting the neighbourhoods, having Muslim immigrants, with different ethnic backgrounds, who will eventually go, into cultural training centres. The government introduced the political plan 'One Denmark without parallel societies – no ghettos by 2030' and enacted the concept of 'non-western' in Danish law.

These 'ghetto neighbourhoods' are defined as low-income areas, and the children, living in them, are called 'ghetto children.'

Currently, there are around twenty-five ghettos, identified by the Danish government.

The immigrants, who live in these ghettos, come from countries, such as Pakistan, Somalia, Lebanon, Iraq, Syria, and Turkey.

Since 1980, immigrants have grown, from fifty thousand to five hundred thousand, till date.

Prime Minister Lars Lokke, the legislative member of *Venstre*, believes that immigration, to his country, is a major problem.

According to him, 'people with the same problems have clumped together, and we have let it go, perhaps with the naïve idea that integration would happen on its own over time because this is such a great country with so many possibilities. But it has not happened. The problem has grown.'

Instead of using phrases of integration, Prime Minister Lars Lokke used provocative phrases, in his annual 2018 New Year's speech, where he warned that ghettos could 'reach out their tentacles onto the streets', by spreading violence, and because of ghettos 'cracks have appeared, on the map of Denmark.'

The government calls these ghettos 'vulnerable areas.' Out of twenty-two, clearly defined cultural reforms, around thirteen, apply to these ghettos. Most of them have been approved, by the parliamentary majority.

According to an article, in the Guardian, written by Michala Bendixen, head of Refugees Welcome Denmark, these laws, are a betrayal, of Danish values. From derogatory cartoons on Prophet Muhammad, and debates on circumcision, to *niqab* clampdown, she believes Denmark has turned Islamophobic, for a decade, or so.

Being a non-westerner is viewed as being inferior. Although, the paradox, she insists, contrary to a hostile government policy, is that many Danes have been seen helping immigrants, get a new job, or helping them, learn a new language. In 2017, there was a sixty per cent rise, in the employability of immigrants, in Denmark.

These laws came into being, after an inflammatory newspaper column, which was written, by Boris Johnson, the former British foreign sectary, who compared *niqab-*

wearing women, to 'letterboxes' and 'bank robbers.' His comments were termed as 'divisive', and 'inflammatory', by the Equality and Human Rights Commission', but the comment helped politicians, in Denmark, for similar campaigning, that included a ban on full-face veils.

The area of focus includes physical redevelopment, crime reduction, and education. The children will be taught Danish values, including traditions of Christmas, and Easter, and the Danish language. From 2019, language tests will become mandatory, in schools, in a government effort, to remove ghettos from the country, till 2030. Its noncompliance would mean that social welfare would be denied, to their parents. They could be convicted, of a four-year prison sentence, if they force their children, to make extended visits, to their country of origin. The government describes these trips as 're-education trips.' It seems that the government will compel immigrant families, to join these welfare programs, and would increase surveillance, and monitoring.

However, the controversial laws include control over, who is allowed to live, in these neighbourhoods, a plan to double the punishment committed for crimes committed, in ghettos, and children attending daycare, at least thirty hours a week, as soon as they turn one.

Some of these laws are defined, as too radical, which include confining children, to their homes, after 8 pm. Some leaders, such as Martin Henriksen, of the Danish Peoples Party, insist that young people, in these areas should be fitted with electronic ankle bracelets. Critics argue that these laws are a vehement attack on equality. Many have compared these policies, with the policies of the Nazis, upon the Jews, in Germany. It was in 16th century Venice when the term 'ghetto' became common, which described areas, where Jews were restricted.

Denmark is now the first country, in the world, which has officially used the term 'ghetto,' for certain residential areas. This argument was endorsed, by The Liberal Party, as well as the nationalist Danish People's Party. The opposition party, the Social Democrats, also supported the deal. The Social Democrats have been accused of adopting a similar far-right manifesto that they overhauled, into 'Together for Denmark.'

Currently, there are discussions, about serving pork, in public schools, and whether Muslim bus drivers can drive safely, during *Ramadhan*. The talks also include fining women who wear *niqab*, and banning the circumcision of boys. The government will also deny citizenship, to any applicant, who refuses, to do a handshake, in naturalisation ceremonies, with their local mayor. It has been seen, as a measure, to target Muslims, in Danish society. An opinion poll has suggested that fifty-two per cent, of people, have voted, against this proposal. Some have deemed it unconstitutional.

Denmark refused its 2018 UN refugee quota, arguing that it will be focusing on the existing immigrants, who have arrived, in the country. In 2016, the country excluded itself, from the UN refugee quota system.

17 October, 2018

49

TRUTH BEHIND JAMAL KHASHOGGI

W<small>HEN</small> PILGRIM WATCHERS OF THE MUSLIM WORLD, went on a killing spree, in Yemen, it shut the mouth, of its cronies, that represented the Kingdom, both regionally, and internationally.

The global media, lately, has gone amok, against the killing silence of the Saudi government, when a mysterious killing, of a Saudi journalist, Jamal Khashoggi, happened, in the Saudi embassy, in Turkey.

Who was Jamal Khashoggi? What threat did he pose to the monarchy? If we dwell into the truth, he was one among many, who was killed, for speaking the truth, against the Saudi kingdom.

Sometime earlier, there had been calls for the beheading, of a Shiite woman, Isra-al-Ghomgham, who represented the rights of the Shiite community, in Saudi Arabia, in the Qatif province, when she was sentenced, in the General Intelligence Prison, in al Damaam, under secret.

Saudi Arabia has been notorious, for its human rights violations. It is now, that a major headache, for the West has started, who enjoy lucrative trade relations, with the country, and balance their values, and diplomatic ties, on this immoral impunity. It is for this reason, the kingdom's offensive, in Yemen, for example, has been majorly viewed, with a long silence, from the West.

Trump has shamelessly called this act an 'inside job,' denying its links to the monarchy, and has given a green signal, to a prospective $100 billion arms deal. In other words, it means that the blood of dissenting Arabs, is cheaper, and diplomatic interest, for oil should be prioritised over it.

On October 2, 2018, Jamal Khashoggi, went inside the Saudi embassy, in Istanbul, to obtain a document, to satisfy, that he had divorced his ex-wife so that he could marry his Turkish fiancée. He went inside the consulate and vanished. His fiancée, Hatice Chengiz, waited near the embassy, for hours.

For over two weeks, the Saudi government denied that he was killed, under mysterious circumstances, and claimed that all reports about his disappearance, or death, were completely 'baseless' and 'false'. Then, after eighteen days, they proclaimed that he died in a fistfight, with a dozen Saudi officials, in a brawl that eventually turned violent.

Turkish officials say that his body has been dismembered, but his chopped remains have not been found yet.

US officials, on the other hand, believe that as Crown Prince Mohammad bin Salman had recently announced an overhaul of his intelligence service and a suspension order for around eighteen intelligence officers, its intelligence agency must have been aware that there was an operation to target Khashoggi.

A prominent journalist, he had reported major stories, on the Soviet invasion, of Afghanistan, the Gulf war, in Kuwait, and the rise of Osama bin Laden, for various news channels, even interviewing him, between 1980 and 1990. In 2003, he was fired after two months, for serving as editor of Al Watan newspaper, because he was overly critical, of the monarchy.

He also served as an advisor, to the Saudi government, and was close to the Saudi family as well, for some time. Since 2017, Khashoggi was living, in the US, in a self-imposed exile, where he wrote bylines, for the Washington Post, criticising the policies of Crown Prince Mohammad bin Salman, and comparing him to Vladimir Putin.

Just three days before his arrest, he had told BBC, 'People are becoming convicts for just having an independent perception, and they are not even dissidents.'

The team of investigators, in white uniforms, barged into the consulate, hours after his disappearance. Some examined the main garden, while some perched, on the roofs, to find the missing body. Luminol, a chemical, which detects traces of blood, was used by laboratory teams. They took soil samples, and DNA samples, for testing, after eight hours of investigation, and even reconnoitred the nearby Belgrad forest, and Yalova province, for any clues. At least thirty-eight people were questioned, by Turkish officials. Three Mercedes cars, operating for the consulate, were also checked.

Khashoggi's children have called the United Nations, to call an independent enquiry, and pleaded, both, the Saudi government, and the Turkish government, find his body, as soon as possible, so that his funeral can be held.

It is alleged that the head of forensics, for the consulate, has been involved, in the murder, and his dismemberment. A three-member team, of the consulate, had been seen surveying the forest, in Istanbul, a day before the murder. They were also believed to be Saudi officials.

In a Guardian article, Wadah Khanfar wrote: 'under the banner of reform and fighting extremist Islam – words with an appeal to Western circles – and by virtue of billions of dollars the new crown prince poured into the coffers of US arms manufacturers, Mohammad bin Salman, was granted full cover to abuse his country and the entire region with impunity.'

Currently, there are efforts, made by the US administration, to rescue Mohammad Bin Salman, from the repercussions, but this biased approach will not succeed, because of the uproar, in the global media institutions, and their insistence, on learning the truth, behind Khashoggi's mysterious murder.

He had appeared, in *al Sharq* forum conference, a week before his disappearance, where he said: 'Change will happen solely because of the grave mistakes committed by the despots.'

28 October, 2018

50

AASIA BIBI'S ACQUITTAL FROM COURT

AASIA NOREEN BIBI, COMMONLY KNOWN as Aasia Bibi, had been kept, in solitary confinement, in a Lahore jail, a space without windows, and with an open sewer, for around eight years. In the prison, she struggled with malnutrition, unattended illness, beatings, and psychological abuse. In one of the most disturbing incidents, she recounts how she had her neck put in a brace that was tightened with a key. It was then pulled about on a chain by guards.

Bibi was accused of blasphemy, in a Muslim country, because, in her village, twenty-five miles, north-west of Lahore, several Muslim women, poor and uneducated, like her, disagreed, that she should draw water, from the community well, as she was a Christian.

Wife of Ashiq Masih, a brick maker, one of the few jobs available, to Christians, in her village, in rural Pakistan, she also made a living, for the family, as making money was hard. The discrimination, in her chore, at a local farm, was such, that she was directed to fill berry baskets, twice, as large, as the Muslim women.

The local fables also make Christians spiritually unclean. If Christians touches the Quran, they are accused of a crime.

After the tussle, with the village women, she eventually lost her job. It was later accused that she uttered blasphemy, against Prophet Muhammad. Days later, she was found beaten, and dragged, around the village. Smeared in blood, she was taken to the police station, where a report was drafted against her. The local *Mullah* had assured her that if she converted to Islam, she would be pardoned, but Bibi, a Roman Catholic, refused. As a result, the local court charged her, with death, on November 8, 2010, after her imprisonment.

In Pakistan, blasphemy laws can persecute anyone, including non-Muslims. According to their official sources, around one thousand four hundred seventy-two people have been charged, with blasphemy between 1987-2016, including five hundred-one Ahmadi Muslims, two hundred-five Christians, and twenty-six Hindus.

Since then, a memoir (Blasphemy, 2013) was also out in her name, co-written by a French journalist, Anne Isabelle Tollet, where Bibi was manifested, as 'a woman of Christian courage', against the odds of injustice.

Bibi wrote: 'I've been locked up, handcuffed, and chained, banished from the world, and waiting to die. I don't know how long I've got left to live. Every time my cell door opens, my heart beats faster. My life is in God's hands, and I don't know what's going to happen to me. It's a brutal, cruel existence.'

The French journalist hired an Urdu-English translator, and waited hours, at her prison gate, for her husband Ashiq, who would tell her Aasia's answers, to her questions.

In one of her email interviews, she wrote: 'Even her husband, and five children, are also suffering from the accusation of blasphemy. They are all living [under] the threat of death, and have gone into hiding, frequently moving house, and unable to go outside, or to work. The children miss their mother badly, and have stopped going to school, for their own safety. The youngest is only 9 years old. Her health is deteriorating, her husband risks being killed every time, he visits her [in jail], and her children cannot see their mother for their own safety'.

Two politicians, Salman Taseer, former Governor of Punjab, and Pakistan's Minister for Minorities, Shahbaz Bhatti tried to come to her rescue, but they soon lost their lives. Bibi had broken down, in her cell, when she heard about their deaths.

In the past, Tehrik-e-Hurmat-e-Rasool, called for only one punishment for her beheading. Some others wanted her to die by hanging. In 2010, a Muslim cleric, Maulana Yousuf Qureshi, put a bounty of five hundred thousand Pakistani Rupees, on anyone who killed Aasia Bibi. He had also warned for speaking against, or changing the blasphemy law, and vowed that the Taliban, or the *Mujahideen*, would soon kill her. Even though the leader of the Peshawar High Court Association, at that time, called these statements as 'words of a madman', this scenario did reflect Pakistan, as a divided, and radicalised society, where the whip of the majority, was to be feared the most.

For assisting Bibi, Rev. Samson Dilawar, a parish priest, had also been threatened, by anonymous callers, for assisting Aasia Bibi. In the past, he saw his Catholic Church burned, to the ground, and was also wounded, by gunmen, in 1997.

Since then, the members of the Christian community, in Bibi's native village, were asked to keep a low profile, particularly, when they moved beyond their streets.

Later, Bibi's husband, Mr Masih relocated to a single-room house, in Sheikhupura, in Punjab province, with his children, from an earlier marriage, that was a little more than a mile, from her jail. But, after Taseer's death, he had gone into hiding. After that, he presumably assumed an imitated identity and lived in some safe house.

Hate crimes against Christians, in Pakistan, are common. These people live in the most ghettoised neighbourhoods, do the most menial jobs, and live the most marginalised social lives. In the past, when two Christian brothers, walked out of a Faisalabad courtroom, facing blasphemy charges, they were shot outside, by gunmen. In 2014, around twelve hundred Muslim men, burned alive, a Christian couple, to death, for insulting Islam.

Several campaigns have been organised, for her release, ever since, to protest her imprisonment, through online petitions.

Ooberfuse, a UK-based Christian pop band, collaborated with the British Pakistani Christian Association and released a song titled 'Free Aasia Bibi', with a music video. She has also been the subject matter, of many documentary films.

Quite lately, one petition, created by the Voice of the Martyrs, an organisation aiding oppressed Christians, received over four hundred thousand signatures, from over a hundred countries.

In her memoirs, Bibi wonders, 'whether being a Christian, in Pakistan today, is not just a failing, or a mark against you, but actually a crime.'

After Aasia Bibi's acquittal from the supreme court,

on 31 October 2018, it is believed that Aasia Bibi is in some protective custody. Her lawyer, Saiful Malook left Pakistan, a week after the verdict, citing security concerns, after receiving death threats.

But, supporters of Islamist parties, such as Tehreek-e-Labaik Pakistan, have not taken it lightly, and riots have paralysed the cities, of Lahore, and Islamabad.

In Lahore, the co-founder of the party, Muhammad Afzal Qadri, called for the death of the supreme court Justice Saqib Nisar, and asserted, 'whosoever has access to the judges, should kill them before evening'.

Conversely, Prime Minister Imran Khan had warned the protestors, not to clash, with the state.

In the country, there are many of her sympathisers, who want Asiya Bibi to live a free life, as she has grappled, with injustice, for many years. Even the Pope had once prayed for her freedom.

10 November, 2018

51

SRI LANKA'S CONSTITUTIONAL CRISES

S RI LANKA SLIPPED INTO CHAOS IN October 2018, when a constitutional crisis, happened, in a matter of fourteen days. It was on 26 October, when President Maithripala Sirisena, removed Ranil Wickremesinghe, and appointed Mahindra Rajapaksa, as the new prime minister.

When people questioned his unconventional decision, as he sacked him, without any parliamentary consultation, he defended this decision based on internal stability, governance issues, and accountability.

He had adjourned the parliament session, till November 16, giving Rajapaksa ample time, to gain support. Eventually, Rajapaksa became the new prime minister and entered the official Temple Trees Residence. But this is something against democratic values, because Wickremesinghe enjoyed a majority, in the parliament.

As two 'non-confidence votes' have already passed. against Rajapaksa, it seems that it is illegal, for Rajapaksa, to stay in power. Parliament had turned violent, as rivals exchanged blows, when these no-confidence votes, were passed, as a reaction.

The Speaker counted votes, based on the voices, he heard, and it seemed that the new leader failed the floor test. Lawmakers, supporting Rajapaksa, threw books, chairs, and chilli powder, mixed with water, to try to block the proceedings.

During these sessions, Rajapaksa insisted that the speaker had no authority, to remove him and that he is continuing his role, as prime minister, as he is directly appointed, by the President.

For years, the change in leadership, in Sri Lanka, has been happening, through sustained democracy, but the present crises are reflecting the country's glaring problems, in its institutions and regional politics.

Sirisena had become president because he allied, with Ranil's UNP. Had UNP not sponsored Sirisena, as a candidate, he would have had no way defeated Rajapaksa as the presidential candidate. Sirisena was not a populist candidate, and nor did he belong to any major political party. Although, part of the Rajapaksa government, he got support from Ranil Wickremesinghe's UNP, and became the next president. But he ousted a prime minister, from power, with whom he had agreed to work, on common grounds. A political betrayal may sound like an appropriate term. This development even surprised Rajapaksa's cadre.

According to an article, by Sonia Seats, in the Guardian, Sirisena has no record, of being a human rights champion, either, and it has not surprised the Western world, because the country is notorious, for its approach, towards handling a sensitive ethnic conflict. As the result, the diaspora population, of the Tamils, has grown, and it is trying to arouse worldwide sympathy, for their aspirations.

When parliamentary elections, happened, in 2015, Ranil was able to form the government. Both had promised accountability and development. But it is unfortunate that Sri Lanka has slipped, into political turmoil, again. The difference between them also reflects a certain political machiavellianism.

As of now, conspiracies have happened. Many regard Ranil's sacking as unconstitutional. It also seems that when Ranil accused India's RAW, to assassinate him, cracks appeared, in the diplomacy, between the two neighbouring countries, something that Sirisena was displeased with.

Rajapaksa has largely built his voter base, on the Sinhala identity. It seems probable that his tenure might deepen fissures. The wounds, of a brutal civil war, between Tamils and Sinhalese, are still afresh. What Sri Lanka needed now, is a reconciliation process, but things have suddenly taken the opposite form. The UN peace process has also not been triggered, either.

During Rajapaksa, a civil war, with Tamil Tigers, ended in a grotesque, the worst of its kind, in South Asia, after the calculated, ethnic cleansing, of Tamils, on a large scale. His tenure was also seen, as one of the most corrupt, as his brothers, were involved, in various corruption scandals.

If Rajapaksa remains in power, he will most certainly put an end, to these infamous corruption cases. As of now, the military, and police officials, are already paying him visits.

During his time, the relationship with China had deepened, and most of the corruption cases had taken place, on Chinese projects. Rajapaksa was trying to shift the diplomatic ties, more towards China. But, Ranil was seeking a middle path. Although, it seems that Rajapaksa, as the incumbent leader, might undo this.

Even many journalists, and activists, have disappeared,

mainly through targeted assassinations. His tenure might incur more fear.

As the result, the minority issue of Tamils, in Sri Lanka, will again stir up. It will also give political mileage, to regional Dravidian parties, in India's south. Quite lately, the Indian state of Tamil Nadu has condemned the capture of Tamil fishermen, by Sri Lanka.

In its ruling, the apex court said the parliament will be suspended, until December 7, and it will review all the petitions, filed on President Sirisena's decision.

According to Colombo-based NGO Centre for Policy Alternatives: 'the Supreme Court's order is a great victory for all those forces in Sri Lanka and anywhere else in the world who believe in the constitution and free and fair functioning of a democracy. The president cannot dissolve the parliament till the court's final orders. He can prorogue the parliament, but cannot dissolve it.'

As parliament is dissolved unexpectedly, new elections might happen soon. But, supporters of Rajapaksa, believe that the counting of votes was not done fairly, and it sabotaged the actual democratic process.

19 November, 2018

52

REPRESSIVE POLITICS IN BANGLADESH

CALLED AS THE IRON LADY, Sheikh Hasina has been acclaimed, by her ardent followers, for doing economic wonders, for the country, for nearly ten years.

As per official figures, in her tenure, as prime minister, per capita income has grown, by over one hundred fifty per cent. The population, living in poverty, has dropped, from nineteen per cent to nine per cent.

In the 2014 election, her party won two hundred thirty-four seats, out of three hundred seats, despite the strong anti-incumbency factor, according to several independent observers. In 2018, her party strongly retained two hundred forty-six seats, in the parliament.

Also, back in 2016, when Jammatul Mujahideen attacked a Dhaka bakery, killing twenty-six people, she was acclaimed for cracking these extremists down.

For allowing the ethnically cleansed, Rohingya refugees, from Myanmar, to stay, in the southeast of her country, her fans believed that she should be awarded a Nobel Peace Prize.

During her rule, she also launched trials, of powerful Islamist opposition, for crimes, committed during the 1971 independence war. When five top Islamist leaders, and the main opposition loyalists, were executed, a strong reaction was witnessed, that launched deadly clashes, and frequent mass protests, in her country. For her critics, Mrs Hasina is an autocrat, who has largely muzzled dissent, in a calculated manner. More specifically, she likes to keep religion-based voters, on trial.

What has led to a series of controversies, pre-election, in 2018, was her unsparing crackdown on people, which ranged from convictions, and arrests, of opposition candidates. Activists and protestors were subjected to harassment and surveillance. There was an initiative of a draconian 'digital security law,' that includes prison terms, for posting 'aggressive and frightening content,' according to statist narratives.

According to this law, Section 25(a) authorises sentences of up to three years, for publishing information that is 'aggressive or frightening'. Section 31, on the other hand, imposes sentences of up to 10 years, for posting information that 'ruins communal harmony, or creates instability, or disorder, or disturbs, or is about to disturb the law-and-order situation.'

During the election campaign in 2018, at least seventeen people died, due to political unrest. Ahead of the election, Bangladesh Telecommunication Regulatory Commission required all telecommunications officials, to shut down 3G and 4G services, in Bangladesh.

Brad Adams, Asia Director of Human Rights Watch said: 'The pre-election period was characterised by violence and intimidation against the opposition, their campaign events, and the misuse of laws to limit free speech. Reports of ballot stuffing, intimidation of voters, and ruling party control of voting locations on Election Day mean that an independent and impartial commission should be formed to determine the extent of the violations.'

Among the eminent Bangladeshis, who had been victimised, by government orders, is the eminent photographer Shahidul Islam, who was jailed for months, after being arrested, in August, for doing a story, illustrating police violence against student protesters, in a Facebook post, and for interviewing with Doha based media agency, Al Jazeera. There had been a huge furore, in the global media, then.

During the same pre-election period in September 2018, the Dhaka-based Odhikar group highlighted a worrying spate of enforced and illegal disappearances, of opposition leaders, students, and activists. The group claims that thirty people were allegedly abducted, by law enforcement agencies without explanation — a sharp jump from a total of 28 in the first eight months of the year.

Of those, who went missing in September 2018, the group says twenty-six were confirmed to have been arrested. Odhikar group even said that three were found dead, and one remained missing. Thousands have also been convicted, for the government's attempt, to crack on 'war on drugs.'

Earlier, in February 2015, a Bangladeshi-American blogger, Avijit Roy, was lynched to death, on the streets of Dhaka. His wife was critically injured, in the same attack. Another related mob incident happened, in Sylhet, in 2015, where another secular blogger, Ananta Bijoy Das, was murdered. None of their killers have been arrested or tried yet.

Now, after the post-poll results, opposition parties, journalists, and voters have alleged serious disparities including ballot stuffing, and restricting access to voters, at polling stations. There have been instances where the ruling Awami League activists, occupied polling places, and the police behaved in a partisan manner, as there were violations, of voter privacy, due to blatant intimidation.

The opposition party, BNP have accused the polling agents were denied access to two hundred twenty-one constituencies, reflecting that vote robbery has been unprecedented. However, contrarily, Chief Election Commissioner Nurul Huda characterised these reports, of violations, on polling day, as 'stray incidents.' On the other hand, Police chief Javed Patwari described the atmosphere as 'peaceful,' which is quite strange.

In a country, such as Bangladesh, ravaged by floods and cyclones, lately, there are media regulatory bodies, such as the Editors' Council, Press Institute, and Press Council, reflecting the times of their country. The activities, in their offices, have been mainly restricted, because it is alleged that they were mainly threatened, by the intelligence agencies, or the police.

Now, it seems, that Sheikh Hasina's every sincere achievement, in ten years, would be overshadowed, by her authoritarian attempts, to make her party interests prioritised above all – even above the people, she represented all these years. Sometime before, she had been accused of misusing the judiciary and the police.

Mrs Hasina, who is seventy-one, is rooted in her country's political culture. Her father, Sheikh Mujibur Rahman, was Bangladesh's first president. She was abroad when he was assassinated.

It was only in 1975, that she returned, in 1981, to take

over the leadership, of the Awami League.

Her party, and the Bangladesh Nationalist Party, led by another powerful woman, Khaleda Zia, locked horns, in the last election, in 2014, which the opposition party boycotted, to protest changes, to electoral procedures. This scenario gave Mrs Hasina an uncontested new term.

When Mrs Zia was recently convicted, of corruption, for seventeen years, Mrs Hasina backed herself, for another term. It reflects that Hasina's undisputed wins, have turned Bangladesh, into a one-party ruling state, as incumbency favoured her. Historically, both these women have been called as 'Battling Begums,' after both disassociated themselves, in 1990, by ousting former military dictator, Hussain Muhammad Ershad. In 2007, both leaders were imprisoned, after a military coup. But the charges were later dropped, and they were allowed to contest the 2008 election.

Bangladeshis, in the 2018 election, had to decide whether to penalise the ruling party, over alleged human rights violations, or reward it, for the steps, it took to grow the economy. According to them, they had to choose a leader with 'lesser evils.'

For Sheikh Hasina, providing food, jobs, and health means providing human rights, and she desists her criticism because she believes that it is blown out of proportion. Mrs Hasina believes that although Bangladesh's urban elite has been at the forefront, of criticising her policies, she wants to represent every section of the society. 'They are trying to please their donors, and are exaggerating, to get more funding,' she said, to The New York Times.

But, BNP, the main opposition, believe that Hasina's

public policies and perceptions are evasive, as around ten thousand, of their party workers, have been arrested, including ten of its candidates. In August 2018, thousands of students, marched the streets of Dhaka, to protest the government, for poor road safety, after a bus killed two children, in a tragic accident.

For many Bangladeshis, economic growth should not be sacrificed for political ideals, and village politics should also take priority, like the politics, reflected in the urban centres. And, above all, many Bangladeshis believe in a grassroots movement, vibrant civil society, and freedom of speech, despite Hasina's attempts at self-serving populism, in recent years. Does it also mean that she has not done much, to strengthen democratic institutions?

Human Rights Watch, has also alleged, that the government, has also failed, to properly enforce women's safety laws, in cases of sexual violence, rape, domestic abuse, and acid attacks, among others. Despite the government committing to end child marriage, by 2041, a law has remained, on the legal books, that allow girls, to marry, before the age of eighteen, although under 'special' circumstances.

Coming back to the recent election, Hong Kong-based rights activist, Mohammad Ashrafuzzaman, working for the Asian Legal Resource Centre, said: the media 'blackout,' during the election, was 'immeasurable and irreparable.'

21 January, 2019

53

OMAN'S DIPLOMATIC CAPACITY

MOST OF THE COUNTRIES PROMOTE diplomacy, on a specific political ideology, and economic interests that are often short-term. Oman, however, relies on long-term diplomacy.

The country believes that peaceful negotiations are pivotal, for its long-term prosperity, and security, primarily because Oman has limited military strength that it uses, for its internal security. That is why, for more than twenty-five years, it is pursuing an independent foreign policy, and has thus become a vital place, for backroom deals, by recognising its scope.

The Omani leader, Sultan Qaboos, has tried several ways, to neutralise internal, and external threats, in his country. His strategy of 'Omani balancing' is unique, but also controversial, because it allows him, to befriend Arab enemies, such as Iran, and Israel.

Conversely, Oman has also pledged, to play a limited role, in providing, military, and humanitarian support, to counter ISIS, but has refused to provide military support, in Yemen.

As per the narrative, in Joseph Kechichian's book, 'Oman and the World: The Emergence of an Independent Foreign Policy' (1995), he mentions that, in 1970, when Sultan Qaboos ousted his father, in a coup, he then, had developed diplomatic world relations, with India, and

England, Qaboos reversed this decision, by establishing new relations, with the League of Arab States (LAS), and United Nations in 1971. It had been an attempt, to end diplomatic isolation, within the region, by mitigating its dependence, on Britain, and achieving internal unity, by dealing with political unrest, in the north, ending the Communist-backed Dhofar War, threatening the Sultanate, since 1965, and addressing Oman's poor standard of living. He believes that due to this firm, pragmatic approach, displayed by Qaboos, he has changed 'an isolated and unstable Oman,' into a leader of Middle Eastern and global diplomacy. The fact that Qaboos encourages even warring countries, to find commonalities, and acceptable trade-offs, speaks of his mindset.

Historically, Oman became one of those countries, which did not break ties, with Egypt in 1977, and more specifically, during 1978, when Saadat approved of US Camp David peace talks, with Israel. Oman also became one of three Arab nation-states, to recognise Israel, and did not attend Baghdad Rejectionist Summit, which condemned Egypt. In 1979, when Khomeini came into power, Qaboos proposed a 100 million-protection plan, for the Strait of Hormuz, to deal with any possible aggression. When five other Gulf States, rejected this idea, he turned to the United States, and signed the 1980 Facilities Access Agreement, for Oman's long-term security interests.

Between 1981-1985, when Iran, and Iraq, were at war, Qaboos helped formed the Gulf Cooperation Council (GCC), which brought six Gulf states together. As Oman had kept a neutral stance, when Iraq and Iran war happened, it received nearly all support, from the Western governments.

During the early 1990s, Qaboos was recognised as a

regional figure, in the Middle East, who could be counted, on by other Gulf states, on security issues. When Iraq invaded Kuwait, in 1990, Omani forces participated, in the UN liberation effort, and Oman granted access, to prepositioned supplies, and facilities, in Oman, via the Facilities Access Agreement, which was renewed, in 1990. At the same time, he put efforts, to end the war, for the good prospects, of the region. In 1991, he also recognised the need for citizen participation, in government matters, by establishing *Majlis Al Shura*, despite holding a strong grip, on every institution, in the country, including the economy, judiciary and the military.

In other words, Qaboos is an excellent example of a personalist dictator, who, even reshuffled his cabinet, during the Arab Spring, to avoid any unrest, in the country.

In recent times, Oman has been a mediator, in the Qatar diplomatic crises, to help facilitate, the signing of the Iran nuclear deal, and offer secret negotiations, between warring parties, in Yemen.

For years, Qaboos has hosted negotiations, between US leaders, and Iranian leaders, often in his own house. Oman let free three abducted American tourists, in Iran. In 2012, the United States requested Oman, to hold its first round of talks, with Iran, concerning its burgeoning nuclear power. These talks were held secretly, until they were revealed, to the public, in 2013. Back then, Oman had become a 'Switzerland of the Middle East', a soft power, almost a meeting point for signatories of the nuclear deal: China, France, Germany, Russia the UK, and Iran.

Oman, under Qaboos, also has intentions to end the standoff, between Qatar, and Gulf Cooperation Council

(GCC), led by Saudi, and the UAE. It reflects Oman being a neutral state, often overshadowed, by Saudi Arabia's regional dominance.

Farea al-Muslimi, a Middle East analyst working for the Carnegie Centre wrote that since the start of the latest war, in Yemen, Oman has played a key facilitation role. It has hosted Houthi leaders, and representatives, of former president Ali Abdullah Saleh. This, as well as its good relations with Iran, enabled it to stake out a middle ground, allowing it to engage, in a political process, to help resolve the conflict.

In May 2015 and November 2016, Oman hosted secret talks, between US officials, and Houthi rebels, to the extent, that Qaboos had convinced Houthis, to attend UN backed peace talks. Though these attempts have not proved successful, for any form of urgent conflict resolution, required in the region, it did set a benchmark, for a peaceful dialogue. Add to that, Qaboos had rejected an offer, from Saudi, and Emirati officials, to intervene, in the civil war, as he had figured out the human costs, involved in the war.

In October 2015, Oman also briefly entered a diplomatic effort, in Syria, where Qaboos dispatched his close aide, and Minister responsible, for Foreign Affairs, Yusuf bin Alawi, to Damascus, to convey a message, from then US Secretary of State John Kerry to Syrian President Bashar Al Assad. Omani Foreign Minister, Alawi, and Kerry had met, before, to discuss Obama's diplomatic initiatives, in Syria.

After that, in early February 2016, Russian Foreign Minister Sergei Lavrov, travelled to Muscat, to speed up the political, and diplomatic settlement, in the region.

This also set the stage, for the meeting between the Syrian Foreign Minister, Muallem, and Oman's Foreign Minister. It was a significant development, considering the rife relations, between Washington DC and Tehran, and Riyadh and Tehran especially when the US, currently, is finding difficult ground, in dealing with Moscow, at a time, when Russians killed an American spy, and his daughter, in the United Kingdom.

In March 2018, US Secretary of Defence, James Mattis travelled to Muscat, for talks, with Sultan Qaboos, regarding how to achieve a resolution, to Yemen's civil war, and ensuring to stop the smuggling of missiles, to Yemen's Houthi rebels, through the Strait of Hormuz.

Following Mattis – Qaboos meeting, Omani Foreign Minister, Alawi also travelled in March, to Tehran, for talks with Iranian President Hassan Rouhani. Analysts say that it might be plausible that Alawi would have carried forward a message pertaining, to the JCPOA (Joint Comprehensive Plan of Action), and the conflict, in Yemen. Some believe, CIA Director Pompeo, also paid a visit to Qaboos, which may come, in handy, on issues pertaining, to JCPOA.

According to Asha Castleberry, a fellow at the American Security Project: 'Oman may be triangulating, between Washington, Moscow, and Tehran, by carrying messages between the various parties, to help unwind Syria's civil war. In the process, Oman would help reduce global tensions, by keeping the various parties engaged, on regional issues, such as Syria and Yemen, while facilitating dialogue, between Washington, and Tehran, on the JCPOA.'

However, despite Qaboos's long list of accomplishments, he still has some controversies, to his name, that includes being an Arab leader, who vows to accept Israel, just like Saudi's Crown Prince, Muhammad Bin Salman, who urged Palestinians 'to accept a peace deal, or shut up.'

2 February, 2019

54

VENEZUELA'S CONTINUING POLITICAL CRISES

WHEN JUAN GUAIDO self-proclaimed himself, as the interim president, in January 23, 2019, it surged new political crises, in Venezuela.

More than fifty countries have recognised him, as the new leader, but Maduro refuses to step down, as he believes, many quarters, from where, he draws support, have not abandoned him.

A country, such as Venezuela, which was discovered, by Italian explorer Christopher Columbus, cannot have two presidents, but a standoff between them has heightened tensions.

In the recent past, many political commentators claimed, that after the fourth successful election, of Hugo Chavez, Bolivarian Venezuela suffered new, often-unstable economic shocks, mainly due to the crumbling oil sales. Gone were the days of the thriving 1970s, when people, on the Caracas streets, drove Cadillacs, and Buicks. This oil-driven economy, sustained its high economic growth, mainly during the mid-2000s.

As socialism was regarded as the most powerful political force, in the country, Chavez's grassroots populist policies, and progressive welfare ideas, were often declared heroic, and even hailed, from every quarter, of the globe. But, due to gradual 'structural inequalities,' as proclaimed by NACLA Report on the Americas, the country went into crises, almost in a continual slump, and then into quagmires of a recession. It is because the Venezuelan economy had a high dependence, on oil, and it paved the way, for its eventual mismanagement.

Over time, crises in Venezuela, heightened, to widespread hunger, hyperinflation, disease, crime, and massive immigration, from the country. All this burdening baggage was succeeded, in Maduro's leadership, after Chavez's death. As per Mercy Corps, around ninety per cent of people, live under the poverty line, currently. And, as per UN data, around 2.7 million people had fled the country, since 2015, for employment, and a better life.

When Ivan Briscoe, travelled with some of his peers, working for International Crises Group, he spoke to various former high-ranking public officials, including Maduro's loyalists, in the Constituent Assembly, his party members from United Socialist Party, and in regional governments. All had thought that the recent developments are giving rise to a fragile political scenario, although it has still not been able to fracture, the ruling coalition.

Despite allegations of Maduro winning the 2018 election, on election fraud, even people such as Bernie Sanders, pointed out that there were democratic operations, running in Venezuela.

In a Foreign Affairs article, Briscoe quoted a former minister in Maduro's cabinet, where he said that, since Guiado self-proclaimed himself, as the new president, 'they have become united, more than they ever were.' Some officials, who never were shy, to provide their critic, to the government, even proclaimed that Maduro's statements were never *bravuconadas* (populist messages), and they were unsure, how there would be a regime change, under the current dismal scenario, when Washington was willing to arrange a coup against Maduro's alleged misrule, through private and public diplomacy, and not through direct action, of invasion, or war.

The Lima Group, an amalgam of right-wing Latin American leaders, endorsed by the Trump administration, wants to drag Maduro, to the International Criminal Court.

Maduro's supporters, on the other hand, view him as a Peronist, a follower of political thought, synonymous, with a populist Argentine movement. In this dismal economic time, his government provides subsidised food containing pasta, rice, flour, and tuna, to around seven million households, which costs around $400 million, a month.

But, this state-sponsored food supply ran into a problem, when the United States put a sanction on Venezuela's state-run oil firm, PDVDSA, which made the largest public currency reserves. Around 8.36 million barrels of Venezuelan crude, worth half a billion dollars, currently, are not finding buyers, as per data, compiled by Bloomsburg. They have even reduced rates as the country ran out of space, to store its oil barrels.

Currently, Venezuela owes much of its oil, for its debt, to countries, such as China, and India, but sanctions prevent them to trade.

According to the head of the Venezuelan Oil Chamber, representing five hundred public companies, Reinaldo Quintero, the country can neither charge, nor receive money, and the public institution predicts huge collateral damage, in the future.

The world is finding it hard to find oil, as Canada has implemented a policy of self-curtailment, while OPEC's rising supply costs, prevent them to trade Venezuela's oil stocks. Then, the Venezuelan Central Bank, removed eight tonnes of gold, for sale in February 2019, to raise its currency. But America has warned all global banks, not to deal with Venezuelan gold. The Bank of England, froze a billion dollars, of Venezuelan gold, which was condemned by Italy, as they expressed distrust, about England, as a 'neutral arbiter.'

These a crisis have increased the price of Colombia's flagship oil, *Castilla*, giving a rise to oil wars, around the globe, directly attributed to America's growing diplomatic interference.

This kind of seasoned American foreign policy has been aggravated, because they simply want Maduro to step down, so that his opposition can put him, in exile, or maybe execute him, for alleged tyranny.

According to an article written by Alan MacLeod, these 'hare-brained' schemes are mostly backfiring. He calls Trump's policies, as 'comically incompetent' because, according to his statistics, seventy-five per cent, of the world's countries support Maduro. And surprisingly, the global media institutions, many a part of the mainstream Western press, largely supporting an 'Americanised prejudice', against the Venezuelan president, almost unreported the UN Human Right Council's condemnations, of the US sanctions, as they have targeted the country's poor.

As per a poll, conducted by Hinterlaces study, recognised as a neutral agency, around eighty-one per cent, disagreed, with the US sanctions.

But, at the same time, it has paved the way, for Guaido's political opportunism. For a campaign against Maduro, the Trump administration also revoked the visas of forty-nine Maduro officials. In this process, the Venezuelan president has tried an alternative source, of income, such as shipping gold, to Turkey, and Russian intermediaries. He is also willing to refine Venezuela's light crude, through Russian, and Chinese companies, as both nations, openly support Maduro. But, at the same time, they want their debts, to be repaid. In its nine-month investigation against *Banesco,* a private bank, for being responsible, for depreciating the Bolivar currency, Maduro arrested eleven top executives.

The US believes that Maduro's Russian support is his biggest 'political weapon.' Their uncalled statements had come, after Russian foreign minister, Sergei Lavrov accused Americans, of buying 'small scale arms, mortar launchers, and anti-aircraft missiles,' stationing them close to Venezuela, for active interference, and supporting a political coup, in the country.

As per McClathy DC Bureau, Elliot Abrams, an individual, responsible, to smuggle weapons, inside Nicaragua, under the guise of aid, was caught smuggling weapons, and arms, inside Venezuela.
According to these officials, Maduro has blamed financial sanctions, imposed by the US, and introduced in August 2017, for the current crisis. There is also a chance that these influential public officials might bog down, to foreign pressure.

Maduro, in the current crisis, has also promoted several army officers, in the hope that these military officers might help him, against the Guaido coup, plotted by outside forces.

It is also unclear whether civil society can topple him. The self-proclaimed, interim president, will try to unite the opposition, but many see him as 'too young' to bring Venezuela, back into a democratic order. Some believe that he can come into power, only with the support, of the military. More than five hundred soldiers have already crossed into Colombia, which also reflects the growing disorder, inside the military.

Until January 2019, eighty per cent of Venezuelans had never heard of Guaido. By many, he was accused of 'labelling the deaths, in his country,' mainly to 'invest in his political future.'
As the political crises continue, in the previous weeks, there were some skirmishes, involving the military, at Brazil and Colombian borders, as some trucks, poised as humanitarian convoys, containing one hundred seventy-eight metric tons, of an essential commodity were blocked to enter the country.

This act, supported by Guaido, was seen, as an ostensible reason, by Maduro, for a US-led invasion. It is an overused strategy, which most people, regard, as a threat to world peace. But, in this entire clamour, the battle for a stable, and prosperous Venezuela, continues.

3 March, 2019

55

TWO FEUDING NEIGHBOURS

WHEN A SUICIDE BOMBER BLEW him up, near Pulwama, in Indian-occupied Kashmir, on February 2019, in an SUV, containing eighty kilograms, high-grade RDX, by ramming into a travelling bus, he caused maximum damage, to his enemy, by killing forty personnel, of the 76th battalion.

The relations, between two feuding nations, in the subcontinent, reached a new low. Indian military officials, in their nationalism whims, assured of an answer within hundred hours.

An attack, on the Indian army, in this manner, reminded us, of the highly volatile war zones, such as Iraq, Afghanistan, Syria, and Yemen, where such retaliatory aggressions, are common.

But, in places, such as Kashmir, suicide bombings, making large causalities, have been largely unheard of, and are uncommon, too. Although, there have been some previous episodes of suicide bombings, turned up, as failed undertakings, in Kashmir valley, especially a failed attempt, near the army cantonment, near Badami Bagh, Srinagar, in 2000.

A similar attack, happened, on the Indian army, in 2010, when Maoists attacked them, in Dante Wada, killing seventy-six personnel. After the Pulwama bombing episode, the images shown, of torn bodies, charred pieces of luggage, burned clothes, and a demolished bus were both grotesque, and horrifying. An incredible number of debris had spread, over the travelling Pulwama highway. The ruins, of the bus, had reached, as high, as the height of the nearest telecommunications tower. The inner walls of the houses, near the vicinity, developed major cracks, and their windowpanes were broken. Life, in the Kashmir valley, came to a standstill, as the tentacles of the conflict, clutched common Kashmiris, all over again.

A war was fought in the TV studios. Pakistan was declared a war mongrel state, once again, by the anchors, and client commentators, almost in an identical manner, that we saw during the 2016 Uri attack. Bollywood actors, and high-profile journalists, soon joined the long crowd of political commentators, and military officials, and made provocative speeches, on social media. It was these Indian journalists, who instigated the jingoism, around the nation.

Although the Islamic Republic of Pakistan assured of an investigation, these overtures were undermined, in India, and the hate, and the political hostility, were rechristened.

However, it was not only the hate that spread. Confusion also spread. Conflicting reports, of the exact location, of Balakote, appeared, as the exact location of the place, was not confirmed initially. Balakot was a place where the Indian army launched a pre-dawn operation as a reaction to the Pulwama blast. The observers, initially, however, were confused, about whether it was a small village, near the Line of Control, or in the Swat valley. But, when Major Ashraf Ghafoor, through Twitter, confirmed the Indian aggression, by showing some pictures, of a dropped payload, it became apparent that it was Balakote, in Khyber Paktunwala, in the heart of Pakistani territory.

As per reports from Al Jazeera, somewhere in the alpine

forests, of Khyber Paktunwala, craters were formed, the trees had fallen, and some civilians, mostly mountain people, such as Nooran Shah, living in shacks, and growing crops, such as wheat, maize, and rearing livestock, for a living, were injured, with dispersed metal shrapnel, and travelling stones.

According to the Australian Strategic Policy Institute, publicly available imagery, acquired by European Space Imaging, the day after the strike, suggested that the buildings, at the camp, were not visibly damaged, or destroyed, and suggested a 'systematic targeting error'. The high-resolution picture showed undamaged buildings' roofs, where the strike was intended.

A day, or two later, it had appeared that no JeM militants were killed, and the whereabouts of a sophisticated operating JeM camp, were, likely, a fabricated lie. In this sensitive time, many international news agencies, also accused the media, of both nations, of broadcasting fake videos. However, as per The Hindu, India's Home Minister, Rajnath Singh believed that over three hundred mobile phones were active, before the operation, according to inputs, given to him, by National Technical Research Organisation.

Although, the Balakote locals, believed that there was a mysterious *madrassa*, which was operated by JeM, and was no longer active. According to them, there appeared, no such highly sophisticated operating compound, where militants trained, on the hills of Balakote. However, a Reuters team was denied access to this compound, by the Pakistani army, citing 'security concerns.' The team visited the area, three times, in nine days.

As IAF dropped their bombs, in hostile territory, Indian media left no stone unturned, in propagating lies. In a high profile, largely neutral Indian news channel, such as NDTV, conflicting reports appeared, about IAF shooting a PAF F16, near Lam Valley, of Nowshera. Pakistani media, never confirmed, any such incident, and international media, also questioned, the authenticity of the incident. A US-based foreign magazine concluded that all PAF aeroplanes were intact.

Disowning your air force men also goes against your morals. The footage, of a captured IAF pilot, Abhinandan was turned down, by many common Indians, as for some reason, they believed, that IAF does not allow pilots, to keep moustaches. Ironical and repugnant, it may sound, but army generals, and other jingoistic commentators, who once threatened Pakistan, of nuking them, kept quiet over Pakistan's gesture of peace, by releasing the captured IAF pilot, some days after. He had been treated well, by the Pakistani army, was shifted to a medical facility, and then released, soon after.

There were many infuriated people, including many Kashmiris, who complained about why India talked about the Geneva conventions, for Abhinandan, and not uttered a word, when a Kashmiri man was tied over a military jeep, and paraded by the army, in the valley, a while back. One might ask: why do these conventions only apply to Indians?

In places, such as Srinagar, shrill sounds of fighter jets, were heard, repeatedly, just like, in north Kashmir, by some local journalists. These activities concerned the Kashmiri diaspora, and almost everyone wanted to hear their families back, at a time, when local Internet was getting snapped repeatedly.

There was artillery seen, getting transported, to the border, near places in Punjab, Jammu region, and Kashmir valley. An IAF chopper, shot accidentally, by IAF authorities, also crashed, in central Budgam, Kashmir. After the event, the locals huddled near the site and chanted '*Jive Jive Pakistan*' (Long Live Pakistan), near police, and army personnel, who tried to drive them away.

But the Indian media believed that twelve Mirage 2000 fighters, backed by 4 Sukhoi 30 MKI, and two AWACS (airborne warning and control system) aircraft, fired by Spice-2000 guided bombs, and AGM-142 (Popeye-2) missiles, destroyed a 'terrorist facility', killing three hundred militants, as per reports, by Times of India.

Despite this strong claim, given by Indian authorities, people in Pakistan, questioned their sheer audacity, because there were no local stories, of the dead bodies of militants, getting buried. Hoax images and stories were circulated, on social media, aiming to mislead people. And, even if people believe the Indian version of the events, then most likely Pakistani government would have collaborated, with the ISI, for any kind of secrecy, post-Balakote operation, which, again, will be a highly controversial accusation.

In a New York Times Op-ed, Pakistani author, and political commentator, Fatima Bhutto wrote: 'Pakistan's recent history has been bloody, and no one has suffered that violence more than its own citizens.' Factually, not only India, but many other countries, especially, in the West, have undermined Pakistan's political, and social problems, lately, including the current problems, it faces, as the country is becoming a laboratory, for religious extremism, and sectarian divide.

Nuclear bullying also started, for some days. Pakistan's Prime Minister Imran Khan had assured: 'if India talks about war, then Pakistan's answer will also be war, and if India talks about dialogue, then Pakistan's answer will also be dialogue'.

There were also speculations, of the Indian army, marching towards Sialkot, and the Indian navy, advancing towards Karachi waters, and people living near its shore, had been advised, by the local authorities, of electricity blackouts, in their communities.

In places like Kashmir, people were seen painting red cross slogans on hospital roofs.

Pakistan's railway minister, Sheikh Rashid Ahmad, known for his provocative speeches, threatened India, and assured that if a war had happened, it would have been a final war. He said: 'if anyone gazes at Pakistan, with an objection, it will be a reason for an all-out war. Pakistanis are ready to die for their homeland. The country is a fort for global Muslims, and is watched by them, from all over the world. After the nuclear war, neither will the birds chirp, and nor will the bells ring, at the temples, after that.'

Former President Pervez Musharraf also talked about the advantage, of the strike-first policy, against India.

But, if a nuclear war happens, between these two feuding neighbours, there will be no holy, and kingly warriors, rather, this war would eventually ignite a serious catastrophe. It will affect half of the world's population. Even the laymen around us, know the devastating aftermaths, of a nuclear war.

In history, politics has often produced warmongers, bloodthirsty criminals, disguised, as leaders. Many see India's invasion, of Pakistan, as an opportunity, for Modi, to cash in Hindutva votes, under the bravados of Hindu nationalism. This misguided strategy, of revenge, will put millions of civilian lives, at stake. It has also projected Modi's image, largely, as a failed leader, around many quarters of the globe.

On the other hand, Imran Khan has been appreciated, for his political maturity, for not letting the situation go out of hand, and for letting the captured air force pilot, return.

11 March, 2019

56

CHRISTCHURCH MOSQUE RAMPAGE

IT WAS A DASTARDLY KILLING SPREE of worshippers shot on a video. In Christchurch, southern New Zealand, an Australian white supremacist, Brenton Tarrant had driven to the Al Noor Mosque in Deans Avenue on 15th March 2019, with a stash of weapons and ammunition, along with petrol canisters. A homicide of Muslim worshippers, including small children, had been on his mind.

After arming himself, with a camera mounted on his helmet, he walked into the mosque and began shooting indiscriminately. In three minutes of rampage, manslaughter, butchery, whatever one might call it, he exited through the front door, and fired random shots, as cars on the highway travelled past him. After some time, he then re-entered the mosque to check for survivors.

Around fifty people were declared dead in this horrifying episode. Prime Minister Jacinda Ardern called it 'one of New Zealand's darkest days.'

Brenton Tarrant was arrested minutes after the massacre. After the incident, it became apparent, that the shooter wanted to create fear of white supremacist ideology in the minds of immigrants living in the region.

Tarrant had written that he hoped that his actions would 'balkanise' the United States 'along political, cultural and, most importantly racial lines.' This thought would hasten the destruction of the current world order, and enable the creation of white, Christian ideas, while give an assault to the values of multiculturalism, at the same time.

New Zealand is isolated and unruffled to violence, possibly because of its location. It was probably the reason the shooter wanted to choose this place for a heinous plot. The attack had invoked major reactions from all quarters of the globe.

After the incident, it seemed that the shooter also wanted attention because he had left a 74-page document, posted on social media, under his name. Beyond his white supremacist views, he claimed to be an environmentalist and a fascist who believed China aligned with his social and political values. He also described contempt for the wealthiest 1 per cent. Regular media reports claimed that he made 'regular, racist, Facebook posts.'

According to Jarrod Gilbery, a senior lecturer at University of Canterbury: 'instead of the traditional bunch of street thugs hanging around on a corner drinking cheap cider and sneering at immigrants, the alt-right gathers together from the privacy of their homes.'

Race Relations Commissioner of New Zealand, Paul Hunt, also ascertained that in some quarters of New Zealand society, there was Islamophobia and a cause towards appealing to the government to bring back some form of 'hate laws.'

Tarrant grew up in a working-class Australian family and described himself as a poor student. He was believed to have worked briefly and made some money through Bitconnect, a crypto currency like Bitcoin. For quite some time, he was a licensed gun owner of five weapons.

In the past four years, Tarrant had spent a little time in Australia, and just had minor traffic offences on his record. He was a personal trainer at Big River Gym, in northern New South Wales, and is believed to have inherited his interest in physical fitness from his father. Gym manager Tracey Gray commented: 'he worked in our program that offered free training to kids in the community, and he was very passionate about that.' Ms Gray said Tarrant did not come across as some individual who had an interest in firearms.

His manifesto also included protracted themes of hatred between people of European descent and Muslims, often framing it in terms of the Crusades.

He had been motivated towards violence, after an episode occurred in 2017, while he was touring through western Europe, when a Muslim Uzbek man drove a truck into a crowd of people in Stockholm, killing five people.

In some cities in France, the scene of immigrants, in the cities and towns he visited, appalled him. He called for the removal of minarets at Turkey's Hagia Sophia Museum and claimed to have donated to far-right white nationalist groups such as the identitarian movement, which originated from France, but he was not an active member of any organisation. However, he admitted having contacts with an immigration group called the Reborn Knights Templar, and it is believed by some that he had got approval from Anders Breivik, himself, for the attack, a claim that has not been verified yet, according to Associated Press. Anders Breivek is a right-wing extremist, who killed 77 people in Oslo, at a nearby island in 2011. But, Breivik's lawyer Oeystein Storrvik told Norway's VG newspaper, that his client, who is in prison, has very 'limited contacts with the surrounding world,' so it seems very unlikely that Breivik had any contact, with the Australian-born shooter. Nevertheless, Breivik was someone who Tarrant admired.

In his puerile assertions, Tarrant also wanted to attack the participants at a Worker's Youth League Summer Camp, who he libelled as 'cultural Marxists.'

Many people might not be surprised that at the upper echelons of power, especially in American politics, a similar watered-down version to demonise leftist intellectuals, journalists, and academia has been happening, especially since Trump branded them as 'enemies of the people.'

According to inputs from the Associated Press, Brenton Tarrant used many hate symbols associated with the Nazis and white supremacy. The number 14, seen on his rifle, was possibly a reference to a white supremacist slogan, attributed in part to Adolf Hitler's *Mein Kemph*, according to Poverty Law Centre. He also used the symbol of *Schwarze Sonne*, or 'black sun,' which has become synonymous with far-right groups.

His manifesto has been compared with an 1893 text by white supremacists around the world titled 'National Life and Character: A Forecast,' a text, which was acknowledged by 'White Australia' policymakers, including Keith Murdoch (father of Rupert Murdoch), who called for racial unity, and former US President Theordore Roosevelt. In other racist texts such as 'The Rising Tide of Colour Against White World Supremacy', a sacred union was called for, that amalgamated together Australians, Africans, Californians, and Canadians. It made thinkers such as W.E.B Du Bois believe that the biggest problem of the 20th century would come from the colour line – the relation of darker-coloured men to lighter-coloured men.

In a Washington Post Op-ed, Khaled Diab wrote: 'if a terrorist were to claim that their attack was intended to add momentum to the pendulum swings of history, further destabilising, and polarising Western society, you might be excused in thinking the perpetrator was an Islamic extremist. But these are the words of a white supremacist and a crusader.' Diab compared his nihilistic perceptions, to jihadis, as they claim to polarise an already divided world - while Islamists vilify secularists as fakes, and often as traitors, at worst, white supremacists, on the other hand, disparage Islamists as hate-spreading pseudo zealots.

Tarrant was also convinced that a society of rampant nihilism, consumerism, and individualism was destroying the Western world. As an individual, he spoke of victimhood, and oppression from elites, much like his jihadist counterparts, despite living in a modern society, founded by European settlers. Although, not sure of his Christian beliefs, his manifesto spoke of Christian imagery, as he justified his crime on religious terms, to many extents, by even quoting Pope Urban II, who initiated the First Crusade.

Reasoned continual immigration has mainly exerted an inferiority complex on white supremacists, mainly because of anti-colonial voices, coming from oppressed people, who have attacked their agenda. Thus, this claim of foreign occupation and oppression are common recurring themes in white nationalist cabals. That is why, it is common to see restricted immigration policies, even for displaced refugees, in places such as Australia and the United States, where current politicians are seemingly born out of these ultra-conservative and radical rightist views. These ideas are evident in their intellectual arena.

According to Indian writer, Pankaj Mishra: 'Trump himself acknowledged as much in January 2017, eight days into his presidency, when he confessed his admiration for Australia's brutal measure of detaining refugees on remote islands. He had called it a good idea, and called for similar measures in the United States.'

This inferiority complex had even let British-educated Australian academic Charles Henry Pearson comment that 'white men were in danger of being elbowed and hustled and perhaps, and even trust aside, by black and yellow races.'

After the incident, more than 10.8 million NZD have been received so far, to help the families of the 50 people killed in mosque shootings. A support fund on the New Zealand site givealittle.co.nz had received more than 91,000 donors, while launchgood.com, a global crowdfunding platform focused on Muslim lives, netted around 2,546,126 NZD from over 40,000 donations.

New Zealand has been holding memorials ever since the massacre happened. At Hagley Park, a crowd of 40,000 people expressed solidarity. Many women were seen wearing *hijabs* as a sign of solidarity, including Prime Minister Jacinda Ardern. She has been hailed for her stances, including banning automatic weapons in the country.

The prime minister has also called for paying for any repatriation charges, if any associated family members of victims, wanted to move away from New Zealand. She said that a Royal Commission, the most powerful probe in New Zealand's history, was needed to find out how a single gunman was able to kill 50 people in a rampage.

Despite the ardent praise Ardern received, post mosque rampage, her critics were not shy enough to take on her political views. While as Ardern was trying to prove that New Zealand is a land of peace and tranquillity, the fact remains that the country too, is built on a horrific past, that includes the genocide of the Maoris, just like the aborigines in Australia, and the native Americans and African Americans in the US.

In New Zealand, the settlers, from generation to generation, used confiscated land from Maoris. Her government is currently keeping an alliance with New Zealand First, a protectionist, populist party, favouring anti-immigration.

In the case of Australia, former Prime Minister Kevin Rudd, had once apologised to the people of Australia, for the massacre of aborigines, but no such official apology has come from any Kiwi politician, lately. There is little reconciliation between a *Pakeha* (white New Zealander) and a Maori in her country.

According to Op-ed writer, Sunil Sharan: 'reaching out to the Maoris damages her political career. Reaching out to the Muslim *ummah*, gives her a worldwide platform, to project her image.'

Numerous calls have gone out for her to be awarded the Nobel Peace Prize. A Nobel for her will obfuscate what the ancestors of the current Pakehas did to the Maoris.

25 March, 2019

57

GIFTING GOLAN HEIGHTS

DONALD TRUMP'S RECOGNITION OF Israel's sovereignty over the Golan Heights on 25 March 2019 marked one of the most controversial foreign policy decisions of his presidency. As reported by Al Jazeera, the proclamation was signed at the White House alongside Israeli Prime Minister Benjamin Netanyahu, and it effectively endorsed Israel's 1981 annexation of the territory captured from Syria during the 1967 Six Day War. The move was unprecedented: no other major power had recognised Israel's claim, and the UN Security Council had repeatedly affirmed that the Golan Heights remained occupied Syrian territory.

The timing of Trump's decision was politically significant. According to Victor Kattan in JSTOR, the proclamation came just two weeks before Israel's general election, providing Netanyahu with a symbolic victory to present to his electorate. In the United States, the announcement coincided with the annual conference of the American Israel Public Affairs Committee (AIPAC), the most influential pro-Israel lobby. Trump's administration used the occasion to attack Democrats, with Vice-President Mike Pence accusing them of being afraid to stand with Israel's strongest supporters.

Domestically, Trump's recognition of the Golan Heights was seen as part of a broader strategy to consolidate support among Evangelical Christians, who make up roughly a quarter of the American electorate. As

CNN polling showed, while 71 per cent of Democrats opposed moving the US embassy to Jerusalem, 79 per cent of Republicans supported it. Trump's team framed Democrats as increasingly hostile to Israel and even to Jewish Americans, with close associates promoting the idea of a 'Jexodus' — a supposed migration of Jewish voters away from the Democratic Party.

The truth is also that Jewish Americans represent only about 3 per cent of the electorate, but Evangelicals were a far larger and more reliable voting bloc for Trump.

This was not the first time Trump had broken with diplomatic orthodoxy. In December 2017, he recognised Jerusalem as Israel's capital, despite the 1993 Oslo Accords stipulating that the city's final status should be resolved in peace talks. As The New York Times journalists Mark Landler and Edward Wong observed, Trump's approach was to shake up long-standing policies that had remained unchanged since the 1970s. The UN General Assembly voted overwhelmingly to declare the US recognition of Jerusalem 'null and void.' In 2018, Trump closed the Palestine Liberation Organisation's office in Washington and passed the Anti-Terrorism Clarification Act, which forced the Palestinian Authority to reject US aid. He also shut down the US consulate in Jerusalem that had traditionally handled Palestinian affairs, prompting one Palestinian official to describe the move as 'the last nail in the coffin' of America's role in peace-making.

International reaction to the Golan decision was swift and overwhelmingly negative. The Arab Parliament denounced it as a violation of UN Resolution 242, which calls for Israel's withdrawal from territories occupied in 1967. Its speaker, Mishaal bin Fahm al-Salami, argued that legitimising Israeli occupation was now the orientation of

US policy. UN Secretary-General spokesman Stephane Dujarric reiterated that the status of the Golan had not changed and that UN policy remained consistent with Security Council resolutions. Leaders across the Middle East voiced outrage. Lebanese President Michel Aoun condemned the proclamation, while Hezbollah warned that similar recognition of Israeli claims in the West Bank could follow. Iranian President Hassan Rouhani declared that no one could imagine an American leader giving land to another occupying country against international law. Russia's Kremlin spokesman Dmitry Peskov warned of negative consequences for Middle East stability. Even US allies such as Canada, Australia, Turkey, and Gulf states including Bahrain, Qatar, and Kuwait rejected the move.

The decision also highlighted the uneasy position of Arab allies of Washington. As Al Jazeera noted, Trump's alliance with Netanyahu, motivated partly by biblical interpretations favoured by Evangelical supporters, placed Arab governments in a bind. Public opinion in the Arab world was angered by what was seen as hegemonic Zionist policy, yet governments dependent on US security guarantees struggled to respond forcefully.

On the ground, the Druze community of the Golan Heights, numbering around 26,000, continued to resist integration into Israel. Nearly all Druze residents boycotted municipal elections in 2018, rejecting Israeli attempts to normalise control. Meanwhile, about 20,000 Israeli settlers live in the territory, alongside UN peacekeepers who have monitored the ceasefire line for decades. For Lebanon, the adjacent Shebaa Farms and Kfar Chouba hills remain disputed, with Beirut insisting they are Lebanese land occupied by Israel.

Trump's recognition of the Golan Heights boosted his

popularity among Israelis. A Pew Research Centre survey showed his approval rising from 56 per cent in 2017 to 69 per cent in 2019. For Netanyahu, the proclamation was a diplomatic gift during a crucial election campaign. For Trump, it was a domestic political tool, reinforcing his image as Israel's staunchest ally and energising Evangelical voters.

Yet the broader consequences were destabilising. By breaking with international consensus, the US undermined the principle that territory cannot be acquired by force.

As Victor Kattan argued, the proclamation set a dangerous precedent, potentially encouraging other states to annex land under the guise of security. It also weakened America's credibility as a mediator in the Israeli-Palestinian conflict.

The recognition of the Golan Heights fits into a pattern of Trump's Middle East policy: symbolic gestures that please domestic constituencies and Israeli leaders but erode international law and regional stability. While these moves won him support among far-right Israelis and Evangelicals, they alienated Palestinians, angered Arab publics, and unsettled US allies. As The New York Times noted, Trump's approach was less about geopolitics and more about domestic politics, shaking up orthodoxies for electoral gain.

Ultimately, the proclamation illustrates the contradictions of US foreign policy under Trump. On one hand, America presents itself as a champion of democracy and peace. On the other, it legitimises occupation, undermines international law, and fuels conflict.

The Golan Heights decision was not just a diplomatic gesture; it was a political calculation that prioritised short-term electoral advantage over long-term stability.

10 April, 2019

58

ERDOGAN'S TROUBLING TIMES

T HE LOSS OF ANKARA AND ISTANBUL in the 2019 mayoral election has proved a major setback, for Recep Tayyib Erdogan.

Many neighbourhoods, in Turkey, were tense lately, as people were glued, to the television sets, in regard, to the recent mayor election outcomes, which reflected, a somewhat changed, democratic mindset.

Erdogan seems to have become aloof, recently, with very few aides, and ministers, hanging around with him, in his presidential palace.

In Erdogan's political lobby, he has been seen as someone, like an Ottoman Sultan, having a kind of imperial presidency, under his name. But, if Erdogan amends the constitution now, to stir up the voter base, then he would not likely enjoy political authority, now.

This mayoral election has been seen, as a referendum, and his overall leadership evaluation, against the backdrop of economic meltdown, in the country.

Supporters of the Republican Peoples Party had been seen in jubilation, in Istanbul, waving the crescent, red flag of their country, when they saw their candidate, just a fraction ahead. In total, Erdogan has lost control, in seven, out of twelve major cities. In eastern Turkey, the leftist *Halkların Demokratik Partisi* (HDP) has also made gains.

In Istanbul, Ekrem Imamoglu, was declared successful at 48.79 per cent, against his closest rival Binali Yildrim, who gained 48.51 per cent. In the capital Ankara, Mansur Yavas won 50.91 per cent of the vote, over Mehmet Ozhaseki, at 47.1 per cent.

Lisel Hintz, a professor at Johns Hopkins University, Turkey believes that the country has a robust, and deep belief, in democratic structures, and a resilient civil society, that has stood the test of time, in the previous sixteen years.

In the last general election itself, the voter turnout was eighty-seven per cent, one of the highest, in the world.

Erdogan's populism has struggled lately, due to Turkey's burdening economic crises, elevated since 2018. Government spending, on prestige infrastructure, rising interest rates, and debt levels, were largely ignored, under his regime. There was a recession, in March 2019. His son-in-law, the Treasury and Finance Minister, announced a series of economic reforms, starting, from the banking sector, but they were met, in a lukewarm manner. Unemployment exceeds ten per cent now, and it is thirty per cent, among young people.

The Turkish Lira has lost twenty-eight per cent, of its value, since 2018, and inflation has soared up to twenty per cent. Government has setup tents, where they sell farmer's produce, at a loss, damaging the retail business. In some areas, traders have hoarded up stocks, which has inflated commodity prices. At large, there have been no long-term solutions, in agriculture, the industrial sector, and the tourism sector.

Despite lodged appeals, for discrepancies, by AKP,

the opposition candidates were still shown ahead. The application, to rerun for Istanbul's mayor's race, is seen by many regional observers, as a final effort, to avoid losing control, in Turkey's two largest cities. By being thirteen thousand votes ahead, it seems Ekrem Imamoglu, nicknamed, 'Turkish Emmanuel Macron,' in the press from the rival opposition, will likely be the new Istanbul mayor.

AKP's deputy leader, Ali Ihsan Yavuz believes that the irregularities, included sixteen thousand votes, for Justice and Development Party, that have been erroneously recorded, for other parties. However, his opponents believe that filing a rerun, for the election race, is a disrespect, to the law. As of now, the AKP party has a divided opinion on whether to accept the result or keep pushing for a new vote.

'The invalid ballots are counted, and it is over,' Imamoglu said.

This is not the first time Turk politicians have been unhappy, with an election result. As per Kimberly Guiler, a research fellow at Harvard Kennedy School of Government's Middle East Initiative, Erdogan called for snap elections, in 2015, as he had a conflict with PKK, to stir up concerns, such as national insecurity, and to swing the pendulums, in his favour, for an election win. There were allegations of the government, tampering with the election result, in 2015.

In his adventures of kleptocracy, Erdogan has insisted that nobody challenges him. There has been only one authority, in Turkey, lately, under his command. It has allowed him, to tyrannise, many sections, of the army, police, courts, and the press. Some analysts believe that Turkey has experienced democratic backsliding, under his rule.

In 2016, there was a failed military attempt, to overthrow him, that he blamed on his rival, Fethullah Gulen, some foreign plot makers, and the US military, but Erdogan, somehow, moved on. However, in the coming time, he fired hundreds of bureaucrats including judges, prosecutors, and lawyers, from their jobs, who did not toe the line of his party's narrative.

Historically, he managed to handle the coups, against him, through *Sledgehammer* and *Ergenekon* court cases, and began negotiations with the PKK political party, until the ceasefire again broke down, in 2015.

Despite having a share of his criticism, people have also applauded his political talents, and some development measures, which largely attributed to his leadership success. There are many foreign honours, and numerous awards bestowed on him. In 1994, he started as a mayor, representing the Islamic Welfare Party, and after that, there was no looking back, for him.

These results will not, however, likely change Erdogan's political behaviour, which includes promoting religious values, over secularism, closer ties to Russia, and the United States, and good relations with NATO. Erdogan has four more years, under his presidency.

As per inputs from Financial Times, a new election would scare away overseas investors, as political and geopolitical issues, would decide trade factors. Also, the ruling government would not try to miss an opportunity, to influence the judiciary, in their favour, for a rerun in the election. It is because the judiciary, in Turkey, has increasingly come under government pressure, in recent years.

For the opposition party, winning the mayoral elections was a time of momentous change. They have been criticised, for a lack of organisation, but during this election, it seems, everything went in their favour. It also allows them to improve garbage collection measures and mass transit schemes.

As mayor, Imamoglu has also promised that he would audit books, for alleged corruption cases, a prospect, that could create new problems, for the AKPs ruling watch.

17 April, 2019

59

ARREST OF JULIAN ASSANGE

A HANDCUFFED AND DISHEVELED Julian Assange was dragged out of the Ecuadorian embassy, in London, in April, 2019 after seven years, of confinement.

The footage showed him heavily bearded, and his silver-coloured hair, tied to his back. He had shouted, 'UK must resist,' before officers escorted him, into a police van.

Before the arrest, Assange had barged past the police officers, returning to his private room, and had commented before them: 'this is unlawful'.

The Ecuadorian government had offered him asylum, after a diplomatic row, with the US Government, over an alleged cable, reflecting widespread corruption, within the Ecuadorian police force.

The Wikileaks founder had reached the tenure limit, of his asylum, since June 2012, and had invited metropolitan police officers, inside the embassy premises, to avoid being extradited, to Sweden, in connection with sexual assault allegations, against him. He was then transferred to Belmarsh Prison, in London.

As per Australian Prime Minister, Scott Morrison, Assange will receive some consular advice, but will not be given any special treatment. Assange's father, John Shipton, who lives in Melbourne, has requested Scott Morrison, to bring his son back, to Australia, 'for some fresh air, and a chance to consider what he's done.'

After his arrest, some other stories, also appeared about the 47-year-old, Australian citizen, violating his bail conditions. He has now been found guilty, of failing to surrender, and faces a charge, of up to twelve months, in a British prison.

He was arrested on a US extradition warrant, but it has also generated worldwide fury, where his arrest is deemed, as an attack, on press freedom, and its right to publish freely. However, according to Ecuador's President, Lenin Moreno, Assange used the embassy, as a centre, for spying on other countries, and alleged that Assange's behaviour, inside the embassy, was questionable, as he insulted the staff, had brawls with the embassy security officials, and accused the embassy authorities, of spying on him.

However, Moreno's statements have been taken, in a hostile manner, in Ecuador. Rafael Correa, his one-time political ally, called him 'the greatest traitor in Ecuadorian and Latin American history.' But many also say that Moreno's recent statement, is a reprisal, against Wikileaks' alleged document leaks, which claimed, his brother had started an offshore company, that included private pictures, of Moreno, and his family.

According to letters, seen by the Guardian, Ecuador President Lenin Moreno, was assured by British foreign secretaries, that Julian Assange would not be extradited, to a country, where he could face the death penalty. These official assurances converge, with British legislation law. These letters were signed on 7th March 2018, and 10th August 2018, respectively.

The letters read: 'you have expressed concern that, should

Julian Assange be extradited from the UK, there would be a risk that he could be subject to the death penalty. I can confirm that under UK law, a person's extradition cannot be ordered if the person concerned will be subject to the death penalty.'

Julian Assange is charged, by the US, with a conspiracy, to commit computer intrusion, and may face five years, in prison, if convicted, and may also face additional charges.

The US is actively seeking his arrest, over allegations, of conspiring with former US military analyst, Chelsea Manning, now in prison, after a 22-year-old intelligence analyst, Adrian Lamo informed the FBI, and the US army, about her alleged claims.

Assange allegedly assisted Manning, in cracking a password, to download material from Pentagon computers, which the US Justice Department has called 'one of the largest compromises of classified information in the history of The United States.'

Some of the selected material, from Wikileaks, was even published, by the Guardian, the New York Times, Le Monde, El Pais, and Der Spiegel.

Assange's lawyer, Jennifer Robinson, told BBC that the conviction of his client sets a 'dangerous precedent' that should concern 'free speech advocates.' Barry Pollack, a US lawyer, for Assange, criticised the arrest and said that Assange would need medical treatment, which he has been denied, for seven years.

A group of doctors believe that the pain, and suffering, inflicted on Assange, is both physical, and psychological, and is in violation, of the 1984 Convention Against

Torture protocols.

Although Theresa May, the UK Prime Minister welcomed the arrest, Jeremy Corbyn, who heads the UK Labour Party, in opposition, condemned his arrest. It also brings important arguments into foray: should Julian Assange be regarded as a criminal or a hero? Some people question whether he should be regarded, as a journalist, a hacker, a whistleblower, or something else. He has denied calling himself, to be a journalist, and rather, calls himself, an 'information activist'. And then, also comes the conspiracy-mongering, such as his support for provocative individuals, living in the West, such as Holocaust denier, Israel Shamir.

Wikileaks believes that under the current scenario, there is a conspiracy, hatched by powerful actors, including the CIA, to 'dehumanise,' 'delegitimise,' and 'imprison' Assange.

Edward Snowden, who has been linked with Wikileaks, and had earlier criticised, the leaking of Pentagon documents, believes that as Ecuador recently got $4.2 billion in aid, from International Monetary Fund, it was a sign that the country was getting close, to the West, and for this reason, the country was adamant, in handling over Assange, to the US authorities.

He also criticised people, who started hating Assange, after the 2016 US election.

Snowden believes Assange's work had 'profound public interest,' which included leaking information, such as the Democratic Party's leanings for Hillary Clinton, over Bernie Sanders, in the last US election.

Daniel Ellsberg, who leaked *The Pentagon Papers*, in the

past, believes that Assange's capture, is an assault, on The First Amendment, the pillar of American democracy. He also believes that unauthorised disclosures have become a kind of lifeblood for the republic and that his country is in danger.

Until now, Wikileaks has published over nine one thousand US military documents, online, including the US Army's protocol, at the Guantanamo Bay detention camp (2007), Church of Scientology documents (2008), and content from Sarah Palin's email account (2008).

Assange first became a hacker, in 1987. Four years later, he was convicted, of hacking into a master terminal, of Nortel, a Canadian multinational corporation. In 2006, he established Wikileaks, which now has over eight hundred occasional helpers, ten thousand supporters, donors, and around forty full-time staff.

As of now, the documents, which Assange leaked to the public, some time back, with assistance from Manning, have once again put American foreign policy, in a bad light, concerning its recent invasions, in places, such as Iraq and Afghanistan.

One of the most damaging documents was an official video, in which pilots of US Apache helicopter machine-gunned civilians, in Baghdad, while making odious remarks like, 'oh yeah, look at those dead bastards,' and 'it's their fault for bringing their kids into a battle.'

As per Guardian Op-ed writer, Jess Philips, Julian Assange's case makes it clear, that when it comes to women's rights, they can wait, until political games are settled. She believes that the political establishment, in the UK, has slapped the feminists, in the face, as two women, linked to Assange's case, have waited, for years, for their cases, to be answered. Assange, to defend his claims, has denounced this charge, as a 'radical feminist conspiracy.'

April 25, 2019

60

BREXIT IMPASSE

IN 2019, THREE YEARS HAVE PASSED since Britain, voted to leave the European Union. However, as a pending Brexit looms, amidst parties trying to lock horns, during May 23, 2019, election, and the European election, there may be some real consequences, that Britain could face.

As of now, the callous, and slothful ways, of the politicians, show a deepening political discord. There is little lucidness, regarding when the eventual Brexit, would occur.

UK Prime Minister Theresa May has agreed, to meet the 1922 committee, of Tory members, of parliament, once more. It might also propel her, to provide final action, on Brexit, in the coming time. The rules, for a new leadership contest, however, within the conservatives, might remain unchanged. Quite recently, in December 2018, several Tory MPs tried to oust May, but they cannot challenge her, for a year, at least. However, all these clauses can change, in the prospective meeting, of the 1922 committee, of Tory members, of parliament.

May has already failed, three times, to get approval, for the Brexit deal, from the parliament that she had brokered, with the EU.

As of now, a roadmap has been chalked out, for her departure. Theresa May may go after the Brexit deal is done.

Britain's two leading political parties, the Labour, and the Conservatives, have also met, several times, to find common grounds, on the Brexit impasse, but no clear blueprint, has been agreed upon. May's deputy, David Lidington, had quite recently commented, that the talks, between the two parties, had been mostly 'difficult,' but 'constructive.'

Labour Party wants the UK, to be part of a customs union, but the Tories, are against any agreements that would halt the country to make its trade deals. It is quite probable that there will be a second reading, of the Withdrawal Agreement Bill 2017-2019, a future bill that will oversee the withdrawal of the United Kingdom, and the European Union, in domestic law, before the European elections, and May 23, 2019, election. A second reading will allow the legislation to pass the first big parliamentary hurdle on Brexit, which has remained ever since the referendum in June 2016.

To stop May's proposals, Labour has been campaigning, against her, for quite some time. Her authority has declined, ever since, she tried to find a compromise deal, her critics allege.

George Osborne, the former Tory chancellor, told Sky that it was time for Theresa May, to quit her chair: 'Eventually, the party has to confront the truth,' he said. 'It needs a new leader, a new agenda, it needs to win over supporters who have disappeared and make an appeal to urban, metropolitan Britain that has turned its back on the Conservatives.'

Tory strategists are also, of the opinion, that if they cannot go forward, with drafting Brexit, they might not win the next election, perhaps. If any sort of hard border, with Ireland prevails, Tory strategists believe that Britain could be trapped, with Brussels, for a customs union, that they do not want.

Brandon Lewis, the Conservatives chairman, also thinks that they might not do well, in the upcoming European elections. Under Corbyn, the Labour, on the other hand, has vowed, to act as a good mediator, between Remain supporters, and Brexiteers. Through Corbynism, Labour has also improved in opinion polls, in recent times, as he is looking for 'alternative arrangements', to ensure an open border, with the EU.

British political commentators believe that if Brexit does not pass the deadlock, a second referendum is inevitable, as many people, will revolt against it.

As of now, there are hardcore supporters, of Brexit, inside the Conservatives lobby, that include the European Research Group, that want Brexit, to pass, without any compromises. Not to forget the newly formed far-right Brexit Party, having a mercurial rise, in polls, led by Nigel Farage, which recently got corporate donations, of around one hundred thousand pounds.

Farage is confident that he will win the European elections, but his sceptics also believe that he will lose, badly. He, somehow, remains one of the most important British politicians, in the two last decades. In the past, he persuaded David Cameron, to call for a referendum, on membership, in the EU. Now, he is trying to persuade May, to deliver, on that referendum. He has been able to do it, without holding a single seat, in the House of Commons, or any seat, around the cabinet table.

A poll published, by UBS Global Wealth Management, found that forty-one per cent of global investors believed that Brexit would have a positive impact, on the local economy. Twenty-four per cent, held a neutral viewpoint, over Brexit. In a report, the firm had also urged British investors, to expand their portfolios, internationally. Currently, the rise of 'zombie firms' present a risk, to the British economy. Conversely, there are some academic forecasters, who believe that the British economy, will get three per cent poorer, over the long term. The National Institute of Economic and Social Research (NIESR), believe that the long-term loss, after ten years, compared to staying, in the European Union, would be equivalent, to around eight hundred pounds, per person, per year.

Pressure has been mounting, on Theresa May, due to her incertitude, which has also impacted, her respect, within her cabinet. The absence, of finality, on Brexit, has bestowed maximum uncertainty, in the regional political lobby, projected, by the media. Of late, British politicians have become full of prejudices, and racism. Conservatives have been charged, with making Islamophobic comments, while Labour, has been accused, of anti-Semitism.

In 2018, a special UN rapporteur said that the Brexit debate, is making people vulnerable, to 'racial discrimination', and 'intolerance.' The Asian community is accused of inculcating gang culture, and British society has been nostalgically perceived, as white. The economic environment has suffered, too. Britain does very little trade, with some of the world's largest food product exporters.

As per ONS, Britain imported seventy percent of its food, worth £30.4 billion, from the European Union, until 2017. Currently, the US, China, and Mexico dominate key global export food markets. Britain might look at China,

Mexico, and Canada, for many commodities, such as beer, apples, crab, lobster, and pears. However, promoting trade, with these countries, might harm the interests, of local British farmers, due to cheap imports. Signing new trade deals, might take some time, and even if Britain leaves the EU, and Customs Union, the policymakers, need to find a solution, for the immediate future, which is short-term policy.

Matt Kilcoyne, a trade expert, at the Adam Smith Institute, said: 'Diversity of imports, is the ultimate food security. If crops fail in one part of the world, imports mean we can all keep eating. It's meant life is both more secure and more affordable. Those who oppose the UK having a more independent trade policy, and support preserving a protectionist bloc on the continent, should explain why they want to drive up the cost of living, keep choice low and scuttle a key benefit of Brexit.'

If Britain, becomes eager, to trade with major trading countries, such as China, in a post-Brexit scenario, the country could become a major advocate, within the West, for China's interests.

9 May, 2019

61

RIVALRIES BETWEEN UNITED STATES AND IRAN

POLITICAL RIVALRIES BETWEEN THE US and Iran have been inflamed, yet again, after Donald Trump, 2015, withdrew from the 2015 nuclear agreement, and reinstated sanctions, on the petrochemical industry, in the Persian Gulf, quite recently.

As a back clash, Iran calls this move a form of 'economic terrorism.'

For a while, Iran has maintained, that its nuclear program, is peaceful, as international investigators have found, several times, when the deal was drafted, that the country, was, in compliance, with the agreement. But this perspective is falling upon deaf American ears, as per Iranians, or perhaps, America wants to isolate them, for abhorrence, of Iran's past actions.

In May 2019, Iran attacked oil tankers, at a United Arab Emirates port, and it was highly condemned, by the United States. Americans, enraged by the threat, during May 2019, had announced that it would rush aircraft carriers, and other assets, into the region. Seeing this, Iran has chosen to 'step back and recalculate', for a likely attack, on the United States, in the Persian Gulf. A top commander, in the American forces, in the Middle East, said, that, it would be too early, to speculate, about a possible Iranian attack, that could prove, as any real trouble, to the United States. He was reluctant, in getting any additional deployments, against Iranian missiles, or other weapons.

In an interview, with three reporters, including one from Associated Press, General Frank McKenzie, involved, in leading America's war, in Afghanistan, and Iraq, said: 'I do not believe that the threat has diminished. The threat is very real. Our country is showing enough force to establish deterrence without needlessly provoking its longtime adversary.'

In the past, Iran also intended, to target US troops, in Syria, and even used drones, against Americans, in a key waterway, near Yemen. There were also speculations, that Iran put cruise missiles, on ships, heightening fears, that it may attack US Navy vessels, with them.

However, he also believes, at the same time, that Iran had been planning, some sort of attack, on US forces, in Iraq.

According to inputs, received by him, Iran was also, in a high state of willingness, with its ships, submarines, surface, air missiles, and drone aircraft, in 2019. Four oil tankers were damaged, in May, near the Strait of Hormuz, a strategic waterway, patrolled by the Iranian navy, through which the world's liquefied natural gas, and almost twenty per cent, of the world's oil production, flow. While two tankers belonged to Saudi Arabia, one belonged to the United Arab Emirates, both enemies, of Iran. But the war games do not stop here. Iran-backed Houthi rebels, in Yemen, launched an attack, on a Saudi pipeline, a few days, after their oil tanker, was damaged. At that time, Iran had told its military leaders, to prepare for war.

United Nations ambassadors, from the Emirates, Saudi

Arabia, and Norway, told UN Security Council Members, that many defence analysts and investigators believed that attacks were led, by foreign agencies, using divers, on speedboats, who planned mines, on the vessels, but, they, interestingly, did not blame Iran.

In fact, in early May 2019, US National Security Advisor, John Bolton announced that the US was deploying an aircraft carrier, some bomber planes, and anti-missile batteries, near the Persian Gulf, in response, to several provocations, from Iran. In April 2019, US Navy fighter jets were seen hovering over the waters, of the northern Arabian Sea, giving a strong signal, to Iran, that US's attempt, at global reach, by involving political supremacies, had also come, near Iran's backyard.

The Nimitz-class aircraft carrier USS Abraham Lincoln, having a capacity, to hold seventy aircraft, was seen streaming, near the waters, of Oman, about two hundred miles, from Iran's southern coastline. But it had not entered the Persian Gulf. Admiral John F.G. Wade, commander of the Lincoln strike group, said, that Iran's forces have adhered to international standards, of interaction, with his ships, and his group.

He went on to comment: 'since we have been operating in the region, we have had several interactions with the Iranians. To this point, all have been safe and professional — meaning, the Iranians have done nothing to impede our manoeuvrability, or acted in a way which required us to take defensive measures.'

The United States has put sanctions, on the Iranian petrochemical industry, and its thirty-nine subsidiaries, because these entities are considered, by the US, as lifelines, for Islamic Revolutionary Guard Corps (IRGC), which the US views, as a terrorist organisation.

IRGC, since its inception, has played a role, in the economy, and it also has a large military force, even having foreign interests, in places, such as Syria, and Yemen. But, the sanctions against them mean that Iran will badly lose, its vital oil exports. According to past *Bloomberg* data, Iran's oil shipment is to tumble, to seven hundred fifty thousand barrels, a day, in April, compared with 1.5 million, in October.

However, Iran has vowed, to trade oil through 'unconventional and secretive means', to divert from US sanctions. They would also not disclose sales figures until sanctions are lifted. As per reports from Al-Jazeera, Iranian investors, and entrepreneurs are turning up to small-scale businesses, such as opening coffee outlets, so that they can churn up profit.

In an interview, Minister for Oil, Zanganeh said that the US has reached 'an evil maturity' by using 'smart sanctions', but he also believes that this act may eventually tighten their noose. Statements, such as these, have come because several officials in Tehran believe that the US is not respecting the dialogue measures, as both countries have various scores to settle, politically. Iran thinks that Trump is not serious about talks anymore, and the country feels isolated, despite assurances for talks.

The US, already, has announced plans to send nine hundred additional troops, to the Middle East, and will extend the stay, of six hundred more, as tens of thousands of others, also, are on the ground, across the region. As a counter-reaction, Iran's influential Revolutionary Guard believes that they are not afraid, of American aggression, and their strategic moves, in their country's precincts, for a possible war, with the US Iranian officials have further asserted that America's military headcount, has not mounted up, under the current scenario. 'The enemy is not more powerful than before,' the Guard spokesman, Gen. Ramazan Sharif, said, in late May 2019. Iran, also believes, that the current policy, of pressuring nations, in the region, is not a fitting policy anymore.

9 June, 2019

62

DEATH OF A TYRANT, MOHAMMED MORSI

AFTER THE DEATH OF MOHAMMED MORSI in June 2019, the global media, is in a stir, as reactions have come from all quarters, of the globe. Cairo Institute for Human Rights Studies, called his death, 'a slow death,' but Morsi also had a dark side and many flaws.

Mohammed Morsi was a pivotal member of the Muslim Brotherhood, which started its political undertakings, from the shadows of Egyptian society.

In his ambitious political resolve, he believed that he could provide a transition for a democratic Egypt, but, in the process, also feared an assassination. A charismatic leader, for his followers, in the Brotherhood, he wouldn't have become a democratically elected president of Egypt, in 2012, and earned a name for himself, in the political clique of the Middle East, and beyond, if the first choice candidate, Khairat Al Shati, disqualified by the electoral commission, for serving a prison sentence, under Mubarak, ran for the presidency.

He had started his presidency, by giving Egypt, a flicker of hope. It had appeared, then, that Egypt might replicate the Tunisian model, for a successful democratic transition, but, after one year, his rule reflected a breach of trust and aspirations. The Tamarod Revolution, triggering million-strong protests, by unhappy Egyptians, had started, and it gave impressions, of a prior concluded Arab Spring, when idealists, anarchists, revolutionaries, feminists, minorities, reformers, and dreamers, all became united, for a cause. Eventually, the interim president, Adly Mansour, replaced Morsi, until the democratic installation of Abdel Fatah el Sisi, in 2014, but Egypt's soaring problems did not end there.

Sisi, who was re-elected in 2018, has stifled democracy, and has become instrumental in banning all forms of protests, shutting down independent media, and even engaging in extrajudicial killings, after the tragic Rabaa Square massacre, during the last days of Brotherhood's political activity. During his rule, he has been accused of cementing military privileges, over a robust, and vibrant civil society.

Before the military coup, when Morsi was in power, his stubborn Islamist policies had no clear recovery plan, for Egypt's economy. In his brief despotism, he failed to reform the security apparatus that continued to kill, harass, and torture people. The economic reserves were slowly plummeting, as expensive food, and fuel subsidies were mainly bestowed, upon his cadre, or precisely, electorates. He had enmity towards Egypt's secular constitution, and towards its liberal-minded people. That is why, his regime-attacked Egypt's Coptic Christians, and Shiite minority, thereby reflecting that his regime was not interested in plurality.

Despite the worldwide condolences, giving him a status of a 'martyr,' or a 'hero,' the fact remains that he was the brain behind different endeavours that killed Egypt's democracy. He purged nothing bad but alleviated it. Due to this perspective, it is not paradoxical to believe that Egyptian liberals, and socialists, looked upon him, as a thorough sectarian.

As protestors against his rule grew, in the past, it also became apparent that he had lied to several youth activists, regarding their inclusion, to reform Egypt's sleazy institutions.

During his rule, he stripped his predecessor, Hussein Tantawi, the army chief of staff, and denied him the right for any consultations, for Egypt's new constitution, which boosted the role of Islam, and restricted freedom of speech, and assembly. The political power, in Egypt, was now looked through the prism of Islamic fascism, and democracy, unexpectedly, turned utopian. His decisions were so authoritarian, that they went beyond judicial review. He replaced regional governors, from the Brotherhood, and one, for Luxor, from Gamaa Islamiya, the dreaded extremist group, responsible for the massacre of tourists, in 1997, in Luxor. In June 2013, he was locking horns, with the Coptic pope, Tawadros II, the judiciary, the police, the army, and the intelligence.

Morsi was the wrong man at the wrong time. Robert Fisk, in an article, for The Independent, wrote: 'Morsi's near-year in power was also second-rate, uninspiring, disappointing, occasionally violent, and tinged by a little dictatorial ambition of his own. Trotting out of cabinet meetings to phone his chums in the Brotherhood for advice was not exactly running a government through *primus inter pare.*'

A former Muslim Brotherhood member told The Atlantic, in an interview: 'In the fall of 2012, thuggish Morsi supporters tortured anti-Morsi protesters on the grounds of the presidential palace, proving even that even minimal hope was unrealistic.' However, Egypt remains in a quagmire. According to journalist, Thananssis Cambanis, who authored The Atlantic article, dissidents are described as a threat in Egypt, irrespective of the fact, whether, they are powerful, minor, Islamist, or secular.

As of now, there are around sixty thousand Egyptians, imprisoned, on various charges, most of them, charged under the Mubarak regime. Cambanis further wrote: 'every notable political faction has been subject to the same indiscriminate sledgehammer, from youth movements to a breakaway alliance of secularists and former Muslim Brothers, as well as the Brotherhood itself, and even politicians, who loyally backed Sisi's coup, but dared to disagree with the new dictator about minor policy matters.'

Morsi joined the Muslim Brotherhood, in 1979. He studied for a doctorate in material sciences, at the University of Southern California, and then joined California State University, where he served as the assistant professor of engineering, in 1982, until returning to Egypt, in 1985. After that, he also remained as an assistant professor, at Zagazig University, where he remained as a professor, until 2010.

After his post-graduation, in 1978, he married his seventeen-year-old cousin, Nagla Mahmoud, who told one magazine, that Morsi, sometimes, used to cook food, for her, and helped her, with the household chores.

When Brotherhood's political wing, the Freedom and Justice Party, was founded during the 2011 revolution, Morsi served as its president.

Now years later, he was eventually put into prison, and convicted for twenty years, for instigating clashes, between his supporters, and anti-Morsi protestors, in Cairo, in December 2012. He was not given the death penalty, initially, as he was cleared of not inciting the Brotherhood, to kill two protestors and a journalist. It may have been his worst nightmare. A month later, in December 2012, he was sentenced to death, after being accused of collaborating, with Hamas and Hezbollah militants, in organising a prison break, during uprisings against Mubarak. In terms of pursuing freedom from his jail, it was the final nail in his coffin. He was later also accused of espionage, for selling Egypt's state secrets, to Qatar, some fraud, and insulting the judiciary. During court hearings, he was compelled to sit in a soundproof glass cage.

During his conviction, he suffered from diabetes, and kidney and liver disease, but Muslim Brotherhood members were not allowed to visit him. However, the poor conditions, at the Tora prison, where he was based, were condemned by a report, of British MPs, as they believed that the jail conditions were below international standards.

Whatever the whimsical reactions, there are, history would not be kind to Mohammed Morsi. In the court, like a Pharaoh, mad in pride, and arrogance, he still believed that he was Egypt's ruling president. And before collapsing, he is reported to have told the court judge, that he knew many secrets that could have harmed Egypt's security.

After the case was adjourned, he was supposed to have fainted and was brought dead to the hospital.

The Brotherhood had accused the government, of a plot, in killing Morsi, through poor living conditions, and regarded him, as a victim of unfair trials.

22 June, 2019

PART V

ENVIRONMENTAL ISSUES

63

INDIA'S DWINDLING FORESTS

THERE HAS BEEN A CONTINUOUS ALLOCATION, of forestland, in the Hasdeo Arand forest stretch, in Chhattisgarh, spanning one hundred seventy thousand hectares, by the local government.

Dubbed India's most pristine, and densest forest area, it has been made accessible, for open-cast coal mining purposes. This plan has again raised concerns, about the future, of the country's ecology.

There has been a fifty-five per cent increase, in forestland diversion, between 2001, to 2008. This is indeed alarming. According to the Committee of Land Reforms, and State Agrarian Relations (CLSR), the total forestland, diverted for non-forest use, in Chhattisgarh, between 1987 to 2003, has been 1.71 lakh hectares, out of which sixty-seven per cent, has been used, for mining purposes.

This committee was formed, in 2008, by the Government of India, which drafted its official report, in 2009. It had raised concerns about India's dwindling forest area including Chhattisgarh. Going by the statistics, the most land diversion, in the country, has taken place, in Madhya Pradesh, followed, by Chhattisgarh, and Maharashtra.

It has been a decade, since then, but there has been no meeting, convened, by Prime Ministerial Office, regarding this matter, and neither has the National Council, for Land Reforms, met even once. To make matters worse, in

February 2019, the apex court ordered the forced eviction, of more than a hundred thousand tribals, and other forest-dwelling households, in sixteen Indian states, after a case, filed by wildlife groups, questioning the validity, of the Forest Rights Act.

As per the research done, by C.R Bijoy, the last eviction, of tribals, took place between 2002-2004, triggered by a Supreme Court Order, that resulted, in violence, deaths and protests, in affected central Indian states, a place where tribal dwellers lived in forest areas.

Interestingly, in 2009, the Hasdeo Arand forest area, in Chhattisgarh, was declared a 'no go zone', for mining, based on a joint study conducted, by the Ministry of Coal and the Ministry of Environment, Forests and Climate Change (MoEFCC). Its inaccessibility had greatly irked the mining entrepreneurs. As the land is now being exploited, for mining purposes, it may be the biggest forest diversion, in India, in recent times, triggering an ecological disaster.

The corporate lobbying for setting up businesses, in the area, has only escalated. As per Chhattisgarh's Ministry for Environment, Climate Change, and Forests, between 2000 to 2015, a total of five hundred eighteen mining projects. had been received, including coal, and iron ore mining, out of which, four hundred thirteen were approved, and forty were rejected.

The hills, that form the Rowghat range, in Chhattisgarh, are believed, to have the second-highest deposits, of iron ore, in the country. It is established that the local government has expressed interest, to exploit this area, for three decades. But it was only, in 2014, when construction of support infrastructure, including railway tracks, to carry iron ore took place. There was also a process, of land acquisition, for housing, schools, and hospitals, for prospective labour. As this plan would require large-scale deforestation, around two thousand, and thirty hectares, of forestland, would get destroyed.

Chhattisgarh has done little, to protect the Scheduled Tribes, and Other Traditional Forest Dwellers, because the state has turned a blind eye, toward Forest Rights Act, passed in 2006, which recognises that the locals have rights, over their land, they have been occupying and have the rights to use forest resources.

In the recent past, non-governmental organisations, such as Disha and Janabhivyakti, have taken the task, of helping the villagers, for rights awareness, where they managed, to file Community Forest Rights documents, in twenty out of one hundred four villages, of the Antagard district. However, many tribals, living in the villages of the Rowghat region, such as Gonds, dependent on forest produce, and agriculture, will be evicted, without any discussions on rehabilitation, or resettlement. They have been given monetary compensation, of thirty thousand per acre, despite the fact, the villagers believe that their land is worth three times more. They also believe that the *dalaals*, or middlemen, have cheated them. These practices signify the desperation of the state, by dodging legislation, and taking matters, into their own hands, gaging democratic values, for specific interests.

Between December 2014, and March 2015, a total of eighteen villages, unanimously passed *gram sabha* resolutions, strongly opposing coal mining, in Hasdeo Arand. In February 2019, one hundred fifty *gram sabhas* came together, in Morga village, to protest the FAC clearance, as per a press release, from the HABSS.

Raksha Kumar wrote, in an Op-ed, in Scroll, that in July 2015, Washington-based think tank Rights and Resources Initiative released a study that found forest rights (both individual and community) have been granted in just 1.2% of the total area that should be recorded and recognised. The Tribal Affairs Ministry's 2015 status report meanwhile says the total area reported to be recognised under Community Forest Rights is only 73,000 hectares, which is less than one-five-hundredth of the CFR potential in India.

In January 2019, Stage I clearance was awarded, for mining at the Parsa coal block, located in northern Chhattisgarh, by the ministry of environment, forests, and climate change. At present, there are two operational mines, in the Hasdeo Arand area: Chotia and Parsa East and Kete Basen (PEKB). The approval for Chotia came in 2011, but it was soon reallocated to Bharat Aluminum Company Limited, in 2015. The approval for Kete Basen came into the foray, after a negotiated agreement, between Forest Advisory Committee (FAC), and then Minister, Jairam Ramesh. Both mines were given clearances, for capacity enhancement, in April 2018. The minister had given his approval, based on the reason, that they were located, on the outer fringe, of the Hasdeo Arand area, and not in biodiversity-rich Hasdeo Arand. As the result, in places, such as Parsa East, and Kete Basen, the farmlands, belonging to villagers, were stripped bare, reflecting illegal practices.

Parts of Hasdeo Arand, rich in sal forests, rare plants, and wildlife species, form an elephant corridor, and the region has recorded human-elephant conflicts, involving property damage, and deaths, lately. To defend its agenda, the state has refused to recognise, the migratory route, of this large mammal. The state, conversely, has called their movements, 'stray movements'. Initially, the area had been proposed, for an elephant reserve, but this initiative was never been developed, by the state government. Moreover, mass deforestation, and mining operations, would impact the flow of the Hasdeo River, one of the most important sources of irrigation, in the northern part of Chhattisgarh.

Despite this, several proposals, for environmental and forest clearances, have been coming up, in Hasdeo Arand. There are around six coal blocks, in Hasdeo Arand, as per inputs published, by The Wire. The region is supposed to have billion metric tonnes, of proven coal reserves. It reflects gross miscalculations, and distrust, by the local government. The Madanpur South Coal Mine has been issued a Terms of Reference (ToR), based on the Environment Impact Assessment Report. Very recently, Paturiya Gidmuri OCM put forward an application, for forest clearance, in July 2018, and it has been considered, by the EAC, for the grant of ToR, in September 2018. The Kete Extension coal block also has been approved, to commence prospective, for coal.

As of now, two cases are pending, in the Indian Supreme Court regarding Hasdeo Arand. A petition, by Chhattisgarh-based lawyer Sudeep Shrivastava has been drafted, seeking the de-allocation of RVUNL's Parsa-Kente Extension coal block (adjoining Parsa open cast mine), in Chhattisgarh, and cancellation of the joint venture, and coal delivery agreement with Adani Enterprises Limited. The other petition is filed by RVUNL, seeking a relaxation of the National Green Tribunal's direction, restricting mining, in certain forest areas, of Chhattisgarh.

15 May, 2019

64

PALM OIL POLITICS

THE MOST WIDELY USED VEGETABLE OIL, in the world, over the years, has become available to consumers, at a harrowing cost.

It is a production that not only makes our planet warmer, but is also destroying the habitat of Sumatran Tigers, Sumatra Rhinos, and Orangutans, driving these species, to near extinction.

Global financial institutions, such as the International Monetary Fund (IMF), have pushed Malaysia and Indonesia, on track, to produce more of this crop, leading to severe environmental degradation, in its low-lying tropical regions, which source rainforest, and peat lands. It is because these leading global institutions view its production, as a poverty reduction scheme. Various Dutch banks, themselves, have provided various loans, to Indonesian farmers, between 1995, to 1999.

The business expansion has been vital, to regional companies, because it not only gives a higher shelf life, to processed foods, available in the supermarket, but is also the least expensive vegetable oil, in the world, due to its crop efficiency, and oil versatility, in comparison, with other sources of vegetable oils. At the same time, it also needs less available farming land than sunflower, soybean, and rapeseed.

Palm oil has been a staple of west Africa, and its origins are artisanal, rather than industrial. Most palm oil, in the past, was produced by workingwomen, by boiling the fruit and pounding it to extract oil, from the pulp.

Palm oil accounts for around thirty-five per cent of the world's vegetable oil. In around nine countries of the world, palm oil production has been a reason, for the country's economic growth, and poverty reduction. But, in Indonesia, and Malaysia, around 4.5 million people have been engaged, in this trade. Both countries produce around eighty-five per cent of the world's palm oil. As the palm oil trade will have a market worth, of around ninety-three billion dollars, by, 2021, there are very fewer reasons for companies, to not engage in this lucrative trade. Zion Market Research puts its growth until 2021, at 7.2 per cent. Due to rising trade, the One Map initiative keeps a sustainable record of ownership, to prevent disputes between plantations, and indigenous communities.

Colombia, right now, is also rigorously, pursuing palm oil production, in areas, where illegal cocoa was grown but has a lot to match its Asian counterparts. Gabon, one of Africa's most forested countries, renowned for exporting *okoume* logs, will also begin palm oil production, on a large scale.

According to an article, written in the Guardian, by Paul Hills, it was a perfect commodity for corporates, because they replaced several of their product's ingredients, with it, at a right time, and that is why, there was no looking back, for its producers. Now, it has penetrated so deep, into the consumer economy, that it has become very difficult to remove it, from trading customs.

Palm oil was a hotly debated topic, in the last Indonesian election. Generally, the populist talk of infrastructure, giving jobs, and lobbying with corporates, are convenient reasons, for politicians, to boost their popularity. The crop has remained active, all along, in keeping a political significance, in the country. In 1982, there were only small-scale Indonesian farmers, engaged in it, but until 2016, it has increased to a whopping forty per cent. By 2030, it might account for around sixty per cent.

As Joko Widodo, won a second term, there are likely chances that deforestation would be escalated, in areas, such as Papua, Borneo, Sumatra, and beyond, besides paradoxically propagating himself, as an environment conscious individual, who battled destructive wildfires, and noxious haze, and propagated several eco-smart measures. Conversely, as Indonesia is also threatening to pull out of Paris Climate Change Protocols, there are widespread breaches of Jokowi's moratorium. In September 2018, Jokowi imposed a moratorium, on new palm oil plantations.

Jokowi, seemingly, also wants to axe the trade with the European Union, by introducing a measure to phase out biofuels, produced from palm oil, by 2030, mainly to improve the country's self-sufficiency. Some say that it is a strategy, to win buyers, in China and India, where the massive consumers belong. Indonesia is also threatening the European Union, to bring the palm oil dispute, to World Trade Organisation's Settlement Body (DSB).
Malaysia, on the other hand, has been encouraging palm oil companies, to file suits, against the European Union, and is also threatening to ban European goods, reflecting a protectionist policy. Indonesia and Malaysia, both, also have been promoting smaller and medium-sized producers, collectively called 'smallholders', to reduce forest loss. But they are the biggest destroyers of forest covers, as they comprise more than fifty per cent of Indonesia's palm oil estate. During work, human rights violations have

also occurred, such as child labour, and forced evictions, that have been generally well documented. However, it becomes farcical to know that a Nigeria-based Institute for public policy analysis, supported by climate sceptics, wants to help these 'smallholders. This scenario reflects the politics, of forest-destroying puppets, and powerful agriculture lobbies.

Malaysia is also looking for new markets, in Africa, for its palm oil, like its rival, Indonesia which is too looking for countries, such as India and China, as its major consumer. Africa is the third largest consumer of palm oil, after Southeast Asia, and South Asia, as thirteen per cent of Malaysian shipments, were reported in Benin, Nigeria, and Tanzania, as per published inputs from Reuters. In its history, when Malaysians realised that Sabah Island, largely devoted to cocoa, had falling world prices, most plantations switched to oil palms. As of now, Sabah produces seven per cent of the world's palm oil.

In sustaining demand, regional politicians often give a green signal, to create forest fires, to clear forestlands. As per Nature Climate Change research paper, published in 2014, Indonesia had the highest deforestation rate, in the world. It has become a top reason, for high greenhouse emissions, particularly in Indonesia.

The other factor, favouring the producers, is all-year-round production, due to exceptional photosynthesis qualities. It also gives the highest yield per acre than other crops. It is the reason, why, from 2001 to 2017, Indonesia lost around twenty-four million hectares, of forest cover, an area larger than the United Kingdom.

Since 1973, nearly sixteen thousand square miles of Borneo, the islands shared by Malaysia and Indonesia, have been logged, burned, and bulldozed, to make way for palm oil production. In Indonesia, the frontier for palm oil production has been mainly the island of New Guinea, where practices are violating the Indonesian moratorium. Nearly one hundred fifty thousand critically endangered Bornean orangutans have perished, between 1999, to 2015, with other reasons, besides palm oil production, logging, and hunting.

The domination of palm oil has been the result of many factors. It has replaced healthy fats, in foods. Producers often keep the price of the produce low. As it is cheaply produced, it has become a staple food, in many Asian countries, where Asians are now known to consume fat, in the form of palm oil.

In history, palm oil has been given importance, due to the fact, that during the 1960s, researchers began to warn, that butter's high saturated fat content may increase the risk of stroke. Companies, such as British-Dutch conglomerate, Unilever, replaced butter's high saturated fat content, with margarine, made with vegetable oils, low in saturated fat. But, in 1990, it became clear, that the process through which margarine was made, known as partial hydrogenation, created a kind of fat, that was even unhealthier than trans-fat. This situation created a dilemma, that researchers needed to figure out, how they could replace this trans-fat, while maintaining its properties, such as remaining solid at room temperature, a necessity for manufactured commodities, like cookies. In the end, it became apparent that palm oil was the only choice.

Palm oil has also replaced personal care products, animal products, and personal care items such as soaps, shampoo, lotions, and makeup. In soaps, animal tallow was replaced by a composition of palm oil, and palm kernel oil, as it contained the same set of fats, as tallow.

In current times, palm oil is bought in Europe and the US. Asia uses it far more: India, China and Indonesia, account for nearly forty per cent, of all palm oil, consumed worldwide. The growth has been the fastest in India, quite recently. It is now a major part of the country's junk food industry, and fast-food market. In the European Union, half of the palm oil goes into biofuel, and it has an advantage over its rival, due to a low price. Currently, palm oil, used in biofuel, in Europe should comply with the standards of the Renewable Energy Package (RED III), adopted by the European parliament. However, the value of palm oil imports has dropped from seventy-seven per cent to only sixteen per cent, since 1990. According to the EU's proposed directive on renewable energy, biomass fuel components will most probably have an exit, by 2020.

Despite its overwhelming production, in Indonesia and Malaysia, palm oil originally originated in west Africa, and had been introduced from there, to Malaysia, in 1875. A Scot named Leslie Davidson, a plantation officer, was pivotal, in discovering the crop's pollination phenomenon, in a Unilever farm, which was carried forward, by insects, that resembled rice weevils. When he was transferred, to Cameroon, by his employer, he observed that pollination occurred, more efficiently, in Cameroon. Initially, he was rebuked for his findings, but, when he became the vice president of Unilever, he recruited entomologists, to observe the phenomenon.

After that decision, Leslie's observations eventually came out to be true. Leslie also concluded that Malaysia, previously, was going with pollination all-wrong. As the result, when pollinating weevils, were distributed all over Malaysia, the country saw an increase of four hundred thousand tonnes of palm oil and three hundred thousand tonnes of palm kernels. He was the man who changed the future of Malaysia and Indonesia. Four years after, Malaysia's independence from Britain, in 1961, Malaysia started exporting palm oil, and replaced its rubber plantation programme, with it. Through various policymakers, they began giving tax concessions.

Palm oil producers have now found profitable uses, for the crop's waste, such as empty fruit bunches, palm fronds, palm fruit peels, and palm kernel shells. But, in the farming process, the soil fertility is reduced, as many fertilisers are needed, for the compensation. The process also results, in an imbalance, between the biomass produced for human consumption, and the quantity left for the ecosystem.

The current debate about palm oil sustainability also rages, now and then. But, the biggest drawback, of sustainability, is its complicated supply chain network. Environmentalists have severely criticised palm oil plantation programmes, but producers need to answer, only their buyers.

Due to this reason, several sustainability programmes have become questionable. But it did not stop the World Wildlife Federation, to create a more transparent, robust Roundtable and Sustainable Palm Oil (RSPO). As a result, around nineteen per cent of global producers have been certified by it. However, the organisation also claims that there is a chance for illegal products to enter these supply chains.

Conversely, in a report, published in Eco-Business, there were accusations that an RSPO-certified plantation is no better than non-RSPO plantations. One of its members, Bumitama, has been accused of clearing Indonesian farmers illegally. Despite this, around eight EU countries have pledged to buy sustainable palm oil, from several major companies.

24 June, 2019

65

EARTH'S PLASTIC POLLUTION

ASIAN NATIONS NO LONGER WANT to be a plastic dumping ground, for rich nations.

It is because innumerable rubbish crates arrive, at the ports, of the Philippines, Indonesia, Malaysia, and Vietnam, from the West.

But these southeast Asian nations are now vowing to end it, by freeing their seas, and lands, that resemble, a giant, clogged gutter, or a place of toxic wasteland. It brings back the adage: We made plastic. We depend on it. Now, we are drowning in it.

That is why Rodrigo Duterte, had threatened to suspend diplomatic ties with Canada if the Trudeau government does not take it back. Earlier, the Canadian government did not agree to take back its sixty-nine containers, containing fifteen hundred tonnes of waste that had been expelled to the Philippines, in 2013, and 2014. Duterte had even said that if the Canadian government did not stop playing petty politics, over this issue, he might forcibly dump the Canadian waste, into their waters, by sending it back, from where it came from.

Other countries, such as Thailand, Malaysia and Vietnam, have now introduced legislation that will prevent foreign waste from coming into their ports. In April 2019, Malaysia declared, after an investigation, which revealed that the UK, Australia, the United States, and Germany were pouring waste into the country, illegally, by disguising the waste, as a kind of economic import. There were five containers, from Spain, discovered at the Malaysian port, quite recently, which have been sent back. Malaysia's environment minister, Yeo Bee Lin, has announced that around three thousand tonnes of plastic will be sent back, to the US, Australia, Japan, France, and Canada.

Poor and developing countries are also rejecting to take plastic, because of poor waste management systems. Interestingly, as more plastic is dumped in the oceans, green NGOs fear their role, in promoting bad policies in the past and they have a chance to come under scrutiny, especially after European Union's Circular Economy Package, which was agreed upon twelve months ago. But this will result in a big problem for European countries, because there is no way that Europe can recycle fifty-five per cent, of its plastic, till 2030, no matter how much money pours in. Companies still seem to use primitive and contaminating methods, especially in recycling electronic waste, as toxic air is whipped in the air, extracted from valuable metals, like lead and copper, that can also poison soil and water.

Around twelve years ago, what happened, in the Italian region of Campania, was that piles of rubbish led to a catastrophe. As there was no space for the waste, to be dumped in, the countryside became polluted with dioxins, and people started making huge bonfires. To curb the crises, waste was transferred to vast incinerators, in other parts of Europe, and there were talks of the expansion of incinerators.

Plastic imports to Malaysia also had tripled, since 2016, to eight hundred seventy thousand tonnes. A Greenpeace report recently found that Malaysia is the new dumping ground, for plastic, for more than nineteen countries.

China banned the import of plastic, in 2018, with rising concerns, within the country, for environmental concerns. It was a recipient of seventy per cent of the world's electronic waste that is recycled on a large scale. The communist country had also accepted paper, metals, including enough rubber, as much equal to ten thousand swimming pools. Lately, it had been found that most of the waste travelled through Hong Kong, due to lax rules. But China banning plastic imports means that many rich countries, from the West, need to worry now. This action has changed the whole landscape.

The US, at the current moment in time, is the biggest offender, as only nine per cent of its plastic was recycled, while the global rate was less than twenty per cent. British rivers, too, are so polluted with plastics, that almost all British rivers have samples of microplastics. The plastic waste in Mersey is choked with the largest accumulation of floating debris, in the north-central area of the ocean, and then there is the Great Pacific Garbage Patch, which lies between Hawaii and California, notorious for accumulating the highest ocean plastic.

The Independent reported that more than four-fifths of the polymers, found by Greenpeace, were polythene, polystyrene, and polypropylene, which are used to make products, such as food packaging, milk and water bottles, and carrier bags.

A new controversy also accumulated, when around sixty containers, of plastic, were found in Indonesia, in the port of Riau Island, for around five months, since early 2019. There were some crates of garbage that had travelled from Australia.

There are environmental strategists, who believe this

attitude by affected nations, is right because it will make the richer nations, in the West, realise that they should be responsible for their waste problems, rather than burdening other countries. As of now, it seems that recycling is the optimum solution, as various global companies are looking for green plastics, sourced from cleaner, more sustainable materials. But, it seems, recycling itself, also causes pollution, as every machine is deemed to make some kind of pollution. In the end, recycling, too, is a complicated issue, and recycling will also not solve plastic pollution.

The global media, in its attempt for arousing attention, is filled with images showing garbage-filled warehouses, containers, trash islands, abandoned factories, landfills, trucks, polluted canals, garbage-filled seas, plastic-laden beaches, or whales, turtles, birds choking on plastics, in the Philippines, in Vietnam, in Thailand, in the Caribbean, in Malaysia, in Bangladesh, in India, and China.

Places, such as India, are also facing incredible waste management crises, as the urban, population is rising. Around fifteen thousand metric tons of waste is collected, in every corner of the country.

Historically, plastic was initially called Bakelite and was invented by a Belgian chemist, Leo Baekeland, in the 1990s. But the first synthetic plastic was created a hundred years ago.

According to an article in ASEAN Today, plastic waste imports grew by one hundred seven per cent, from 2016 to 2018, to over two million tonnes, signifying an accumulation of over twenty-five per cent of the world's plastic imports.

In 2018, The Conversation reported a breaking news story,

where a strange looking two thousand foot, floating 'pool noodle', was seen drifting slowly, through the central-north Pacific Ocean, through the Great Pacific Garbage Patch, containing about five trillion pieces of plastic, driven by wind and currents, and it will accumulate more plastic along the way, creating a massive environmental problem, impacting our ecosystem, health, and economies.

At this precarious time, Ocean Cleanup, a Dutch organisation, has given a solution, where a passive system is developed, using natural oceanic forces, to catch, and concentrate the plastic, carried by the current. The wind and waves propel this passive system. According to the law of nature, waves, winds, and currents move the plastic, in a certain way, and the solution uses these same forces, that will act on Ocean Cleanup's roaming system. The plastic sits beneath the floater, just above the surface of the water. On their website, the organisation has estimated it cleans up fifty per cent of the Great Pacific Garbage Patch, every five years.

Due to this reason, in the Basel Conference, of the Parties, from April 2019 to May 2019, governments amended the Basel Convention, to include plastic waste, in a legally binding framework, intending to make the trade, more transparent and better regulated. It also vowed to prohibit non-recyclable and contaminated plastic, to be dumped in developing southeast Asian nations, without their consent. The Bangkok Declaration has also been signed, as per inputs from Agence France-Presse (AFP), which, significantly, will aim to reduce ocean debris. There are some existing theories, put forward by experts, where they believe that the amount of plastic will weigh more than the number of fish in the ocean, in the future. Each year, around a hundred thousand animals, and seven hundred species, in the sea, are killed by plastic. The situation has become concerning for our planet.

To help ease the crises, countries, such as Germany, Norway, and Sweden, currently, have a bottle deposit scheme, and it helps those countries, that recycle over ninety per cent of their plastic bottles.

25 June, 2019

PART VI

UNREMEMBERED HISTORY

66

AN UNTOLD SOUTH KOREAN GENOCIDE

SOUTH KOREA HAS ITS PROBLEMS of genocide, in its history. It is mainly, due to the fact, that the country, has hosted several military dictatorships.

For decades, the Bodo League massacre, an unknown massacre, in the minds of historians, part of lost political history, had become unknown to the world. It was part of South Korea's least known 'the forgotten war' and had happened, in a place called Daejon, mainly in October 1950, now an industrial city. Some people believed this systematic massacre, was started, two months earlier.

In 1991, a construction worker, preparing a concrete foundation, at some place, south of the city, discovered something, which shattered the fabric, of South Korean society, in the times to come.

Amidst the soil, he found the human skull, of a child, with several bullet holes. These human remains were not the last one, in the debris, to be unburied, from beneath. After contacting the manager of his company, the later discoveries, revealed, hundreds of sites, with hundreds of skeletons, smothered beneath the soil, some with peasant clothing on them, while others had military uniforms. These were human remains, of civilians, including infants, and children.

When a thorough investigation was done, by archaeologist, Park Raegan, he concluded that more than a hundred thousand civilians were estimated, to be massacred, in and around Daejon. A local Truth and Reconciliation Commission estimated a figure, of around four hundred thousand.

With time, it gradually came forward that the people, who were massacred, were Communism sympathisers. It is a huge embarrassment, for a country, that calls itself a bastion of democracy and development. It is because, for decades, the government concealed, its savage feats, the survivors were not allowed to talk about it, and public revelation, if carried out, by locals, was warned with brutal torture, and even death.

When American troops landed, in September 1945, they were adamant against nationalisation, and distribution of land, to peasants, local councils, and labour unions, a similar revolution of reform that had happened, in North Korea. As the result, there was an abolition of the Democratic Republic of Korea, with a military decree. Officials, serving the government, were assassinated, and buildings were bombed, for several months.

The United States installed its military establishment, in the country, which aroused sentiment against them, from the Japanese empire, despite allowing them, to keep several bases.

Around eight thousand workers, in Busan, lead a strike that spread to other towns, and cities. When around forty policemen, were massacred, including twenty Japanese officials, by the rebels, martial law was declared. Hundreds of demonstrators were fired. Eventually, in 1948, the name South Korea was constituted, from the First Republic of Korea. Exiled Syngman Rhee, an anti-communist, and nationalist, was flown to Seoul and made president. In his internal force, he kept hundreds of communist partisans, in internment camps, where they endured torture, and worked as slaves, for many years. He diverted the social welfare of people, into arms sales, in the international arms market. His paramilitary personnel, froze to death, during harsh winters, when their winter uniforms were sold, to the black market.

The Yesou-Suncheon Rebellion followed, in which three thousand soldiers, rebelled against him, flying red flags. A capitalist government had been formed, on mass killings, and terror, that sustained itself, for coming years.

Years later, South Korean President, Syngman Rhee, in 1950, had about twenty thousand imprisoned. This movement was carried, by Korean jurists, who had collaborated, with the Japanese. Many thousands, were shot, by the Korean State Forces, for their alliance, with North Korea. These executions were carried out, by President Syngman Rhee, without trials. There was brainwashing, in academic institutions, and the media machines.

According to official US reports, some US army soldiers witnessed and photographed the slaughter. One military police investigator, Sergeant Pearce, wrote, in his report, for the command centre, that people were getting killed, for being 'spies.' Some were shot, in the back of their head.

'About three hours after the executions were completed, some of the condemned persons were still alive and moaning. The cries could be heard coming from somewhere in the mass of bodies piled in the canyon,' Sergeant Pearce wrote, in his report.

The US government labelled it as an internal matter. At one point in time, the US government called the act 'illegal', and 'inhumane.' Around forty people, had their backs broken, with rifle butts, while many others were tied together, and thrown into the sea. In 2008, there were some trenches discovered, in Daejon, where dead remains were found.

In a BBC report, Lee Bok Ryong, who lost his father said, 'Our first goal is simple, to let the world know that this massacre of a gigantic scale took place.'

A generation of villagers, in the Dokchon area, remember truckloads of civilians, tied together, and brought, to the hills, for execution.

Conversely, the defenders, of the regime, had other opinions, which were harsh, and unjustifiable. When one of the retired South Korean admirals, Nam Shang Hui, was interviewed, in New York, in 2000, by the Associated Press, he said: 'I authorised three ships to carry two hundred people out to sea off the eastern port of Pohang. There, the police shot them and their bodies were thrown into the sea, weighted with stones.

'There was no time for trials for them. Communists were streaming down. This kind of summary execution was a common practice at that time. It happened during a critical situation for South Korea. We should not judge these incidents through the standards of peacetime.'

3 July, 2018

67

ITALIAN CLANS

For DECADES, ITALY'S PRINCIPAL CRIMINAL clans have hardened into vast, multinational syndicates, driven not merely by territorial ambition but by a belief in what scholars often describe as an extreme, self-serving strain of neoliberalism. The pursuit of monopoly, deregulation and unrestricted capital flows has shaped their behaviour so profoundly that they now exert influence over political, social, and economic spheres. Yet, in recent years, a quieter but consequential shift has emerged within these organisations: a widening generational conflict.

The older generation of clan leaders was known for carefully cultivated relationships with politicians, union heads, and business intermediaries. According to long-time Italian correspondents writing for La Repubblica and Corriere della Sera, these older bosses viewed diplomacy, silence, and patience as vital tools of survival. By contrast, younger clan members, raised in a globalised and fast-moving economy, tend to lack the mediating skills needed to orchestrate corruption discreetly. Their impatience for rapid wealth accumulation has weakened long-standing networks of patronage that once ensured steady income through union influence and public-sector contracts.

This rift has had visible economic effects. As the Financial Times reported in its coverage of Italy's logistics industry, the clans' loosening grip on unions has disrupted their hold on the transportation sector, where they once fixed prices and controlled distribution routes. The erosion of this influence has caused revenue streams to slow, frustrating younger members who see themselves as inheritors of a lucrative empire. At the same time, the clans resist any outside interference in their traditional strongholds, demanding operational ease even as their capacity to enforce it diminishes.

Despite these internal tensions, Italian organised crime remains extraordinarily powerful, both domestically and internationally. In the mid-2000s, for example, clan members even offered journalists cash in exchange for favourable coverage, a detail widely reported in Italian and international press. The scale of the phenomenon is reflected in figures published by Italy's statistical agency, Istat, which attributed more than 12.5 per cent of national GDP, or around €189 billion annually, to organised crime until 2017.

The relationship between the state and the clans has long been described as mutually dependent. Though the Italian Senate passed a law against mafia vote-buying in 2014, political analysts writing in La Stampa noted that enforcement has remained weak. Roberto Saviano, the journalist whose investigations brought global attention to the Neapolitan underworld, observed in Gomorrah (2006) that 'the system's economic grip is not born out of direct criminal activity, but out of the ability to balance licit and illicit capital'.

When Gomorrah first appeared, it became not only a bestseller, selling over 600,000 copies in Italy, but also a cultural shock. Saviano 'tugged a loose thread in the fabric of Italian bourgeois respectability, and kept pulling until nothing was left,' wrote Rachel Donadio in The New York Times. His revelations about the Camorra's entanglement with Naples's garment industry and its command over the city's port, through which an estimated 1.6 million tonnes of Chinese goods pass annually, exposed the global reach of the syndicates. Some analysts told Il Sole 24 Ore that the trade volume at the port had become so immense that quantifying illicit flows had grown nearly impossible.

Imitation has since become a marker of Italian mafia prestige. International investigative reports, including those by The Guardian and Der Spiegel, have observed that Albanian, Nigerian, and Russian criminal groups model their hierarchies, investment strategies, and migration patterns on Italian prototypes. Naples remains a preferred marketplace for cocaine, even for Turkish networks who trade weapons in exchange.

Much of this commerce depends on *putante*, the capital advanced by clans to purchase cocaine. Saviano notes that *putante* circulates rapidly because Italian clans guarantee distribution, sparing producers the risk of excess stock. The returns are staggering: a clan can earn almost four times its initial investment.

Operation Tiro Grosso, a major investigation conducted by the Neapolitan Carabinieri and the Italian border force, exposed a new architecture of global trafficking. Authorities discovered that brokers, not traditional clan members, were now central to the cocaine trade. These brokers travelled easily, held multiple passports, and operated through import–export firms that masked shipments of cocaine in consignments of pineapple slices, bananas, or sealed wiring. As Saviano explained in Beauty & the Inferno (2006), their form of trafficking was 'simple and businesslike', involving narcos, couriers, clan intermediaries, and street-level pushers, yet almost no participant knew anyone beyond their immediate contact.

This model allowed the network to stretch through Spain (Barcelona, Madrid, Malaga), France (Paris, Marseille), the Netherlands (Amsterdam, The Hague), Belgium (Brussels) and Germany (Münster). Couriers, often undocumented migrants, handled routes across Eastern Europe, Turkey, Latin America, and US cities such as Miami. Their vehicles were modified so intricately that detection required dismantling entire chassis. Phones and SIM cards were discarded after each journey, leaving investigators with little to trace.

Other clans extended their reach into infrastructure. The Casalesi clan, named after Casal di Principe, built an empire under Michele Zagaria, known as *'Capastorta.'* Journalists from *Il Mattino* frequently reported that he wielded influence over the Naples–Rome railway line and hoped to shape future developments including the Naples–Bari route and the transformation of the Grazzanise military airfield into a civilian airport. His strength lay in undercutting competitors, accelerating construction projects, and resolving bureaucratic obstacles with remarkable efficiency.

By the late 2000s, the Casalesi clan had diversified into slot machines and online gambling and was estimated by Italian financial investigators to be worth around $47 billion. Yet betrayal lurked even in its highest ranks: Antonio Iovine, *'O' ninno'*, once paid €100,000 per month and bound by ritual oath, turned state witness following his 2010 arrest.

Perhaps the most notorious sphere of mafia profit has been waste management. The consortium Ecocampania, once linked to the Camorra, exemplified how public–private partnerships became monopolies feeding clan interests. Politicians gained votes; clans accumulated fortunes by manipulating contracts, inflating invoices, and burying toxic waste, especially in Campania. Saviano has repeatedly argued that Italy's compliance with EU waste-management standards was effectively propped up by illicit disposal channels managed by the Camorra. Medical research has echoed the consequences: Lancet Oncology reported, in 2004, a 24 per cent rise in liver tumours near waste dumps, with women disproportionately affected.

The environmental devastation has been documented starkly. In the film *Biutiful Cauntri* (2007), directors Esmeralda Calabria and Peppe Ruggiero show cattle dying, orchards poisoned and seas polluted as toxic waste from northern companies was buried illegally in the south.

Some clans operated in even stranger fashion. The Russo brothers, heirs of Carmine Alfieri's empire, reportedly conducted operations from the sea rather than the land, living aboard in vessels in the Mediterranean to evade detection.

Together, these stories illustrate how Italian organised crime evolved into a flexible, globalised capitalist enterprise, shielded by generational change, political ambiguity, and the capacity to merge the licit with the illicit so seamlessly that, as Saviano warned, the system came to resemble the economy itself.

31 March, 2019

68

YEARS OF CULTURAL GENOCIDE IN
CANADA

For MORE THAN A HUNDRED YEARS, the First Nations Peoples, of Canada, were forced to learn in an educational framework, designed to remove all evidence, of their native identities.

As Canada became one hundred fifty years old, in 2017, many people believe that it was their celebration of genocide.

While Canada was willing to spend billions of dollars on events marking Canada's one hundred fifty years, in 2017, essential social services for First Nations people were underfunded.

Pamela Palmater, in a Now Toronto Op-ed, wrote, on March 29, 2017: 'arguably, every firework, hot dog, and piece of birthday cake in Canada's 150th celebration will be paid for by the genocide of Indigenous peoples and cultures.'

In the recent past, a damning report, that took a remarkable six years to produce, details how five hundred thousand children from aboriginal families were forced to attend over one hundred thirty Christian boarding schools, between the nineteenth century, and the 1970s, intending to integrate them in Canadian society. In this process, at least four thousand people were estimated to have died, in these schools, and many were buried in unmarked graves. This residential school system is a violation of the United Nations Genocide Convention.

According to Truth and Reconciliation Commission, cultural genocide is the destruction of those structures, and practices, that allow the group, to continue as a group. States that engage in cultural genocide set out and destroy the political and social institutions of the targeted group. It is a mass action, where spiritual leaders are persecuted, spiritual practices are forbidden, languages are banned, and objects of spiritual value are seized, and destroyed. And families, at large, are prevented in the transmission of cultural values and identity, from one generation to the next. TRC has reported that Canada, as a nation, has done all these things, including people who amounted to cultural, biological, and physical genocide.

Supreme Court Chief Justice Beverley McLachlin believes that Canada attempted to commit 'cultural genocide' against aboriginal peoples, in what she calls the worst stain on Canada's human rights record. In her working past, she has often cited laws that barred Indians from leaving reservations, widespread starvation, disease, and denial of the right to vote.

In Canada, despite the historic animosity against First Nation peoples, there have been National Inquiries. There have been important antecedents, such as the 1991 Aboriginal Justice enquiry, the 1996 Royal Commission on Aboriginal Peoples, the 2001 Aboriginal Justice Implementation Commission, the 2015 Report of the Truth and Reconciliation of Canada, and the 2019 Reclaiming Power and Place, the final report of the National Inquiry. But, unfortunately, due to myriad reasons, this twelve-hundred-page final report has fallen upon deaf ears. For this reason, a good future for long-oppressed indigenous people remains uncertain. But, Trudeau, has promised to pursue a strategy, that would be quite different from that of former Australian Prime Minister, John Howard.

The historical complexity of this issue will also raise bars for another debate: if Canada keeps on claiming to be a plural, multicultural, tolerant, immigrant-friendly country, then under what right, does it claim to be a champion of integration, especially when it has committed genocide, since the nineteenth century.

As Canada has a rich colonial past, several of its educational institutions, have come under sporadic vilification. In Halifax, a school was voted to change the name of Cornwallis Junior High School. The school was named after an individual, who was responsible for putting bounties, on the heads of Mi'kmaw people, reflecting in many deaths. Also, in Toronto, Ryerson University has come under opposition as well, because it is named after Egerton Ryerson, a strong supporter of residential schools, where thousands of indigenous children died violently, through torturous deaths. The 'Famous Five' women, celebrated in Canada's history, have also been questioned, for their heroic stature, as champions of women's rights, because they favoured sterilisation against indigenous women.

Canadians, and the world, at large, should not be shocked. In history, the 'Indian policy,' which was based on obtaining lands and resources, in larceny, and reducing financial obligations, to indigenous peoples, resulted in the primary aim of 'assimilation,' or 'elimination,' of these First Nation tribes. These acts included confining indigenous peoples to tiny reserves and forbidding them to hunt, fish, or provide food to their families, forcing them to live, on unhealthy, and insufficient rations that caused their ill health, and death from lack of food. These inhuman policies were a product of Canada's legalisation process, through the state and the judiciary, which include the Gradual Civilisation Act of 1857, the Gradual Enfranchisement Act of 1869, and the Indian Act of 1876.

Today, more indigenous children are taken from their families and put into foster care. The indigenous population, now, comprises only four per cent, but in some prisons nearly contains hundred per cent, of indigenous inmates. The federal government, in an unhinged attitude, by not displaying any sympathy, has continued with its policy of little intervention. For these reasons, Canada has remained vulnerable to genocide probes, and the scholars, the Hague, and other institutions, who knew about it, remained firm in their belief, that Canada, has a serious face-saving exercise to consider.

Several experts on human rights and culture believe that Trudeau had no right to speak on National Aboriginal Day, in 2016, about the importance of reconciliation, and the process of truth-telling, until he makes some necessary amendments, especially with the kind of institutions they have. In fact, as an amount of token, there was no good gesture, and compassion, to include indigenous art, songs, and dances in Canada's one-fiftieth celebration. Due to gross neglect, most indigenous languages are becoming extinct, of around sixty. Although, there are some political scientists, who believe that the responsibility, now, rests upon indigenous peoples, themselves, to narrate their experiences through colonial languages, in terms of English and French, so that the cultural divide is broken down.

As indigenous peoples used to live under their own

tribal, self-governance systems, the colonial structures, that slowly replaced them, gave a sense of statelessness, to them. Under the current scenario, these First Nation Peoples have no interest, in learning about political liberties, national identity, and what the pillars of a modern democracy stand for in Canada. These same systems have been used to destroy their political, and social aspirations.

27 June, 2019

69

CLIMATE APARTHEID

As EXTREME WEATHER CONTINUES TO FORCE the earth, into more drought, floods, and hurricanes, a time will come, in our world, when the poorest people would be forced to choose, between migration, and starvation. The overall scenario has been termed as 'climate apartheid.'

This term got the limelight after the UN Human Rights Council, published a report that received worldwide attention, and was widely quoted in the global press.

The report rests on the figures from the World Bank, and the Intergovernmental Panel on Climate Change, among others. It imagines a world, after a few decades, with 2° C (3.6° F) of warming above pre-industrial levels. It says this could impact hundred to four hundred million people, who are at risk of hunger, and one to two billion will have no access to adequate water.

Crop yields, in reality, could drop by thirty per cent, by 2080, while malnutrition, malaria, diarrhoea, and heat stress, could cause an additional two hundred fifty thousand deaths, per year, by 2030.

According to this report, written by global poverty expert, Philip Alston, the poorest people of the world are only responsible for ten per cent of the world's greenhouse emissions, while the rich are responsible, for around half. Many people have become rich, exploiting nature, without paying for its costs.

The report alleges that the lifestyle of the wealthy, who have wider access to life-saving resources has augmented climate change, in the wrong direction, indicating that humanity will face greater troubles, difficult to overcome, in the future. There will also be an abnormal rise, in sea levels, and other possible disasters, are in the offing, as well, such as wildfires.

Attacking the US, the biggest producer of emission, Alston, wrote: 'President Donald Trump has placed former lobbyists in oversight roles, adopted industry talking points presided over an aggressive rollback of environmental regulations, and is actively silencing and obfuscating climate science.'

Unmoved by climate change, US President Donald Trump also has recently taken his country, out of the Paris Agreement, in June 2017, which around two hundred nations are signatories. The G20, it seems, is also giving a cold shoulder over climate change, as per inputs, from the Financial Times.

Besides the United States, the problems of emissions are widespread. Despite ending its reliance on coal, China has been still exporting coal-fired power plants and failing in its target, to reduce methane emissions. Currently, Brazil's President Jair Bolsonaro has planned to open the Amazon rainforest, for mining purposes, triggering the demarcation of indigenous lands, and resulting in weakening environmental protection. In terms of climate change, there is a major drought situation, in north India, and south India. The southwest monsoon, responsible for eighty per cent of India's rainfall, has been delayed in 2019. According to Indian Drought Early Warning Systems, more than forty per cent of India is under drought crisis. As per a Scroll article, India is experiencing a serious drought-like situation, since 2015.

To make matters more serious, researchers from Stanford University believe that climate change is making countries poorer, thereby widening the social inequalities of the world. In a 2017 science journal, it was also projected that the poorest states, in the United States, will see the most economic damage, from events, such as droughts and hurricanes. Since 1980, the United States, alone, has suffered two hundred forty-one weather, and climate disasters, costing one billion American dollars, or more, at a cumulative cost of $1.6 trillion. The cost of climate change, suffered at a global level, is something, that has wider and more profound ramifications.

This pertaining climate crisis is giving rise to new movements, all over the world, such as fighting for green economic transition, labour rights, and poverty reduction efforts. The example of the rich, preventing themselves from climate apartheid was recently explained, by a report, from Al-Jazeera, where they highlighted the strategy of Goldman Sachs, where its headquarters were prevented, by tens of thousands of sandbags, and power, from its generator, when Hurricane Sandy hit in 2012. It reflected the economic power of the wealthy private sector, preventing itself from sea rise.

According to an IPCC report, commissioned by CVF countries, the world is becoming hotter, with an increase of 1.5°C, which can be only prevented through rapid uptake of renewable energy sources, phasing out of fossil fuels, and a systematic shift, in the mindset of our societies.

Global climate change should be viewed personally, and solutions and measures must be provided, by every country. That has been another issue discussed at the

Climate Vulnerable Forum, as there are around forty-eight countries, which will likely have grave climate impacts, and in Africa, alone, around sixteen countries have been identified as climate vulnerable.

In fact, in countries such as Bangladesh, Nepal, and India, torrential rains and floods have directly impacted around forty-one million people.

Although, there have been some positive developments, with renewable energy prices falling, coal becoming uncompetitive, and emissions getting a slump, in forty-nine countries, seven thousand cities, and two hundred forty-five regions. There are around six thousand companies, committing to climate mitigation, as per inputs from Al-Jazeera.

Despite this positive development, the world at large needs stronger legislation, that will inject reform in institutions, of countries, suffering from this massive environmental problem

25 June, 2019

NOTES

I.   *'Kashmir's Struggling Peace'* has been previously published on Kerala-based portal, *Counter Currents*, on July 1st, 2019.

II.   *'War Crises in South Sudan'* has been previously published on *Rising Kashmir*, on February 11th, 2018.

III.   *'Surging Refugees of DRC Conflict'* has been previously published on *Rising Kashmir*, on 16th February 2018.

IV.   *'Kosovo Turns Ten Years Old'* has been previously published on *Rising Kashmir*, on 24th February 2019.

V.   *Syria's Newest Graveyard'* has been previously published on *Rising Kashmir*, on March 9th, 2018.

VI.   *'Resource Wars in Nigerian Farmlands',* has been previously published on *Kashmir Images,* on June 29th, 2018.

VII.   *'Unfreedom in Thailand'* has been previously published on *Kashmir Images*, on July 3rd, 2019.

VIII.   *'An Afghan Ceasefire That Didn't Last Long'* has been previously published on *Kashmir Images*, on July 5th, 2018.

IX.   *'An Untold South Korean Genocide'* has been previously published on *Kashmir Images*, on July 7th 2018.

X.   *'Obrador Wins Mexican Presidency'* has been previously published on *Kashmir Images*, on July 14th, 2018.

XI.   *'Imran Khan's Uneasy Crown'* has been previously published on *Kashmir Images*, on August 20th, 2018.

XII.   *'Australia's Erratic Leadership Changes'* has been previously published on *Kashmir Images*, on 20th September 2018.

XIII.   *'Syria's Last War Zone'* has been previously published on *Kashmir Images*, on 3rd October 2018.

XIV.   *'Truth Behind Jamal Khashoggi'* has been previously published on *Kashmir Images*, on 29th October 2018.